# Theatre, Social Media, and Meaning Making

Bree Hadley

# Theatre, Social Media, and Meaning Making

palgrave
macmillan

Bree Hadley
Queensland University of Technology
Brisbane, QLD, Australia

ISBN 978-3-319-54881-4  ISBN 978-3-319-54882-1 (eBook)
DOI 10.1007/978-3-319-54882-1

Library of Congress Control Number: 2017937917



Cover credit: Zoonar GmbH/Alamy Stock Photo

Printed on acid-free paper

This Palgrave Macmillan imprint is published by Springer Nature
The registered company is Springer International Publishing AG
The registered company address is: Gewerbestrasse 11, 6330 Cham, Switzerland

# Acknowledgements

One of the best things about writing this book has been the opportunity to bring several traditionally separate strands of my scholarly work in performance studies, cultural studies, disability, race and gender studies, and arts, cultural and creative industries management studies together in one text. Though the concept of transdisciplinary research on a topic, problem or issue in contemporary industry practice is increasingly popular in academic circles, the practice itself can meet with challenges when it comes to reviews, readings and critiques of contributions in relation to the respective scholarly fields invoked. I am as a result grateful to my many colleagues in transdisciplinarity-friendly scholarly communities such as Performance Studies international (PSi) and the Australasian Association for Drama, Theatre and Performance Studies for their encouragement of this investigation of engagement with social media across the aesthetic, critical, audience development and evaluation domains of theatre practice over the last three years. I am particularly grateful to Gunhild Borggreen, Laura-Luise Shultz and their colleagues at the University of Copenhagen in Denmark for the opportunity to share some of the content of this book with an international audience at their conference on telematic performance as part of the PSi #22 global conference in 2015.

Closer to home, I am grateful to Paul Makeham and Joon-Yee Kwok for the invitation to join their project using the now 10-year-old AusStage Australian Theatre Database to map the health of local theatre ecologies almost 5 years ago, and for the impact that collaboration has come to have on the development of sections of the concluding chapter of this book. This work on local Brisbane theatre culture, and the way online technologies influence its evolution, provides an excellent extension to the recent work on US, UK and European theatre cultures considered here, and some salutary reminders about mistaking volume of activity for value of activity that can benefit all working in this field, and I have relished the opportunity to cite some of our shared articles in this area. I have also appreciated the chance to point those who are interested in evaluating the cultural value of theatre practices to work with another collaborator with whom I completed an evaluation for the Brisbane Festival some years ago, Sandra Gattenhof. Our work looked at the ways in which these specific characteristics of our local Brisbane theatre ecology sit within recognised stages in the evolution of evaluation criteria, processes and protocols for Australian theatre more broadly over the past 50 years. In both cases, inflecting my reading of global trends in uptake of social media in drama, theatre and performances practices in terms of locally specific issues has improved the contribution of this book. I have also appreciated the friendship, collegiality and critique of my fellow audience, spectators and spectatorship studies scholar Caroline Heim throughout the production of this book.

Finally, my gratitude to these research colleagues, peers and collaborators sits together with that to a great many others I cannot name here, including a large number of my students. The first audiences for the content in this book have frequently been my students and my teaching colleagues in the Bachelor of Fine Arts—Drama, Bachelor of Creative Industries, and Master of Creative Industries programmes in the Creative Industries Faculty at Queensland University of Technology in Brisbane, Australia. I am grateful to those I have taught with in our performance, digital media, and social media innovation subjects in particular, including Elizabeth Ellison, Linda Olsen, Michael Klaehn, John Banks, Sharon Altena, Samantha Harrington-McFeeter, Alison Quin and Hyacinth Steele, who have been supportive in allowing me to test the measure of some of this content with students, and in some cases fellow travellers in investigating new ways to use some of the technologies mentioned here to teach this sort of content. Though I cannot name all of the students who have been partners in those learning experiences, their questions have kept me honest about the pros, cons and perils of uptake of this technology over the years, and, above all else, I am looking forward to seeing what these emerging practitioners do with these technologies in their own drama, theatre and performance practices in their careers to come. If their work proves as thought-provoking, inspiring and innovative as the many fantastic artists, artsworkers and critics whose work I have been fortunate to spend the last three years immersed in, the uptake of these new technologies in the theatre industry may well prove to be the game changer many are looking for as they strive to make sure that theatre remains relative to the society it shapes and is shaped by.

# Contents

CHAPTER 1

# Introduction

Theatre has always been an ephemeral artform. This means that theatre makers have always had to engage their audiences in conversations, commentary and critique to ensure that their shows have meaning, impact and a lasting place in the public imagination. Historically, theatre makers in the West have asked audiences to make meaning of their shows through cheers, cries and clapping, conversations after the show or, more recently, commentary in the press and other public records later collected in library catalogues and archives. These records capture changes in theatre's style, theatre's relationship with its spectators, and thus theatrical meaning making over time. In pre-modern times, in European culture as in many African and Asian cultures, theatre was often integrated with social, ritual or religious practices. Spectators played an active part in making, and making meaning of, these festivals, carnivals, parades or other open stage practices. In modern times, Richard Butsch (2008), Susan Bennett (1997) and others note, Enlightenment philosophy came together with a European policy, industrial and production climate that saw theatre as an instrument for instructing spectators in the conventions of a civilised society to change Western conceptions of theatre. A closed stage, in combination with footlights, blackouts, a fourth wall, tiered seating in the dark, and other new technologies allowed theatre makers to transmit messages to a more affluent set of ticket-buying spectators. The paid professional critic became the spectators' spokesperson, the arbiter of what the show, the season or the theatre industry as a whole meant for a civilised society. They served as the spectators' representative, in the same way politicians



B. Hadley, *Theatre, Social Media, and Meaning Making*,
DOI 10.1007/978-3-319-54882-1_1

served as representatives of a presumed-to-be affluent, white, male, heterosexual, able constituency in a civilised society. The new technologies emerging in and after the Enlightenment—from electricity, to lighting, to print media—were thoroughly implicated in the social elite's efforts to encourage what Bennett calls "the more sedate behaviour of audiences" (1997, 3). The new technologies drove a transition away from the participatory, rowdy, riotous or confrontational relationships between producers, spectators, sponsors and the press that characterised some theatrical encounters of the past towards more controlled encounters.

In the twenty-first century, new technologies with the potential to create equally profound changes in theatre's style, theatre's relationship with its spectators, and the production, distribution and reception practices that determine theatre's influence in the social field are emerging. Among the most important of these fast-evolving new technologies is social media. In the broadest sense, a social media platform is any interactive internet-based platform or application that allows artists and audiences to debate a theatrical encounter's meanings before, during or after the ephemeral event. Social media are often called Web 2.0 media (O'Reilly 2005), participatory media or user-produced media because artists, audiences and the public at large can all create content on them. The internet has long been characterised as an "interconnected infrastructure for multiple forms of communication" that has unlimited possibilities as a "public sphere" (Dowling 2001, 202). When it first emerged from its military and industrial origins in the twentieth century, though, a certain amount of skill, software and money was required to create rather than just read content. In the twenty-first century, the advent of social media has allowed the internet to move beyond being a database, bulletin board, and basic search engine (Web 1.0) and become a more interactive, democratic, user-driven communication medium (Web 2.0). The emergence of social media has allowed all internet users to become what Axel Bruns (2006) has called "producers"—participants able to both produce and use content. As produsers, theatre artists, theatre audiences and the public today can use these new social media platforms to make, manage, manipulate and contest theatre's meanings together.

## Theatre, Social Media and Meaning Making

In the theatre industry, many have cast social media as a platform with the capacity to bring about revolutionary changes in the way artists and their audiences come together to make, and make meaning of, plays, performances and events. Victoria Doidge, Director of Marketing and Development at the Sydney Opera House in Australia, has characterised use of social media in theatre as a "game changer" (cited by Blake 2010). For advocates, the appeal lies in the fact that social media is driving a shift from the mass media paradigm that dominated in the twentieth century to the more co-creative, collaborative and democratic media paradigm that is becoming dominant in the twenty-first century. Accordingly, social media has the potential to expand the ways in which spectators engage a theatre work, and, equally importantly, the range of spectators engaging a theatre work. As Cat Hope and John Ryan say, "The ethos of democratisation includes the belief that every person has the right to engage in the arts" (2014, 13). Important to many contemporary theatre makers, this ethos emerges from a desire to address "the historical trend in which involvement in the arts was primarily the domain of the middle and upper classes" (2014, 13–14). By making new mechanisms of production, distribution, reception and critique available to consumers, and making the relationship between producers and active citizen consumers more equal, social media can assist theatre makers looking to engage with new audiences in new ways. It can make opportunities to create, view or critique theatre practice, or records of theatre practice, available to a wider audience, and make these opportunities available to audiences that have historically been marginalised on the basis of class, gender, race or ability.

For advocates, there is a strong synergy between social media and the popular, alternative and political theatres that have always existed alongside the more conservative mainstage theatre. Both are socially, institutionally and technologically convergent platforms that use a range of forms and formats to present news, entertainment or emotionally engaging stories. Both are cheap, accessible platforms that can be used to get a marginalised group's message out into the public sphere. Both are ephemeral forms, their impact reliant on their ability to make spectators stop, think about the issues raised, and then share their thoughts on the issues raised with family, friends, colleagues and acquaintances. In both cases, this means that the spectators' celebratory, confused, outraged or insightful reactions to the content can often overtake the original content in the public imagination. In both cases, the platform allows participants to act in ways they might not normally act—as some spectators did in the famous theatre riots that Bennett (1997) and Butsch (2008) speak of—making the encounters messy, rowdy and unpredictable. In the political sphere, social media is credited with playing a role in everything from the election of the USA's first black president in Barrack Obama to the birth of uprisings against dictatorial government during the Arab Spring (Pérez-Latre 2013, 49–50). In theatre industry there is a hope that social media might be similarly impactful, central to what Christopher Balme calls the "next stage of engagement" between theatre and the public sphere (2014, 66)—a next stage in which theatre will refind its relevance to modern audiences by addressing them in direct, individuated and accessible ways.

With this hope in mind, mainstage theatre makers, independent theatre makers, activist artists and their audiences have all begun experimenting with social media. The experimentation is taking different forms, and taking place across the aesthetic, critical, marketing and audience development domains of theatre practice. The technology is allowing theatre makers to offer their audiences more creative shows, more choice in when, where and how they see these shows, more chance to comment on these shows, and more insight into what is happening behind the scenes of these shows. It is also changing the content of shows as theatre makers start to take the relationships between family, friends, co-workers, companies and politicians playing out on social media as stimulus for the plot, dramaturgy or scenography of their work. The effect of this experimentation goes beyond simply conveying the same messages by means of a new media channel. As twentieth-century media theorist Marshall McLuhan argues, a new communication technology—be it the printing press, radio, film, television or social media—"not only carries, but translates and transforms, the sender, the receiver, and the message" (2001/1968, 97–98, 5). To change the medium is to change the message—the signs, the symbols and the meanings they convey, as well as the co-creative relationships between author, actor and audience that contribute to meaning making. The uptake of social media is changing the way theatre makers inform, educate, entertain or proselytise on stage. It is changing the way spectators perceive and interpret what they see on stage. The language of tweet-seats, polls, competitions, sharing pictures of creative development, rehearsal, frontstage and backstage activity, and following other companies, sponsors, media and spectators is becoming part of day-to-day theatre practice—as is the potentially anxiety-producing prospect that a member of the public's offhand comment on Twitter, Facebook, Instagram or YouTube might carry more weight than a critic's review in a mainstream newspaper. The uptake of social media in the theatre has the potential to upset the status quo for artists, arts organisations, audiences and the public at large. Whether the impact will be as significant as that of the uptake of other technologies in the theatre is still to be seen. The potential to produce a substantial shift in what Western theatregoers expect from theatre makers and companies is, however, clear.

The uptake of new media technology has often been accompanied not just by utopian fantasies but by what Leo Becker and Klaus Schoenbauch call "fears and anxieties" (1989, 8) about its personal, social or professional impact. Fears about social media to date have focused on distanced, disintegrated online communities destroying the fabric of society, privacy, bullying and dumbing down of social debate. In the arts, fears about social media have recalled concerns raised in Theodor Adorno and Max Horkheimer's culture industry thesis (1944/2002). In their oft-cited accounts, Adorno, Horkheimer and others in the Frankfurt School so influential in the 1920s—including Herbert Marcuse, Walter Benjamin and Jürgen Habermas—raised concerns about mass media, mass consumption and mass inculcation of taste among audiences. They worried that the shift to mass media might lead the arts to lose the "aura" that comes from their authentic, physical and ephemeral presence, and teach audiences to favour crass, commercialised content targeted to appeal to the lowest common denominator of spectator sensibilities. They worried that what Jay David Bolter and Richard Grusin (2000) have subsequently called the "remediation" of past artforms in the present media would necessarily diminish them. Similarly, the uptake of social media in theatre today has led some commentators to raise concerns about the future of a fundamentally live artform (Trueman 2012). This includes concerns about whether audiences will pay what it costs to produce live plays, performances and events when they can stream content instead. For advocates, the global reach of social media platforms is positive, making it possible for theatre makers to share their work with a worldwide audience. For detractors, the global reach of social media platforms has the potential to produce a proliferation of poor quality content, with little relation to the live experience that has traditionally been central to theatre's effectiveness. Using this technology to promote theatre, promote theatre performers, and promote the vernacular creativity of amateur audiences who produce their own versions or mashups of well-loved scenes is interpreted, as Stephen O'Neill notes in his study of Shakespeare on YouTube, "as a kind of schlock or regarded as reflecting the "external sameness" of the culture industry and the depthless culture of postmodernity" (2014, 5). For advocates and detractors alike, the uptake of social media in the theatre industry has the potential to impact significantly on its status in the public sphere. But, as Balme suggests, while theatre makers are increasing the scope, scale and frequency of their experiments with social media, it is still "difficult to predict what kinds of creative interchange will emerge between theatres and social media using publics" (2014, 68).

In this context, it is not surprising that the uptake of social media in the theatre—as in most other fields—is not progressing along smooth, straightforward, teleological paths. The stakes for theatre makers and companies investing their time, effort and energy in experimenting with this new technology are high, even in countries such as the USA, the UK and Australia, where social media use is high and highly accepted in the culture—not least because most theatre makers and companies in the West still rely on government subsidy to sustain their theatre practice. Across the US, the UK, Europe and Australasia, funding agencies are asking all theatre makers and companies to make at least some use of social media to attract new audiences, ask for feedback and account for their impact on their audiences (Conner 2013). The rapid changes in social media platforms and practices can, however, leave theatre makers and companies caught between old forms and new forms. There are theatre makers who create Facebook, Twitter, Instagram and YouTube accounts that they rarely use, lack the human resources to use well, or worry about using well. There are theatre makers who use these platforms more regularly, but risk disappointing audiences looking for the more co-creative, collaborative activities advertised because they are simply replicating the same old offline aesthetic, critical, marketing or audience development activities via the online platforms. There are theatre makers who struggle to integrate aesthetic, critical and audience development activities online, or to fully involve audiences in such activities.

With so much at stake, a broad-based survey of this emerging field as it evolves is overdue. As Patrick Lonergan argues, "it seems reasonable to suggest that social media is here to stay, and that its impact upon theatre making and theatre-going merits continued attention" (2016, 63). The task at this stage of the technology's emergence is to examine how uptake of social media in the aesthetic, critical and audience development domains of theatre practice is effecting theatre makers' efforts to engage fellow artists, audiences and society. Is the uptake of social media in theatre facilitating a return to a past in which theatre practices were active, interactive and at times downright rowdy, and the word of the published critic had yet to take over the responsibility for making meaning? Is it reinvigorating the vernacular creativity of past social, ritual and theatre cultures that, according to Lonergan (2016), constitute important precursors to today's social media cultures? Is it facilitating a shift towards a new form of active, interactive, co-creative theatre culture for the future? Or is it simply a good way to get spectators to produce testimonials, commentary or self-created versions of shows they are no longer watching? The changes in aesthetic, critical, marketing and audience development practices that social media makes possible are many and varied, but not yet very well understood, making it a field of practice worth fuller investigation.

## Studying Theatre and Social Media

There are many news reports, industry reports and training resources offering tips on how theatre makers might tackle social media available today (e.g. Bravo 2009; Weidner 2009; Blake 2010; Zarella 2010; Crittenden 2012; Mackrell 2012; Trueman 2012; Brown 2013; Mandell 2013; Vargas 2014). Intriguingly, however, there are not nearly as many scholarly articles, chapters, books or textbooks on social media and theatre. This is an imbalance I want to address here, via a more scholarly analysis that investigates the uptake of social media in the theatre, and the uptake of social media across the aesthetic, critical, audience development and evaluation domains of theatre practice.

To note the imbalance between industry and scholarly accounts of this emerging field is not to suggest that analyses of theatre and social media are absent from the drama, theatre, performance and dance studies landscape. There are already many useful case studies of theatre makers who use social media in making or marketing their work available. This includes books and articles on Shakespeare online by Stephen O'Neill (2014), Christie Carson (2014), W.B. Worthen (2014), Geoffrey Way (2011), and Kate Rumbold (2010), articles on activist online performance by Jonathan Gray (2010, 2011, 2012), chapters on contemporary works, such as Christoph Schlingensief's *Please Love Austria*, Rimini Protokoll's *Call Cutta in a Box* and Marina Abramovic's the *Artist is Present* in Christopher Balme's *The Theatrical Public Sphere* (2014), and chapters on Rimini Protokoll's *Call Cutta in a Box* and Tim Price's *The Radicalisation of Bradley Manning* in Christina Papagiannouli's *Political Cyberformance* (2014). If the term "social media" is taken in a slightly broader sense, to mean any technology that allows two-way interaction between artists and audiences, then there is also some engagement with this topic in texts that trace the uptake of new technology in theatre more generally. These include the oft-cited *Virtual Theatres* (2004) by Gabriella Giannachi, *Digital Performance* (2007) by Steve Dixon, *Performance and Technology* (2006) and *Digital Practices* (2007) by Susan Broadhurst, and *Theatre and the Digital* (2014) by Bill Blaike, as well as articles in journals such as *International Journal of Performance Arts and Digital Media* and *Body Space Technology*. The usefulness of these accounts notwithstanding, lengthier analyses that offer a broad-based survey of social media across the aesthetic, critical and audience development domains of contemporary theatre practice have been slow to emerge. The closest include Christopher Balme's *The Theatrical Public Sphere* (2014) and Lynne Conner's *Audience Engagement and the Role of Arts Talk in the Digital Era* (2013), along with the articles of Toni Sant (2008, 2009, 2013, 2014), one scholar who has consistently written about the affordances, interactivities and aesthetics of social media in the theatre, including an overview chapter in the *Routledge Handbook of Social Media*. Patrick Lonergan's *Theatre & Social Media* (2016) in the Palgrave *Theatre &* series of resource texts has also made a useful contribution to the study of social media as a platform for sometimes highly theatricalised identity performance for professionals, amateurs and the public at large. Together, these texts and their authors have become touchstones central to this study of theatre, social media and meaning making: Lonergan to the sections on self-performance online, Sant to the sections on aesthetic performance online, and Balme and Conner to the sections on criticism, marketing, audience engagement and evaluation.

Though these texts represent a significant start to the study of theatre and social media, the fact remains that the majority of research into social media practice to date still comes from media, communication and cultural studies. These studies tend to concentrate either on specific social media platforms (e.g. Trottier 2012), on social media's role in self-presentation, self-performance, relationships and storytelling (e.g. Baym 2010; Page 2012), on social media's role in politics, revolution, crisis management or civic engagement in particular communities at particular times (e.g. Parmelee and Bichard 2012), or on new ways of capturing social media informatics (e.g. Lovett 2011). There is also a growing body of research that concentrates on social media's role in marketing products to consumers; (e.g. Albarran 2013; Anderson 2010; Berger 2012; Brogan 2010; Handley and Chapman 2012; Kerpen 2011). Accordingly, these also feature prominently in the definitional work, discussion and analysis in the chapters to come, providing insights beyond those available in the arts-based literature thus far.

Though how-to industry texts still outnumber scholarly texts on social media in the theatre—and, most importantly, social media used across the aesthetic, critical, audience development and evaluation domains of theatre practice—the studies that are available offer a firm base for a broad survey of this evolving area of experimentation in the performing arts.

## Book Content

In this book I offer a broad-based survey of the emerging field of theatre and social media, and the first major attempt to chart this new territory. I focus throughout on how artists and their audiences are working with and within a fast-moving curve of technological adoption, adaptation and experimentation to make, and make meaning of, theatre and theatre-related content presented through social media platforms. The book is thematised around the areas of aesthetics, criticism and audience development to enable engagement with the widest range of ideas about how the uptake of this technology is changing meaning making in the theatre. I use examples from the USA, the UK and Australia—including performance texts and para-performance texts such as previews, reviews and comment pages—to provide a snapshot of the field and the way artists and audiences are working in it. In the later chapters, I use textual analysis of comments, conversations and controversies on social media platforms to examine the way the technology is influencing the evolution of the practice and the way the practice is influencing the evolution of the technology in potentially unexpected ways. The result is a timely set of insights that shed new light on the questions that some other scholars have already begun to raise about the uptake of this new technology in the theatre, together with some more tentative assertions about potential paths forward.

In Chap. 2, "Social Media: Platforms, Networks and Influences", I provide a communication model that captures some of the distinctive features of the producer–performer–spectator relationships that play out on social media platforms. I examine the types of action, interaction and affordance that—according to current literature in the field—facilitate success or failure in these fast-based, overpopulated, unpredictable communication platforms. I begin linking these actions, interactions and affordances to the ways in which theatre makers are using social media platforms across the aesthetic, critical and audience development domains of theatre practice.

In Chap. 3, "Social Media as Theatre Stage: Aesthetics, Affordances and Interactivities", I consider the way social media is being deployed in the aesthetic domain of theatre practice, to produce, disseminate and popularise performance works. Here, social media impacts on what Bennett (1997) would call the "inner frame" of theatrical production, inside the auditorium, or whatever street, shopping mall, offline/online public space is serving as the auditorium for a particular performance work. In Bennett's initial conceptualisation, "[t]he inner frame contains the event itself and, in particular, the spectator's experience of a fictional stage world" (Bennett 1997, 2), though, of course, the spectator's experience is always informed by the ideas, discourses and ideologies they bring from the real world into the fictional world. In the current climate, social media is being used in the production, documentation and dissemination of theatrical performances in dozens of different ways—as a topic or a thematic driving the style, dramaturgy or scenography of a show (as in Adam Cass's *I Love You Bro*, Liesel Zink's *Various Selves* or The Builders Associations *Continuous City*), an archive or anti-archive (as on sites such as the Hemispherica database of Latin American performance, the AusStage database of Australian performance or the *Anarcha* Anti-Archive), a means of sharing a show with audiences near and far in "as live" broadcasts (productions of historical works such as *Hamlet*, *Othello* and *Timon of Athens* by the National Theatre Company, or contemporary works such as *The Radicalisation of Bradley Manning* by the National Theatre of Wales), or, in some of the most innovative uptakes, a fundamental feature of the aesthetics of immersive, telematic, networked and online performance, participatory performance or activist performance (from touchstones in telematic performance such as Paul Sermon's *Telematic Dreaming* or Blast Theory's *Desert Rain*, to Ian Upton's *Ritual Circle* on Second Life, or other works on virtual performance platforms such as UpStage or Waterwheel, to the RSC's *Such Tweet Sorrow* with Mudlark and *A Midsummer Night's Dreaming* with Google Creative Lab, to integrated live and online works such as Punchdrunk's *Sleep No More* or New Paradise Laboratories *Fatebook: Avoiding Catastrophe One Party at a Time*, to Jeffrey Cranor's tweet plays, to La Pocha Nostra's *Ethno-Cyberpunk Trading Post*, Wafaa Bilal's *Domestic Tension*, Brian Lobel's *Purge*, Sarah Rodigari's *Reach Out Touch Faith*, to @Platea's *Co-Modify*, or artist Ai Wei Wei's broadcasting of his life under house arrest online).

In Chap. 3 I consider these and other works as examples of the ways in which theatre makers are using social media to share work which embodies an aesthetics of play, participation, games or contemporaneous commentary that can become part of the conversations that unfold in the work. I note that uptake of social media in the theatre frequently blurs the boundaries between fictional world and real world, and thus shifts the relationships between producers, performers and spectators. I suggest that, though examples of innovative uptake of social media exist in both mainstage and independent performing arts practice, concerns about the impact of the technology mean that mainstage producers often use social media events as "transmedia marketing" for their primary program, rather than as their primary programme.

In Chap. 4, "Social Media as Critical Stage: Controversy, Debate and Democracy", I consider the way social media is currently being deployed in the critical domain of theatre practice, as a platform for rating, review and commentary by and for the benefit of audiences. Here, social media impacts at the nexus of what Bennett (1997) calls the "inner" and "outer" frames of theatrical production, between what happens in the auditorium and what is said about it in post-show talks, in the press, or in documentation and archives. In the eighteenth, nineteenth and twentieth centuries, paid professional critics have taken up the role of the representative spectator, providing readings of theatrical performances designed to influence perception, interpretation and taste, and, therefore, the way theatre has an impact on the public sphere in the short, medium and long term. At the turn of the twenty-first century, social media platforms are allowing theatre going public to challenge this, allowing more and more people to share their opinions, push for their own readings of a theatrical performance, and thus play a part in shaping the impact of this performance in the broader public and political spheres. In this chapter I offer a detailed examination of examples of conflicted response to contemporary performance work on online platforms, including responses to Brett Bailey's *Exhibit B*, Peta Brady's *Ugly Mugs* and Rita Marcalo's *Involuntary Dances*, all controversial for their depiction of marginalised identity positions that some spectators and social players took issue with. I consider what these examples reveal about the way in which social media commentary replays, replicates or replaces the role of traditional theatre criticism and review. I look at the strategies spectators-become-critics deploy to try to inform the way their fellow spectators and society at large interpret a work via commentary on social media platforms. I observe that, though traditional criticism operates on a logic of authority, this new user-created criticism operates on a logic of authenticity, of the sort seen in much social media networking, rather than on traditional economies of production, distribution, and reception and criticism.

In Chap. 5, "Social Media as Cultural Stage: Co-creation, Audience Collaboration and the Construction of Theatre Cultures", I consider the way social media is being deployed in the audience development domain of theatre practice. For mainstage and independent theatre companies and makers alike, social media holds a lot of potential to help them in their efforts to encourage the public to follow their personal, social and professional lives, and their motivations for producing their work, so that they will be more interested in coming along to their shows. Social media makes more tools for establishing, managing and maintaining a relationship with an audience in what Bennett (1997) calls the "outer frame" of theatrical production, outside the theatre. At its best it enables theatre makers to invite their public into their processes, not just of making particular shows, or seasons, but of making the ecology of the theatre industry in a city or country. In so doing, though, it also makes more records for evaluating the value of people's engagement with artworks, artists and other audience members more available to theatre makers, and to the funding bodies that support them, to assist in the continuous improvement of production, distribution and reception practice. This can make many mainstage theatre makers nervous. I consider examples of attempts to get a theatre community talking online in my own local context in Brisbane, Australia, what they tell us about what sparks meaningful engagement with communities online, and what they tell us about factors on either the maker or the spectator side that might limit meaningful engagement.

In the Conclusion I reflect on the fact that the uptake of social media in theatre is a remarkably rare case where advice about how to work with the technology is potentially outpacing work with the technology in theatre practice, and in theatre theory, and what this means for those hoping to use it to reconnect theatre with broader cultural debates.

Clearly, the aesthetic, critical and audience development domains I consider in this book are not the only areas in which social media is prompting changes in theatre practice in the twenty-first century. For example, social media is also impacting on the technology that stage managers use to communicate with cast, crew and stakeholders, the technology that scenographers use to share draft stage designs, and the technology that performers use to share their show reels, all aspects of its uptake that have yet to be examined at any length in the literature. It is also, as O'Neill (2014) and Lonergan (2016) emphasise in their examinations of theatre and social media, becoming a platform for audiences and amateur performers to present their own versions of characters, scenes and songs for public consumption. The focus here, however, is on aesthetics, criticism, audience engagement and evaluation because these are the areas in which the uptake of this technology is effecting artists' and audiences' efforts to make meaning and, in doing so, make a meaningful impact on public debates about important issues.

As noted, I use terminology drawn from across theatre, media and marketing studies to ground my analysis of theatre and social media throughout the book. Indeed, I have already introduced terms central to the study that require further definition to firm up their meanings in this transdisciplinary study. In addition to drawing terminology from a range of sources, I typically use theatre, media and marketing terms in their broadest possible sense. I define "social media" as any two-way interactive online platform, and I define "social media networking" as any activity of any actor, agent or participant—from a like, follow or share to a more extended interaction—on such a platform. I define "technology" as any tool that humans create to enable them to achieve their aims in communication or any other area. Accordingly, I describe the uptake of social media in the theatre as the latest in a long list of technologies that have influenced theatre practice, including lighting, sound, staging, print, photography, projection and other technologies. The impact the affordances of this technology are having on meaning making is the core focus throughout the text—affordances being what O'Neill characterises as "the material, physical attributes of a given object and the actions those attributes facilitate" (2014, 6). This said, I do describe social media platforms not just in technological but also in social terms. I cast social media platforms as a part of the public sphere, by which I mean the shared space or place—conceptual rather than concrete—in which new ideas about identity, society, social institutions and their meanings are negotiated. I describe these negotiations using terms such as "performance", "self-performance", "frontstage performance" and "backstage performance". In this sense I use the term "performance" in a social instead of a purely aesthetic sense, where I understand any statement, action, interaction or strategy that a social actor uses to try to gain influence, authority, power or status in a social group as a performance. As a result, I apply the term "performance" not just to the aesthetic activity in focus in Chap. 3 but to the critical, marketing and audience development activity in focus in Chaps. 4 and 5. I do not strongly differentiate between live performance and mediated performance. As Gray argues in his study of social media and theatre, while some might see unbridgeable definitional differences between live performances and social media platform performances, the networked nature of these new online platforms means that the forms are likely to be "increasingly porous and blurred" (Gray 2012). Similarly, I do not differentiate strongly between performance texts and para-performance texts. These too are traditionally separate texts (one occupying the inner frame of theatrical production and the other occupying the outer frame of theatrical reception) that are becoming increasingly porous and blurred in the examples I consider here. Indeed, I focus a lot of attention on transmedia texts that deliberately transfer characters, plots or messages from one medium into another to make them accessible to new audiences in new ways. Instead of separating these texts, I investigate how artists and audiences work with them in interesting new combinations on platforms where collaboration, co-creation and reciprocity are required to create a sense of a community, as an imagined collective of which a participant is a member. I contrast monologues designed to instruct such a community with dialogues designed to initiate negotiation within such a community. I characterise the latter as likely to make social media platforms, and the performances presented on and through them, accessible—in a conceptual as much as a concrete way—to those historically excluded on the basis of class, race, gender or ability. I engage with examples of aesthetic, critical, marketing and audience development practices that specific communities find controversial, scandalous or exclusionary. The examples come both from mainstage theatre and more independent theatre—by which I mean theatre made by people or companies not in receipt of anything beyond project-by-project funding from government agencies or authorities—and thus primarily from professional theatre practices. I look at examples where the context collapse that characterises social media—the convergence of different communities with different values, and, as a result, different definitions of access, inclusion and thus, colloquially speaking, democracy—creates debate and conflict, and thus risk challenging the status quo for theatre producers, theatre spectators and the social field in which they sit. Together these terms provide useful tools to analyse aesthetic, critical, marketing and audience development practice on social media in a thorough way. Indeed, as the analysis progresses, the examples that become most interesting are those that trouble traditional boundaries, and the traditional terms, concepts and theories applied to them, as the places where innovation is most likely to take place. It is these moments—rather than simply the presence or non-presence of social, mobile or locative media in a theatre—that are the real subject of this book.

In collecting the material that I consider over the course of the chapters in this book, I have looked at a lot of content posted to social media platforms, including that of producers, spectators and the public at large. In several chapters I refer to material that people have posted as part of their social or professional engagement on social media platforms, of their own volition, rather than in interviews, surveys or experiments that I have set up. I refer to the textual, visual and video information people have uploaded to sites, and other people's commentary on that information. Although it might have been possible to ask people to participate in direct research—or, indeed, experiments to produce direct research data—I have, in developing this book, taken on board Justin Lewis's (1991, 74) suggestion that setting up such experiments to seek information about making or seeing theatre on social media sites would change the interactions so much that they would no longer be so useful. Using real information, rather than information gathered in constructed research conditions, does raise ethical questions. For this reason I have adopted the approach that has become standard in social media research in that I refer only to posts on publicly available pages, platforms and sites, which are visible to anyone with an internet connection, not just a few "friends" or "followers" of the poster. These pages are public documents where participants contributing to or commenting on them would not have had any expectation that they were private, or that permission would be sought to quote them (Page 2012, 20). They are therefore quotable. The semi-private sites that are only visible to a few friends via their personal passwords are not, so they are not quoted here. The quoting is in some instances necessary because while most sites were available at the time of writing, and many sites may still be available in some form another for many years to come, others are more ephemeral, so "their longevity cannot be guaranteed" (iv, 20).

The examples I have collected here do not provide a definitive summary of theatre that is using social media at the present time. The volume of information passing on these fast-paced, ephemeral sites, together with the fact that researchers can only engage with them intermittently, means that aiming to study all cases, or all the best cases, or all the information about the best case, would be doomed from the start (Bell 2001, 200). Moreover, as David Kociemba (2010) notes, it is not possible to tell whether even the best information on the best social media site is what it seems to be on the surface. One-off posters, vocal minorities or mischief makers posting under anonymised or pseudonymised handles may skew action, interaction and conflict unfolding on these sites in their own ways and for their own reasons. This poor netiquette on the part of some posters may not be visible to a researcher, but may impact on how ready other more regular posters are to contribute to a site, platform or episode. As Ruth Page notes, profile information, posts and other offerings therefore have to "be treated as performances rather than attributes that map onto 'real world' qualities" (2012, 19). Moreover, the performance texts, para-performance texts and spectator relationships I look at are largely US, UK, Western European or, as a result of my location, Australasian in origin, in the English language, on social media platforms popular with English-language speakers—I have not, and could not, offer similar analyses of practices unfolding on, say, a Chinese platform such as Weibo. As Lynne Conner notes in her study of audience engagement in the digital age, "[m]any of the issues associated with Western arts reception are not shared by non-Western cultural traditions" (2013, 8). This means that the examples considered and conclusions made in this book cannot necessarily be extrapolated out into these non-Western contexts, where theatre makers, spectators and societies have their own theatre traditions, their own media traditions and their own meaning-making traditions.

These necessary cautions notwithstanding, analysing the uptake of social media platforms as stages for performing arts practice here provides useful insights into a set of practices that is still evolving. As Elizabeth Evans argues, "[t]echnology does not become part of daily life instantly, and so studying moments of emergence can illuminate the ways in which this process is undertaken" (2011, 81) in ways that later analysis sometimes cannot. "I feel certain," as Conner does, "that new modalities for arts appreciation are being invented right now, online, in ways I don't know about yet" (2013, 170). But, given that uncertainty, changeability and constant updates to suit new user needs and interests are at the core of these new technologies, this should not preclude any study providing a snapshot of particular practices at a particular moment in time. While not all of the examples studied here will have a lasting place in the historical record, they do allow for analysis of trains of thought, negotiations and contestations within theatre practice at this moment in time.

## References

Adorno, Theodor, and Max Horkheimer. 1944/2002. *Dialectic of Enlightenment*. California: Stanford University Press.

Albarran, Alan B. (ed.). 2013. *The Social Media Industries*. London: Routledge.

Anderson, Eric. 2010. *Social Media Marketing: Game Theory and the Emergence of Collaboration*. Portland: Springer.

Balme, Christoper. 2014. *The Theatrical Public Sphere*. Cambridge: Cambridge University Press.

Baym, Nancy. 2010. *Personal Connections in the Digital Age*. Cambridge: Polity Press.

Becker, Leo B. and Klaus B. Schoenbach. 1989. When Media Content Diversifies: Anticipating Audience Behaviour. In *Audience Responses to Media Diversification: Coping with Plenty*, ed. Lee B. Becker and Klaus B. Schoenbach, 1–27. Hillsdale: Lawrence Erlbaum Associates.

Bell, David. 2001. *An Introduction to Cybercultures*. London: Routledge.

Bennett, Susan. 1997. *Theatre Audiences: A Theory of Production an Reception*, 2nd ed. London: Routledge.

Berger, Christopher. 2012. *The Social Media Strategists: Build a Successful Program from the Inside Out*. Boston: McGraw-Hill.

Blaike, Bill. 2014. *Theatre and the Digital*. London: Palgrave Macmillan.

Blake, Elissa. 2010. Geeks, Tweets and Bums on Seats: How Social Media Is Shaping the Arts in Australia. *The Sydney Morning Herald*. July 10, 2010. http://www.smh.com/au/entertainment/theatre/geeks-tweets-and-bums-on-seats-20100709-103g8.html. Accessed 9 Aug 2013.

Bolter, Jay David, and Richard Grusin. 2000. *Remediation: Understanding New Media*. Cambridge: MIT Press.

Bravo, Britt. 2009. 5 Ways Theatres Can Use Social Media. *Cultural Entrepreneurship Blog*. Global Centre for Cultural Entrepreneurship, 10 August 2009. http://culturalentrepreneur.org/blog/5-ways-theatres-can-use-social-media. Accessed 5 Aug 2013.

Broadhurst, Susan. 2006/2011. Performance and Technology: Practices of Virtual Embodiment and Interactivity. London: Palgrave Macmillan.

Broadhurst, Susan. 2007/2011. Digital Practices: Aesthetic and Neuroesthetic Approaches to Performance and Technology. London: Palgrave Macmillan.

Brogan, Chris. 2010. *Social Media 101: Tactics and Tips to Develop Your Business Online*. Hoboken: Wiley.

Brown, Ismene. 2013. Only the Artists Can Save the Arts Critics. Culture Professionals Network. *The Guardian*, 2 August 2013. http://www.theguardian.com/culture-professionals-network/culture-professionals-blog/2013/aug/02/only-artists-can-save-critics. Accessed 7 Jan 2015.

Bruns, Axel. 2006. *Blogs, Wikipedia, Second Life, and Beyond: From Production to Produsage*. New York: Peter Lang.

Butsch, Richard. 2008. *The Citizen Audience: Crowds, Publics and Individuals*. London: Routledge.

Carson, Christie. 2014. Creating a Model for the Twenty-First Century. In *Shakespeare and the Digital World: Redefining Scholarship and Practice*, ed. Christie Carson and Peter Kirwan, 226–237. Cambridge: Cambridge University Press.

Conner, Lynne. 2013. *Audience Engagement and the Role of Arts Talk in the Digital Era*. London: Palgrave Macmillan.

Crittenden, Stephen. 2012. Now Everyone Really Is a Critic. *Global Mail*, 6 February 2012.http://www.theglobalmail.org/feature/now-everyone-really-is-a-critic/23/. Accessed 3 Feb 2015.

Dixon, Steve. 2007. *Digital Performance: A History of New Media in Theater, Dance, Performance Art, and Installation*. Cambridge: MIT Press.

Dowling, John. 2001. *Radical Media: Rebellious Communication and Social Movements*. Thousand Oaks: Sage.

Evans, Elizabeth. 2011. *Transmedia Television: Audiences, New Media and Daily Life*. London: Routledge.

Giannachi, Gabriella. 2004. *Virtual Theatres: An Introduction*. London: Routledge.

Gray, Jonathan. 2010. Social Media Roundtable: Open Forum and the Library of Congress. *Hyperallergic*, *Facebook*, 16 April 2010. http://www.facebook.com/topic.php?uid=90675054811&topic=13770. Accessed 19 Aug 2013.

Gray, Jonathan. 2011. Following Piece 2.0—Day Four, *Bungy Notes*, 30 October 2009. http://bungynotes.blogspot.com/2009/10/following-piece-20-day-four.html. Accessed 19 Aug 2013.

Gray, Jonathan. 2012. Web 2.0 and Collaborative On-Line Performance. *Text and Performance Quarterly* 32 (1): 65–72.

Handley, Ann, and C.C. Chapman. 2012. *Content Rules: How to Create Killer Blogs, Podcasts, Videos, eBooks, Webinars*. Hoboken: Wiley.

Hope, Cat, and John Ryan. 2014. *Digital Arts: An Introduction to New Media*. New York: Bloomsbury.

Kerpen, Dave. 2011. *Likeable Social Media: How to Delight Your Customers, Create an Irresistible Brand, and Be Generally Amazing on Facebook (and Other Social Networks)*. New York: McGraw-Hill.

Kociemba, David. 2010. "This Isn't Something I Can Fake": Reactions to Glee's Representations of Disability. Transformative Works and Cultures, 5.http://journal.transformativeworks.org/index.php/twc/article/viewArticle/225/185. Accessed 19 Aug 2013.

Lewis, Justin. 1991. *The Ideological Octopus: An Exploration of Television and its Audience*. New York, NY: Routledge.

Lonergan, Patrick. 2016. *Theatre & Social Media*. London: Palgrave Macmillan.

Lovett, John. 2011. *Social Media Metrics Secrets*. Hoboken, NJ: Wiley.

Mackrell, Judith. 2012. Dancing with the Digits. *The Sydney Morning Herald*, 2 August 2012. http:///www.smh.com.au/digital-life-news/dancing-with-the-digits-20120802-23hrt.html. Accessed 19 Aug 2013.

Mandell, Jonathan. 2013. Social Media on Stage: Theater Meets Twitter, Facebook, Youtube, Tumbler, Soundcloud. *New York Theater*, 3 January 2013. http://newyorktheater.me/2013/01/03/social-media-on-stage-theater-meets-twitterfacebookyoutube-tumbler-soundcloud/. Accessed 27 Nov 2014.

McLuhan, Marshall. 2001/1968. *Understanding Media: The Extensions of Man*. London: Routledge.

O'Neill, Stephen. 2014. *Shakespeare and YouTube: New Media Forms of the Bard*. London: Bloomsbury.

O'Reilly, Tim. 2005. *What is Web 2.0: Design Patterns and Business Models for the Next Generation of Software*. Sebastapol: O'Reilly Media. http://oreilly.com/web2/archive/what-is-web-20.html. Accessed 19 Nov 2012.

Page, Ruth. 2012. *Stories and Social Media: Identities and Interaction*. London: Routledge.

Papagiannouli, Christina. 2014. *Political Cyberformance: The Etheatre Project*. London: Palgrave Macmillan.

Parmelee, John H., and Shannon L. Bichard. 2012. *Politics and the Twitter Revolution: How Tweets Influence the Relationship Between Political Leaders and the Public*. Lanham: Lexington Books.

Pérez-Latre, Francisco. 2013. The Paradoxes of Social Media: A Review of Theoretical Issues. In *The Social Media Industries*, ed. Alan B. Albarran, 46–59. London: Routledge.

Rumbold, Kate. 2010. From "Access" to "Creativity": Shakespeare Institutions, New Media, and the Language of Cultural Value. *Shakespeare Quarterly* 61 (3): 313–336. http://muse.jhu.edu/journals/shq/summary/v061/61.3.rumbold.html. Accessed 22 Aug 2013.

Sant, Toni. 2008. A Second Life for Online Performance: Understanding Present Developments through an Historical Context. *International Journal of Performance Arts and Digital Media* 4 (1): 69–79.

Sant, Toni. 2009. Performance in Second Life: Some Possibilities for Learning and Teaching. In *Learning and Teaching in the Virtual World of Second Life*, ed. Judith Molka-Sanielsen, and Mats Deutschmann, 145–166. Trondheim: Tapir Academic Press.

Sant, Toni. 2013. Theatrical Performance on the Internet: How Far Have We Come Since Hamnet? *International Journal of Performance Arts and Digital Media* 9 (2): 247–259.

Sant, Toni. 2014. Art, Performance, and Social Media. In *Routledge Handbook of Social Media*, ed. Jeremy Hunsinger, and Theresa M. Senft, 45–58. London: Routledge.

Trottier, Daniel. 2012. *Social Media as Surveillance: Rethinking Visibility in a Converging World*. Abingdon: Ashgate Publishing Group.

Trueman, Matt. 2012. Noises Off: Will Social Media Change the Face of Theatre. Theatre Blog. *The Guardian*, 16 April 2012. http://www.guardian.co.uk/stage/theatreblog/2012/apr/26/noises-off-social-media-theatre. Accessed 27 Nov 2014.

Vargas, Vivianna. 2014. The Big Merge: Internet and Theatre. *HowlRound*, 14 September 2014. https://dramalit.wordpress.com/2014/09/14/the-big-merge-internet-and-theatre/. Accessed 28 Nov 2014.

Way, Geoffrey. 2011. Social Shakespeare: Romeo and Juliet, Social Media, and Performance. *Journal of Narrative Theory* 41 (3): 401–420.

Weidner, Ashley. 2009. Social Media in Theatre. *TheatrePeople.com*, 9 August 2011. http://theatrepeople.com.au/features/social-media-theatre. Accessed 29 Nov 2014.

Worthen, William B. 2014. *Shakespeare Performance Studies*. Cambridge: Cambridge University Press.

Zarella, Dan. 2010. *The Social Media Marketing Book*. Sebastapol: O'Reilly Media.

CHAPTER 2

# Social Media: Platforms, Networks and Influences

Theatre makers have always been eager to embrace new media technologies. These include technologies that help them provoke emotion, entertain, educate or proselytise in the auditorium, as well as those that help them share their message beyond the auditorium, in posters, flyers, programmes, previews, reviews and other records. Even in the pre-modern era, when direct communication between actors and a local audience co-present in the same space was the defining feature of the theatrical experience, theatre was already a multimedia artform with image and movement being integral to its aesthetic. In the modern era, advances in light, sound and imaging technology have led theatre makers to develop new modes of communication with their audiences, including the darkened auditorium, which has become central to the Western public's perception of what theatre is. The concurrent rise of print media has seen the connection between actor, audience and community increasingly influenced by programmes, previews, reviews and other records of theatrical events. Throughout the twentieth century, as Gabriella Giannachi (2004) observes, theatre makers in forms as diverse as biomechanics, Dada, Bauhaus, Fluxus, other sorts of live art, performance art, body art, bioart, intermedia art and installation have all taken an interest in new technology, incorporating sound, light, image, music and, eventually, video and digital media to extend theatre's capacity to convey meaning in and around the auditorium.

The uptake of social media in theatre is in this respect the latest in a long line of uptakes of new technology in the theatre, and



B. Hadley, *Theatre, Social Media, and Meaning Making*,
DOI 10.1007/978-3-319-54882-1_2

as the work of Giannachi (2004) and other new media theatre theorists shows it certainly is not the only uptake of new technology in the theatre today. As a new addition to the arsenal of technologies available to theatre makers to communicate and make meaning with their many and varied audiences—fellow artists, spectators, critics, sponsors and the government, which in some economies subsidises the work—social media is the latest in a long line of technologies that have the potential to produce an evolution, if not a revolution, in theatre's ephemeral form, ecology and mechanisms for making meaning.

The best starting point for an investigation of how social media is impacting on theatre practices is to look at the communication processes or "models" that underpin social media platforms (Fiske 1990). That is the aim of this chapter. It identifies factors typically associated with the uptake of social media, the types of social media available, and the types of communications taking place on social media platforms, to establish themes and terms of reference for the discussion to come. It sheds light on the technology's affordances, and the changes in style, scope and interactivity these affordances allow, as an addition to the many technologies already deployed in theatre's communication with its audiences. It notes how these changes are starting to effect the ecosystem of theatre production, distribution and reception now and, thus, potentially in the future.

## Social Media Platforms, Applications and Affordances

As noted in the Introduction, the term "social media" can be applied to any Web 2.0 platform or application that has affordances that allow two-way communication, which is at once widely available to all but also niche and narrowcast in the sense that it can be filtered to a user's preferences. This includes but, as Ruth Page (2012, 5) notes, is "not limited to" blogs such as WordPress, microblogs such as Twitter, social networking sites such as Facebook and LinkedIn, media sharing sites such as YouTube, rating and review sites, crowdsourcing sites, and comments applications at the bottom of webpages. It includes branded platforms, as well as bespoke applications and platforms. The distinctive feature of these technologies is that they allow artists, audiences and the public at large to engage with, debate and determine the meaning of a show, a season of shows or the theatre industry as a whole. They are often called "participatory media" (Cann et al. 2011, 7) because they allow artists, audiences and the general public to participate in the creation of content, and the distribution of content, not just the reception of content. They allow participants to do this collaboratively, with all the tensions and conflicts that this can entail. This collaboration occurs in the public context of a network of friends, followers or fellow users (Page 2012, 6). As Clay Shirky contends, these collaborating "[p]articipants are different" from passive readers, viewers or spectators. "To participate is to act as if your presence matters, as if, when you see or hear something, your response is part of the event" (2008), he says.

Artists, audiences and the public at large can all use social media sites to tell their own stories about their life, work, leisure, relationships or their own reading of important social issues. "Social media platforms thus provide a space in which individuals and institutions offer performances of themselves for public consumption," as Lonergan puts it (2016, 32). But, he clarifies, "[o]ur social media identities are not just a representation of *who we think we are*, but a performance of *how we wish to be seen* by others" (30, original emphasis). Social media users deploy text, sound, images, video and a range of other formats to tell specific stories in specific ways and so, as Ruth Page (2012) says, construct a specific identity and claim to status within a social network. They tell the truth, half-truths or lies that suit what theatrically oriented social theorist Erving Goffman (1963, 1973) would call their "impression management" prerogatives. Users do this in private, semi-private or public domains. They produce and perform their beliefs, attitudes and behaviours for specialist networks of people or for more generalised networks of people. They do this well, do this poorly, or make mistakes that cause unexpected hurts, harms, controversies or crises within the networks of fellow users they connect with. They thus wittingly or unwittingly expose themselves, others or society. Their self-performances have the potential to disrupt social roles, relationships and ideas—for better or for worse.

These characteristics of social media are often defined in terms of their difference from the mass media that preceded them—"Traditional media, such as television, newspapers, radio and magazines, are one-way, static, broadcast technologies," as Dan Zarella puts it. So "[i]f you disagree with something you read in the newspaper [or see on television or on stage], you can't just send the editorial staff instant feedback" (2010, 1–2). Your role, and your response, is not immediately visible to the producer, fellow spectators or the public at large, so your presence does not really matter. With social media, by contrast, you can share your feedback with producers, fellow spectators and society, and you can also create, present and promote your own alternative content. Your role and your response is much more immediately visible. As Zarella puts it, “New web technologies have made it easy for anyone to create—and, most importantly—distribute their own content. A blog post, tweet, or You Tube video can be produced and viewed by millions virtually for free” (2).

In theory, Francisco Pérez-Latre argues, social media allows almost anyone to have “a global audience” (2013, 50). It enables almost anyone to develop an online community, which may or may not have links to offline communities, for entertainment, education, political action or whatever other purpose. “Its tools to support collaboration have existed for decades,” as David Goff notes. “But social media technologies, such as social networking [sites], wikis and blogs, enable collaboration on a much grander scale and support tapping the power of the collective in ways previously unachievable” (2013, 17). It continues the trend that, according to Daniel Schackman (2013, 106), started when technologies such as video recorders began to take control of who views what, when, where, why and how away from radio, television and film distribution networks. But it takes that trend further, allowing media industries, media makers and private individuals to post content, feedback, ratings and reviews, crowdsource ideas or sponsors, pick and choose what they want to engage with when, where, why and how, and, in doing so, feel like their presence, and the part they play, matters. The power that these applications, platforms and their affordances offer is for Paige Miller and other commentators why the uptake of social media is “staggering in comparison to [that of] users of other communication media” (2013, 86). It is why the increased uptake of social media seems, as Goff (2013, 16–17) puts it, to herald the “beginning of the end” for mass media communication, and the communication, industrial and regulatory practices that characterised it.

This emphasis on community, collaboration and participation relations means that social media is, as I noted in Chap. 1, fundamentally co-creative. People work together to produce identities, social statuses, relationships and content, and, in the process, they play a part in determining the ideas, ideologies and discourses that will come to be dominant in the public sphere.

For this reason, John Dowling (2001, 202) argues, many commentators have cast social media platforms as a sort of contemporary “agora” or public sphere. As Asa Briggs and Peter Burke (2009) have noted, all new media contribute to the construction of the public sphere, and have done since the earliest emergence of new media technology, which tends, in media studies history, to be tied to the emergence of the printing press more than 500 years ago. All types of media contribute to the construction of a space—conceptual, as much as concrete—where, as Christopher Balme puts it, "private citizens [can] engage in debate on issues of public interest" (2014, ix). In Jürgen Habermas's initial and still influential theorisation (1962/1989), the public sphere is an open, participatory, public domain in which all people can contribute to the construction of the dominant ideas that come to be taken up by state institutions. Habermas (1989, 221) argued that after a shift from a feudal public sphere, where familial relations provided a few people with the right to participate in debate, to a more critical public sphere, where the capacity to make rational comment on an issue provided more people with the right to participate in debate, twentieth-century citizens were witnessing a dumbing down of that rational debate as a result of modern mass media. He sought to reclaim the public sphere for rational, critical, consensus-building debate. His formulation was, though, too utopian and too reluctant to recognise the inequities in access to public debate for most contemporary theorists (Briggs and Burke 2009, 6). Today, commentators tend to talk of the public sphere in terms of plural public spheres, plural counter-public spheres, developed and maintained among groups that share affinities based on gender, sexuality, race or ability. For commentators who are interested in access to public debate for all, in counter-public spheres, or more complex networks of public spheres, social media is important. It is seen as part of the paradigm of alternative or radical media that, as Dowling puts it, "express[es] an alternative vision to hegemonic policies, priorities, and perspectives" (2001, v). It allows a wider range of contributors to access communication channels, and, more importantly, circumvent the blocks and barriers that elite, establishment and mass media puts in place to maintain control of traditional communication channels. It thus allows more and more diverse people to become active players in public debate, not mere passive recipients of what Antonio Gramsci (1982) calls the hegemony, undermining the hegemony's ability to control the circulation of ideas (Dowling 2001, 8–9).

As I noted in Chap. 1, although understandable, this enthusiasm for social media as an alternative, radical or anti-authoritarian media does have to be tempered with a realisation of its realities. As Dowling warns, "although some Internet enthusiasts have hyped its democratic essence, we need to retain caution, thinking of its potential in this regard as partially realized but also as constantly in danger of being foreclosed" (2001, 202). Online media, including online social media, are like any alternative media. They are always interwoven with elite and mass media in the policy, industrial and production environment. They are always susceptible to power plays from individuals, institutions or groups looking to claim control over the ideas that dominate in a given culture at a given time. In this sense, although social media may be more open, active and anonymous than other media, this does not mean that it is more reliable, or more resistant to power plays, perspectivality, partiality, decay and conflict. These issues are highlighted by the increasing presence of corporate interests, vocal minorities, thieves, mischief makers and trolls online. Although the initial development of the internet may, as Tim Jordan (1999, 45) notes, have been driven by grassroots communities as much as by the military industrial complex, the forces of capitalism, commercialism and consumerism have played a major part in its development since that time, including in the development of social media as a new defining feature of the internet's functionings. As Stephen O'Neill suggests, though a social media site such as YouTube, Facebook or Twitter present itself "as a community-based network that encourages self-expression, the site's function as a user-generated technology is enabled by its political economy (as evidenced by its dependence on advertising, promotion of industry content and commercial partnerships)" (2014, 13). There are, as a result, many who critique any tendency to fall prey to claims about social media's democratic potential without considering the issues of access, authority, power, status, gatekeeping, privacy, intellectual property and so forth that put social media's potential democratic promise in danger of being foreclosed as swiftly as that of any other media (Carr 2010; Keen 2007). As Pérez-Latre (2013, 50) observes, many of the issues "already existed in analogue media", but they are amplified in these new digital media platforms, and thus also need to be part of any modelling of communication practices that take place through them.

## Social Networks and Networking

The potentials and potential challenges of social media come out of the "networking" at the core of its technological and social characteristics. Though different social media platforms function differently, they are all defined by a network structure of one sort or another. They are set up to help facilitate the personal, social or professional networks—in this study, theatre community networks—that are, as theorists such as Manuel Castells (2001) argue, so critical to success in life today.

In studies of social media networks, the relationships between individuals, organisations and institutions that a social actor can leverage to their advantage on a platform are usually mapped on a hub-and-spoke model which shows the centres, clusters and outskirts of power in a network. In social media, social actors are represented in profiles and posts, and the links, likes, friends or follows that they use to connect with others. The purpose of social media networks—like other human networks—is to inform, communicate, empower, encourage collaborations between or, in some cases, challenge the opinions of other players in the network (Rainie and Wellman 2012). In social media theory, the social actor, or the user, is seen as a "node" that has "ties" with other users, which may be "weak ties" or "strong ties". When many users form ties, they create a "cluster", "hub" or community, which can be "centralised" (if it involves a limited set of people, who share a limited set of characteristics, who come together, but have few ties or "bridges" out to other types of users and communities) or "decentralised" (if there are a lot of ties or "bridges" out to other communities). Though the nature of online networks differs, they are, as Bell (2001, 94) argues, often thought to be more akin to what Ferdinand Tönnies (1955) would call *Gesellschaft*, the temporary communities of association that come about in cities that people have to work hard to turn into true communities of affinity, than to what he would call *Gemeinschaft*, the traditional communities in small towns where family, feudal or other longstanding relationships establish connections and mutual obligations from the start. Though family, friends and direct coworkers might form the basis of a user's earliest connections on a social media platform, these tend to expand quickly, to incorporate a much wider set of connections that a user can call on to acquire social, cultural or financial capital.

Functioning in this way, social media networks are subject to the same powerplays seen in any human network. In any analysis of social media networks, it is immediately clear that different users develop a different status, and thus develop a different level of ability to succeed in achieving their aims via the network. In general networking theory, the different roles or statuses that a social actor can hold in a network are already well recognised. Toby Stuart and Olav Sorenson (2007, 212), for example, suggest that status in a network is influenced by an actor's reliability in terms of the information they share, their position as a regular sharer at the centre of the network rather than someone out at the outskirts, their willingness to reciprocate with fellow users who want to give or get help within the network, their trustworthiness, their credibility, their reputation and whether or not they have been subject to sanctions for failing to uphold the relationships within the networks. This means that some actors in a network are seen as authoritative, credible, likeable and ready to reciprocate with others—without giving away all their valuable insights, information and connections for no return—and have high status. Others are not—and, indeed, may even "burn bridges" as a result of bad behaviour—and have low status. Each of these permutations results in a change to the level of what Robert Putnam (1995) calls social capital—the trusting, reciprocal relationships that can be leveraged to advantage—that a social actor holds in a network. In social media theory, these phenomena are typically talked about in terms of influence, influencers and the idea that some successful social media actors become "influencers" (Wong 2014)—that is, the idea that some successful users act as hubs around which clusters or communities come to exist in the network, and hold sway over others in the network. This is a status that can be achieved in a range of ways—for example, by broadcasting information, communicating information, commenting on it, or advocating for or against it, amongst other strategies (Klout 2012).

In marketing-oriented social media theory, discussion of influencers is particularly prevalent. Influencers are cast as respected players within a network, be it personal, professional, social or interest-based, without much reflection on how they come to have that status or power. These influencers are seen to have the power to circulate their opinion widely, create opinions and convince others in the network to adopt those opinions, in politics, relationships or purchasing decisions. The presumed capacity of influencers to drive opinion and purchasing decisions is co-opted as part of social media marketing strategy, in the performing arts as in other industries (Wong 2014). It is seen, for example, in the use of "ambassador" programmes in which mainstage theatre companies give students free tickets if they will comment on the show to try to "influence" their peers to attend. The power attributed to influencer-based social media marketing is the focus of most industry-based guides on the use of social media to attract audiences (e.g. Albarran 2013; Anderson 2010; Berger 2012; Brogan 2010; Handley and Chapman 2012; Kerpen 2011;

Zarella 2010), and, as a result, central to the approaches to audience development that I discuss in Chap. 5. Although the dollar value of what is given in the theatre industry is low—it rarely goes beyond the dollar value of the free ticket—in other industries the value of celebrities or customers becoming brand ambassadors is recognised in larger payments or sponsorship. The hope for the companies is that their recommendations will "go viral" (Nahon and Hemsley 2013) and thus give their opinion (in a political, social or aesthetic context) or their product (in a commercial context) a boost in and across markets. The importance of this aspect of social media networks and networking has seen open-source software such as Wolfham (which visualises Facebook networks), Socilab (which visualises LinkedIn networks), Mentionmapp (which visualises Twitter networks) and Gephi (which visualises a range of more complex networks across social media) emerge to allow even casual users, artists, arts workers and arts organisations to map influence within their networks.

Critical social media theorists such as Henry Jenkins (2009), Jenkins et al. (2013) are more suspicious of the power of influencers. As Eytan Bakhsy et al. (2011) have noted in a study of Twitter, the hype about the strategies that influencers use to become superconnected, high status and high value is not necessarily backed up by concrete evidence of their capacity to change minds. Indeed, they suggest that content that goes viral via social media is in fact more often started by a regular user, and then a critical mass of regular users, so such individuals often have more impact than celebrities. These critical theorists acknowledge the powerplays and manipulations that come into play in these processes, including how easy it is for people to jump on the bandwagon of an opinion or a product they do not completely understand. It is a phenomenon I discuss further in Chap. 4, on the uptake of social media platforms for critical response to performances, including in some cases by spectators who have not seen those performances live.

With these issues in mind, social media theorists regularly return to networking theory to show the ways in which complex, fast-changing relationships on social media can fall prey to fluctuations, manipulations, powerplays, flows and blockages. They note issues that can create what David Holmes (1997a, b) has called "anomalies of digital reciprocity", where behaviours that bring results in offline networks do not bring the same results in online networks. On the one hand, social media does promote both direct and non-direct reciprocity. As Martin Nowak (2011, 51–67), Alex Bentley and collaborators (2011) and others note, whereas, historically, human beings have been more likely to help those they have a direct relation or tie to, on social media sites, helping strangers is a norm. This happens in gaming, mummy blogger and, of course, certain professional communities. For example, in Australia there is the "Drama Peeps" (i.e. "Drama Peoples") group on Facebook, which regularly sees help afforded to fellow drama teachers whether they have ties or not. On the other hand, social media does involve a lot of non-reciprocation too. In a professional context, users can put a lot of effort into leveraging weak ties through social media, sharing valuable information to show authority, amiability and value as a collaborator, with no guarantee that this will be seen, or reciprocated, or produce the same results as in an offline network (Granovetter 1973). In online networks there is a larger range of people, issues and ideas competing for attention. These flow by in a feed so fast that there is less than 10s to get the attention of the audience (Crunch.net 2014). Contributions can be missed, particularly if they come from those who, as a result of their social background or ability, or other factors, cannot convey their message according the rules of such a fast-moving format (they do not have the bandwidth to present very visual posts, they do not have the visual ability to create or receive text embedded in visuals, etc.). There is scope for mistakes, misreadings, controversies and conflicts, as well as consensus building, as I discuss in the chapters to come. There is also often a suspicion that people are taking advantage of the psuedonymity, anonymity or opportunities for overtly constructed self-performance, which online as opposed to offline communications make possible, to present themselves as something they are not, or as doing something they are not.

In the theatre industry the archetypal example of an "anomaly of digital reciprocity" is the "Yes, I will attend" button on Facebook event pages, an RSVP function that fails to align with actual attendance at a theatre event at all. Clearly there are others, which will emerge in the chapters to come. In this context it is easy to see how a theatre maker could share their time, expertise and ideas with fellow users, only to find that these users forget where the ideas that sparked a conversation came from, forget which friend shared content to create a buzz around it, or take advantage of friends' ideas without disclosing when, where and how they will be used. In other words, that these users never reward or reciprocate the value that has been given. Indeed, if networking theorists such as Breda McCarthy (2006) are correct, theatre makers can be particularly susceptible to this problem. In the performing arts the project-by-project nature of the work means that people quickly start behaving as if they trust each other, a swiftness that may or may not benefit them in the longer term. The increasing importance of social media as a tool for artist-to-artist, artist-to-audience and audience-to-audience communication in and around the theatre industry, as in other industries, can make the process of judging one's place in a network—what one is giving, what one is getting and whether it is worth it—more difficult. Accordingly, though McCarthy (2006) does not write about social media networks, her research suggests that theatre makers should consider their place in such networks with a more critical eye to avoid personal, social or professional disappointments. Failure to take account of the anomalies and challenges that characterise social media communications can lead to confusion, frustration and a sense of failure.

Mapping out how social media platforms work, and how success and failure on such platforms typically plays out, is thus necessary to contextualise the discussion of theatre practice to come—to set up the themes and terms of reference before proceeding to an analysis of shows, attempts to engage new audiences, successes and failures in specific uptakes of social media in theatre.

## Types of Social Media

There are dozens of different social media platforms, applications and technologies. Indeed, there are dozens of platforms that have already come and gone as the field has evolved in just the first decade since its emergence. There are generalist platforms for mixed communities. There are specialist platforms for specific communities, such as professionals, or daters or gamers. There are platforms that incorporate a lot of features. For example, Facebook includes blogging, chat and media sharing functions. There are platforms that are oriented to a single specific feature. For example, Instagram is primarily for pictures, while YouTube is primarily for videos. There are also platforms that allow users to download applications that in themselves meet the definition of social media in their ability to supportuser connections (Henderson et al. 2013, 54–57). For instance, although Facebook does not pitch itself primarily as a games platform, there are games that users can download, usually made by outside developers rather than the Facebook developers.

A summary of the main sorts of social media that have emerged since the late 1990s would include at least a dozen distinct types of

**Table 2.1** Types of social media platforms

| *Type/orientation of site* | *Examples* |
|---|---|
| Personal communication and networking | Microblogs, blogs, social networking sites (e.g. Twitter, Facebook, WordPress, Blogger, Mashable, Weibo) |
| Professional communication and networking | Social networking sites (e.g. LinkedIn, Google+) |
| Real-time communication and conferencing | Text, visual, video conversation sites (e.g. Skype, Snapchat) |
| Content collaboration | Document and project-management sites (e.g. Googledocs, Dropbox, Basecamp) |
| Content curation | Tagging, bookmarking, pinboarding and Wiki sites (e.g. Wikipedia, Instagram, Pinterest, Delicious, Tumbler) |
| Content presentation and sharing | Live or delayed sharing/streaming sites and apps in sites (e.g. YouTube, Vimeo, Flickr) |
| Publishing | Text-sharing sites (e.g. Scribed) |
| Location tracking | Geomapping sites and apps in sites (e.g. Foursquare) |
| News, reviews and ratings | Reviewing sites [e.g. Reddit, Digg, Buzzfeed, Yelp, TripAdvisor, Zomato (formerly Urbanspoon)] |
| Virtual worlds | Games, simulations (e.g. Second Life, Sims, World of Warcraft) |
| Crowdsourcing | Pledging sites (e.g. Pozzible, Kickstarter) |
| Petitioning | Petition sites (e.g. Change.org) |
| Dating and relationships | Dating sites (e.g. Tinder, Grinder, MeetUp) |

platform—for blogging, microblogging, social networking, content sharing, content curation, reviewing, rating, gaming and a range of other purposes within their respective communities (see Table 2.1).

In general, use of social media sites is on the rise. In a 2015 survey, Duggan and collaborators found that the use of such sites by American adults is rising. Facebook is still most popular, with some 70% of adults using it, along with nearly 30% of adults on LinkedIn, Pinterest or Instagram, and just a little over 20% on Twitter. More than half of these users were using more than one social media site too (2015). For many, usage is daily, or near daily—for instance, 70% of the overall 70% of adults using Facebook log in daily (2015), while for more specialist sites, such as LinkedIn, logins tend to be less frequent.

Clearly Table 2.1 does not offer a complete list of social media sites, their functions and their usage statistics. Social media site availability is changing constantly—in the branded sites, in the more bespoke sites that some organisations create for themselves, and in the way they allow integration between them. What the list does show, though, is that although Facebook has been the star performer (Trottier 2012, 15), there are many different social media sites doing many different things—from communication and networking to content creation, curation and sharing—for many different communities. While it is not possible to consider all of these in detail, it is possible to say that they are evolving as a result of technological factors, and as a result of human factors, all the time. These evolutions in uptake and practice are, Geoffrey Way explains, "shaped by two separate yet intertwined aspects: a site's technological constraints and active members practices and culture" (2011). Some have become so prominent that they have been the subject of whole books—for instance those by Parmalee and Bickard (2012) on Twitter, Trottier (2012) on Facebook and O'Neill (2014) on YouTube. Some are based on synchronous communication and some on asynchronous communication. Some are based on short form, fast communication and some on longer forms. Some are widely adopted and some are exclusive. Some are tied to offline communities and some are online only. The practices and relationships that users pursue on these sites are diverse, dependent on lifestyle, life stage and other factors. There are some users who are on one site, and others who are on many, as suits their purpose and their attempts to communicate with personal, social or professional networks. For instance, while up to 70% of adult users mainly network through Facebook, there are also up to 30% of users who network through Facebook and through Twitter, Pinterest, Quora or other sites too. There are users who have one main site and replicate content across their more peripheral sites. There are users who link all their sites and others who keep them separate. There are users who post regularly and prolifically and those who post only rarely. There are users who follow a lot of fellow posters and some who follow only a few. For instance, a famous actor on Twitter may post updates to a lot of followers but may not follow them back. There are users who post mainly personal content and users who post mainly advertisements, endorsements or entreaties to try a product, along with others who post a combination of the two. There are users who use one name or handle only, and some who use multiple names or handles for various personal, social and professional communications on various sites for various communities. There are users who engage with social media platforms mainly on their personal computer, or mainly on their work computer, or mainly on their mobile devices, or on a combination of the three. There are users who move from platform to platform as their lifestyle and life stage changes, or as the status of the platform changes. For instance, a theatre maker on maternity leave may start engaging more people across more platforms more frequently, or in more different ways, to maintain networks while having or minding the children at home. The media platforms themselves also constantly evolve, based on the platform creators' preferences, the app creators' preferences, the advertisers' preferences, the users' preferences, adoption and abandonment patterns, as well as technological, social, political and economic changes. This is what Nancy Baym calls the "shared behaviours" by which "norms of practice are displayed, reinforced, negotiated and taught" (2010, 80). Platforms also change as a result of less predictable controversies, concerns over privacy, mistaken performances of personal, social or professional identity, or other incidents. Or as a result of activists, rights groups, political groups, criminal groups, or terrorist groups—from citizen journalists to jihadists—using the platforms in unpredictable ways. Or as a result of a policy maker, parent, teacher or other advocacy group pressure to open up or shut down particular usage options and patterns. In this sense the technologies and the users exist in mutually productive relationships. "The successful new applications are" therefore, at least according to Way, "those that provide enough structure to render the ritual intelligible while allowing enough flexibility to be appropriate by the users" (2010).

## Succeeding and Failing on Social Media

Together, identification of the issues typically associated with uptake of social media, the social media available today and the behaviours that users participate in on social media allows mapping of some of its common traits—from immediacy, brevity, simultaneity and sociability to the ability to circulate content into new contexts, or to the ability to create memes that seem to take on their own life—onto a communication model. As Brent Ruben and Lea Stewart (1998) have shown, communication modelling began with efforts such as Shannon and Weaver's simple "INFORMATION SOURCE—TRANSMITTER—(Signal)—CHANNEL—(Signal)—DESTINATION model", with "NOISE SOURCE" added below to indicate factors that might stop a message from moving smoothly from source to destination, or from sender to receiver (Shannon and Weaver 1949/1989). Others subsequently added additional concepts to indicate factors that might help or hinder transmission of a message, including audience, context, field, redundancy and entropy. They created what John Fiske (1990) characterises as increasingly complex models to try to capture the complexity of human communication. Based on the analysis of social media

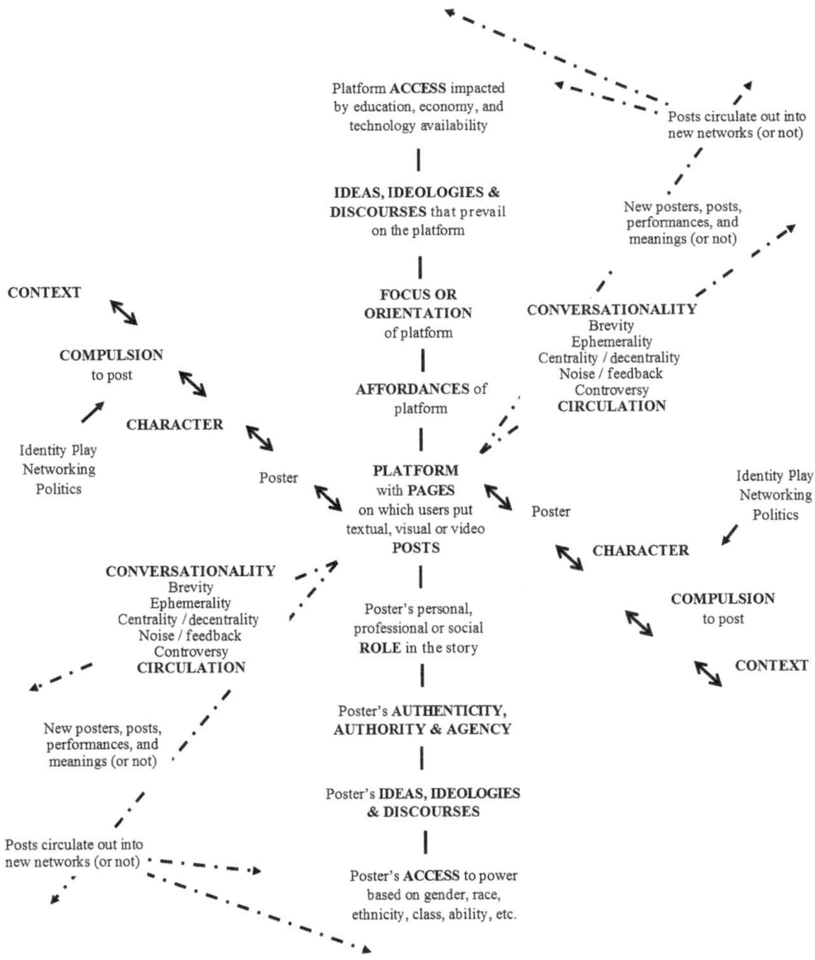


**Fig. 2.1** Communication on social media platforms

platforms' features, and using the format and features common to these historical communication models, a basic model of communication via social media might include the features in Fig. 2.1 above.

Although basic, this model already shows a host of factors that can influence communication on social media, success and failures.

## Context

The first factor that influences communication success on social media is context—or, more accurately, as Alice Marwick and dana boyd (2011) articulate it, the audience that users imagine they are speaking to via a social media platform. One of the distinctive features of social media platforms is their capacity to cross boundaries between online and offline contexts, and between personal, social and professional contexts, so that communications that might once have been shared only with one group of acquaintances in one context become visible to a lot of acquaintances in a lot of contexts. This "context collapse" (2011) phenomenon occurs because, for most users, there will be a combination of family, friends, colleagues and acquaintances in their "friend" or "follower" network. They forget who is in this network. They also forget what sort of privacy settings have been set up to filter the flow of information to whoever is in this network. Moreover, there is no way to control who is in a friend's "friend" network, or a friend's friend's "friend" network, and so on. This can cause problems as users' performance of personal or social identity becomes visible to professional networks, or vice versa.

In the theatre industry, this can happen via posts about companies that produce poor quality shows, are slow to pay, are nepotistic or otherwise problematic. These comments might be fine at a backyard barbeque among family and friends but not in a foyer in front of the general and marketing managers of that theatre company. Even in cases where a user believes they have limited their network to social friends, it only takes one to circulate a comment to professional contexts and cause problems. For instance, at the Matilda Awards for Theatre in Brisbane, Australia, in 2010, a theatre maker took offence at a portion of one year's show—a physical theatre company, the Brides of Frank, performed a masturbatory action with giant cardboard scissors in a scene commenting on concepts of female domesticity—only to see a "friend" copy it across to the public and then popular Our Brisbane Theatre Blog run by local playwright

Katherine Lyall Watson. For a day or two it was a talking point, after which other news pushed it from people's minds. Though the incident passed quickly, it had the potential to have a lasting impact on the reputation and relations of those involved. This blurring of personal, social and professional identity and context happens on social media in ways that were not possible on previous media platforms. It thus influences when, where, why, how and what users will post on social media, particularly in a small industry such as the theatre industry, because prompts to post coming from one context may not align with prohibitions to posting in other contexts, and social media can make it challenging to separate and balance the two.

## Compulsion to Post

The next factor that influences communication success on social media is compulsion to post. This can come from ideas, issues, incidents or things to share from a user's personal, social, professional or political life. Users will post to perform their identity, socialise, gossip, play, gain status in a social group, share or seek information about personal, social, professional, political or other issues, or to sell products. In the example above, the theatre maker took offence at a provocative image, which prompted him to post, and his motivation came mainly from a personal desire to share concern, frustration and something of his own values with his friends. The perceived motivation for the post changed when a "friend" circulated the post more widely, and social and professional reputation became the prompts to post rejoinders to a wider network. For some theatre artists, the personal compulsion to post is clearly strong, and they can post five, ten or more times in a day. For others, the personal compulsion to post is not strong, and they may post weekly, monthly or even less frequently as professional responsibilities for staging, promoting or assessing a work demand. Regularity, visibility and contribution to a network's shared conversations are considered to be factors in success. For those posting mainly as a result of professional motivators, the likelihood of accidentally sparking controversy by sharing too much personal opinion in a "collapsed" personal, social and professional context is typically less, though more sporadic posting can cause other problems.

## Character While Posting

The next factor that influences communication success on social media is to do with character while posting. The character or identity that a user performs while posting can be personal, social or professional, depending on what prompts them to post. The user can take on the role of a new member in the network, or an outsider asking a question, asking for information or looking to form a relationship. The user can take on the role of an experienced member in the network, an insider providing information, or a hub for the flow of information. They can be a protagonist, antagonist, or bystander in the story that the post tells—for instance, the protagonist of a story in which they tell of a job they are auditioning for, the antagonist of a story in which they tell of a show they did not like or a bystander to a story in which they recount something they overheard in a foyer. Complex relations between Is, yous, wes and theys can evolve. For theorists of identity performance on social media, Toni Sant notes (2014, 49), Erving Goffman's (1963, 1973) use of theatrical terminology to investigate social self-performance, impression management and backstage preparation for performance are useful in understanding some of the complexities of communicating online. Indeed, investigating social self-performance online has become among the more popular areas of research into social media (Baym 2010; Page 2012; Pearson 2009). "In picking a username on social media sites," Sant argues, "most people don't think they are creating a fictional character but a version of themselves that is close to their true self, or at least an image of themselves they have for themselves and/or want others to see" (Sant 2014, 49). In theatre there is a greater tendency to fictionalise, for professional purposes, even before theatre makers start embodying characters on social media in the online performances that I consider in Chap. 3. Many theatre makers cultivate characters in their online communications. For instance, comedians cultivate cynical, silly or "stupid me" characters, burlesque artists strong, sexy, sex-positive characters, disability and transgender performance artists strong, resilient and politicised characters and so forth. Many also give more or less constructed insights into what Goffman (1973) would call the backstage components of their professional identity (training, rehearsals, auditions and other behind-the-show aspects of the theatre industry) online. For example, some artists use social media sites as a sort of creative journal, documenting their work in progress, and their twists, turns, discoveries and disappointments. Less frequently, theatre makers will perform a character from a show, as well as their own constructed character as comedian or artist or critic, on their social media profiles.

As Sant notes, "to create a fictional character online, especially one intended to deceive others that this is not a role-play, is an exercise in what performance theorist Richard Schechner (2002) calls 'dark play'" (Sant 2014, 49; cf. Schechner 2002). It raises the stakes, complexity and uncertainty of self-performance online. Whatever the motivation—whether it is for impression management, networking or what in much social media theory today is talked about in terms of personal or professional branding Kelly (2010)—self-performance seen online is not always stably aligned with the self-performances seen offline. This means that maintaining even the thinnest of fictions in an online context can be challenging, and become more so when it comes to the sorts of fictions the artists I consider in Chap. 3 attempt to create in their social media performances.

Many social media guides encourage theatre makers to build a strong personal and professional brand—via their profile, their posts, the fellow users they link to—to better their chances of becoming an "influencer" online (Kerpen 2011). Like any brand, it should be clear, consistent and appealing but at the same time differentiated from others users so there are clear reasons to connect and co-create with this over other superficially similar brands (Ries and Ries 2002, 7). In practical terms, this means a consistent name and a complete profile on the platforms that best suit a theatre maker's purpose, as well as sending out "catchy" snippets of information (cf. Kawasaki and Fitzpatrick 2014). In reputational terms, this means demonstrating credibility, engagingness, enthusiasm and other socially valued traits (Nowak 2011). In the theatre industry, where "portfolio careers" that see a person working in multiple and at times conflicting career roles are the norm (Bridgstock 2011), and creating fictional characters online may be necessary at some points too, this can be challenging. Performance problems—portraying an identity, brand or image other than intended, particularly when messages to one imagined audience get mixed up with messages to another—can become an issue (Marwick 2010; Marwick and Boyd 2011). As I have argued elsewhere (Hadley 2014), when it comes to the performative construction of identity—online or offline—the characteristics audiences project onto theatre makers are as important, if not more important, as the characteristic the theatre makers themselves attempt to project out to the audience. Users need to understand their audiences, and, while open-source visualisation tools such as Gephi might tell them the basics about who and how many these are, they can never capture their full detail and diversity.

## Conversational Appeal of Posts

The next factor that influences communication success on social media is the conversational appeal of the content that a user-become-producer posts. As noted, a user needs to share short, sharp, appealing content to become an "influencer" in a context where the time available to attract attention is limited (Crunch.net 2014; Handley and Chapman 2014; Kawasaki and Fitzpatrick 2014). The optimal length of posts can range from less than 50 words on Twitter to more than 100 on Facebook, then less than 1500 words on WordPress, less than 2 min on YouTube and less than 20 min on Ted Talks or other podcasts. Increasingly, having visual content is seen as being critical to one's success as an "influencer" on social media (Moritz 2013).

Technical factors, together with human factors such as contemporaneousness, clarity, length and the types of interaction that users on a platform favour, all influence the appeal of a post. On the technical side, the availability of the platform to users from different educational, economic or geographic backgrounds, the affordances and features of the platform, and the discourses, ideologies and moralities that prevail on the platform can all influence whether a post will or will not be appealing enough to start a conversation. For instance, for users in countries where the autoplay function that Facebook currently puts on video posts does not work well as a result of limited bandwidth, for instance, it can be frustrating rather than fun to see a snippet of a show. On the human side, the character telling the story, the part they play in the story, their proximity to the core of the story, their claims to the agency, authority and authenticity to tell the story, their status, and their familiarity with the discourses, registers and genres typically used to tell such a story can all influence whether a post will or will not be appealing. This is influenced by gender, race, class, ability and other identity markers. As Page argues in her analysis of social media and storytelling, "although social media is collaborative, this does not mean that all discursive contributions are equal, and that the burden of story is evenly distributed between multiple participants" (2012, 12). If a user cannot participate fully because of personal factors such as disability, economic factors such as lack of access to bandwidth, or political factors such as suspicion that posting specific content will have consequences, this will impact on their agency on social media.

In one recent episode, for example, the media reported that a main-stage theatre company, the Queensland Theatre Company, was cutting a joke out of *Australia Day*, the play opening its 2013 season, for political reasons. Many users commented on the media reports, but the appeal of their comments differed depending on whether or not they were posting as an actor in the rehearsal room. Those at the core of the incident, with greater claims to authority to tell about it, became the hubs of the conversation, with their posts having more appeal than those of people on the peripheries of the incident. This appeal was, of course, influenced by the content of their posts. If they had been posting about more mundane matters, such as the quality of the coffee in the rehearsal room, the fact that they had a strong claim to authority to tell still would not be enough to make their posts appealing. Here, the slightly scandalous content was appealing, but, at the same time, some of the social actors with the greatest authority to post also clearly felt constrained in what they could say while in the employment of the company in question. As this example shows, on the content side, mundanity, importance, controversy and scandal all impact on a post's appeal. Page (2012, 11) talks about these factors in terms of tellership, tellability and the moral stance of a post, and cites these as features that can raise or reduce appeal. Certain combinations of tellers, stories told, from specific character positions, or contextual positions, in more or less open, exciting or scandalous ways can lead to more or less success in creating a post with conversational and, as a consequence, circulatory appeal—a factor that impacts on critical response to performances online of the sort that I consider in Chap. 4.

## Circulatory Appeal of Posts

The next factor that influences communication success on social media is the circulatory appeal of posts—that is, the degree to which liking them, sharing them and sending them on to others to create an ongoing conversations appeals to users. Social media sites may be spaces in which people perform their own identities but, as Patrick Lonergan argues, successful self-performance online depends not just on what a user posts but on "the connections that [they] have forged with others"

(Lonergan 2016, 3). On social media platforms, a content-based broadcast approach alone does not work—users expect that multiple voices, including their own, will be an integral part of the communication. As Jonathan Gray puts it, "Users in *Web 2.0* expect interaction," and look for "information exchange rather than purely linear information dissemination" (2012). Content that does not create opportunities for conversation is not likely to get the circulation from user to user, network to network, platform to platform—the going viral—that typically characterises success on these platforms.

This means social media—unlike past computer-mediated communication platforms—is characterised by ephemeral, open-ended and at times uncertain circulation of posts. This is what makes modelling the communication that takes place on them so complex. "Using these parameters," Page explains,

> we might judge the structural narrativity of social media stories to contrast with canonical examples of literary narrative or spoken narrative elicited in interview situations. For example, the episodic, ongoing nature of a sequence of blog entries or an archive of Facebook updates in [*sic*] not organized around a predetermined, single end point. (Page 2012, 10)

Some posts circulate in current contexts, to current communities of users, and so continue to be the subject of communication/conversation among that set of users. Other posts circulate out into new contexts, and new communities, and so become the subject of communication/conversation among those new sets of users too. Such posts can circulate again and again without a fixed end point to the narrative or the dramaturgy that drives the narrative. In this sense, Tom Abba argues, "digital media offer the potential for content to be transported from their original form and be reconstituted to new ends in a networked ecology" (2009). A post with high circulatory appeal can build new networks, with new participants, new performances and new meanings, and it can even become disconnected from its initial context, and then develop a new purpose, performance structure or meaning in a new context. In 2009, for instance, a group of Australian theatre makers used social media to protest the lack of opportunities for women in the "boys club" Australian theatre industry. The issue that sparked anger on this occasion was the launch of the 2010 season at Company B at Belvoir

Street Theatre in Sydney, along with the ongoing practice of other mainstage theatres, such as the Melbourne Theatre Company, to employ few or no women directors in their mainstage programmes. Discussions on the Australian Women's Directors alliance blog (www.australianwomendirectorsalliance.blogspot.com.au/) and on other blogs, such as *Theatre Notes* (theatrenotes.blogspot.com) and *7-On Playwrights* (sevenon.blogspot.com.au), together with a roundtable at the annual Philip Parsons Memorial Lecture on the topic (*Australian Stage* 2009; *Australian Plays* 2009), culminated in mainstream press coverage (Abela et al. 2009; Bailey 2009; Collins 2009; Usher 2009a, b), including international coverage (Wilkinson 2009), that went on for some years (*The Australian* 2012; Borland 2010; Elkin and Harper-Cross 2012; Hobson 2014; Neutze 2014c; Supple 2011). The complaints, which began with one group of women in one network, circulated out to new users in new parts of the country, and even in new contexts, as this theatre industry issue met with other similar issues in legal, political and academic industries. The all-in participation in the social and news media debate made them impactful enough to prompt the Australia Council for the Arts to commission Elaine Lally and Sarah Miller to report and recommend new policy on the topic (Frew 2012; Lally and Miller 2012). This in turn encouraged mainstage theatre companies—despite their initial instinct to cite as defence issues in training, development and independent practice before directors develop the profile to be part of mainstage programming as defences—to look at their programming. These phenomena can also happen offline as gossip circulates through the theatre industry. With social media, though, the technology, affordances and interactivities are set up to privilege this sort of circulation from the start, and are in fact a definition of the success of a post.

Great circulation—going viral—is considered to be a good thing in social media communication precisely because it can bring these outcomes. However, it is both easy and difficult to achieve: easy in the sense that the platforms are based on network structures, with hubs and spokes that connect to other hubs, other spokes and so on; difficult in the sense that posts are brief and ephemeral, swiftly heading to the bottom of the feed where they will not be visited again in a crowded, noisy, communication context. If posts do not have high conversational or circulatory appeal, are one-offs or lack feedback from other users, the chances of them being seen, shared and circulated are minimal. The nature of the platforms means that users look only at what is being posted, liked or shared largely synchronously. This means that less successful posts can disappear before they start to circulate because they have been overtaken by more appealing posts. In a social media context, a post needs the right combination of the factors outlined here to capture attention, cultivate circulatory appeal and radiate out into networks. Though old material is archived, and can come back to bite a user if it is controversial in nature, it is not a normal feature of a user's engagement with social media, and in most cases day old content has already lost its currency and will not be considered again.

With these factors in mind, the barriers to successful communication via social media platforms become clear, particularly if success is defined—by a person, a community or a company trying to promote its shows or seasons—in terms of massive numbers of likes, shares and circulations. Each time a user posts, they are dealing with a range of different adoption patterns among other users, filters, format issues, as well as appeal factors within an overcrowded economy of supply and demand, reliability issues, relatability issues, and netiquette dilemmas. They are dealing with the risk of making mistakes as they try to communicate in a crowded, multimedia, multichannel and multicommunity context. In some communities and contexts they are also dealing with the risk of coming into contact or conflict with trolls, mischief makers or anonymous players with agendas to push. Together, these factors all impact on the success of uptake of social media in theatre's aesthetic, management, marketing, audience development or critical activities.

## Uptake of Social Media in Theatre

As the anecdotes shared here suggest, understanding the factors that influence theatre makers' choices on social media only becomes more challenging when the many different aesthetic, critical, audience development, marketing, management or assessment aims that a theatre maker might be trying to achieve—together or separately—via social media platforms are taken into account.

As noted in the Introduction, in this book I focus on the three domains in which theatre makers are making the most use of social media platforms, starting with the use of social media in the aesthetic, production and distribution domain in Chap. 3, followed by the use of social media in the critical domain in Chap. 4, and then the use of social media in the audience development domain in Chap. 5.

The possibilities that social media provides in the aesthetic domain of theatre practice are very varied. They range from the uptake of social media as a topic, or impetus for textual, dramaturgical or design features of a performance, or a tool for workshopping, devising and developing new work, to use of social media to document, disseminate or archive plays and performances, and to use of social media to create what I will describe in Chap. 3 as remote, immersive, telematic, virtual, networked and participatory performances in online or offline public spaces and places. Though each of these uses slightly different two-way interactive technology, in slightly different ways, the emphasis tends to be on the potential that these technologies have to engage spectators in different stagings and restagings of reality in different ways. To engage spectators in plays being performed on the other side of the world—for instance, via programmes such as the National Theatre's well-known NT Live programme in the UK, as a sort of modern scaling-up of the salon-based "theatre phones" of a century ago (Curtin 2013). To engage spectators in modern remakings of traditional performance forms, as, for instance, when the London Royal Opera House presented *Twitterdemerung: The Twitter Opera* as a people's lyric opera in 2009 (Blake 2010). To engage spectators in communities on the other side of the world—for instance, via Rimini Protokoll's well-known *Call Cutta in a Box* in 2008 where players at the Willy-Brand Haus (Berlin) and the Schauspielhaus (Zurich) were invited into a 60-min smartphone conversation with a call centre worker in Kolkata, India, walking through to the city to eventually meet with a digital projection of the worker on screen, in a reflection on identity, relationships and digitised realities in a networked work (Balme 2014). To engage spectators in activation of public space, as in *The Attendents* (2011), by Chance Muehleck and US company Nerve Tank, where spectators were asked to text or tweet to ask seven performers in a storefront cube at the World Financial Center to carry out specific actions over a six-hour period (Mandell 2013). Or to engage spectators in consideration of the way digital technologies are changing life, love and relationships, as, for instance, UK artist, academic and author Dani Ploeger does in his *Ascending Performance* (2013) for smartphone porn app MiKandi, where swiping fingers over the touchscreen allows the spectator to progress through pictures of the artist's growing erection, in what Ploeger describes as a comment on use of this technology "as a masturbatory act" (2013). Or, indeed, to engage spectators in artists' politicised performances of self—for instance, via Ju Gosling's performative staging of a debate about access to a gallery exhibit on her website for all the world to see (Hadley 2015).

The possibilities that social media provides in the critical domain of theatre practice turn on the technologies' potential to engage anyone and everyone in networks of commentary, review and critique about a show or a season or the industry as a whole historically reserved for paid professionals. To allow them to share their view on content, casting decisions, staging decisions, or any other aspect of theatre practice, as, for instance, when La Jolla Playhouse in San Diego in the USA cast its production of Hans Christian Andersen's *The Nightingale* with mainly white actors, resulting in scathing commentary on its social media cites, and forcing the company to post an update on its site, defining and defending its policies, to try to defuse the furore (Zara 2012).

The possibilities that social media provides in the audience development domain of theatre practice build on the aesthetic and critical possibilities to try to engage spectators and society at large in the life of a theatre maker company beyond a specific moment, show or season. The hope, in this domain, is that a theatre company or maker's social media networks can become a co-creative community that stretches out across decentralised networks to include not just fellow artists, audiences, critics, media, sponsors and other stakeholders but a much broader community—a community that, because it has had an increased opportunity to engage with the work, becomes interested, invested and involved in the industry, and the impact it has on society, advocating, advising and, where necessary, challenging to continually improve the work, and the ecology around the work.

The hope in each of these domains is that social media technologies and networks will allow theatre makers to collapse barriers between historically separate roles, contexts, media and communities, and, as a result, reactivate the relations between producers, spectators and society at large. The reality, of course, is the degree to which uptake of social media in theatre moves from familiar forms, to reconfiguration of familiar forms, to new forms, is dependent on a whole range of factors—from theatre makers' ability to understand how the technologies and networks function, to their ability to keep up with the pace of them, to their anxiety about the risks of trying new things, to their financial resources. As media theorists caution, the uptake of social media in theatre, as in politics or any other part of society, can exert new forms of control over practices as readily as it can liberate them. The creative citizen-journalists, community makers and influencers finding new forms of expression and social engagement online can easily sit together with groups who continue to feel excluded and invisible. This summary of how communication via social media networks works is as a result useful as a starting point for analysis but it has to be considered in light of how practices are actually playing out on overcrowded, contested social media platforms where new forms of engagement can fade as fast as they flicker into life. In the chapters to come I offer this more detailed consideration of examples where theatre makers are using social media to innovate in, blur the boundaries of and blend aesthetic, critical and audience development practices in interesting ways. Equally, I offer more detailed consideration of examples where theatre makers fail to do this, which can become just as educative about the way they are working with these new technologies to try to extend the impact of their work.

## References

Abba, Tom. 2009. Hybrid Stories: Examining the Future of Transmedia Narrative. *Science Fiction Film and Television* 2(1): 59–75. http://muse.jhu.edu/journals/science_fiction_film_and_television/summary/v002/2.1.abba.html. Accessed 13 Aug 2013.

Abela, Donna, Vanessa Bates, Hilary Bell, Noëlle Janaczewska, Verity Laughton, Ned Manning, and Catherine Zimdahl. 2009. Whats Going On Here? *7-On Playwrights*, June 17. http://sevenon.blogspot.com.au/2009/06/what-is-going-on-here.html. Accessed 13 Aug 2013.

Albarran, Alan B. (ed.). 2013. *The Social Media Industries*. London: Routledge.

Anderson, Eric. 2010. *Social Media Marketing: Game Theory and the Emergence of Collaboration*. Portland: Springer.

Australian Plays. 2009. Where are the Women? *Australian Plays*, Nov 20. http://australianplays.org/parsons. Accessed 5 Jan 2015.

Australian Stage. 2009. Philip Parsons Memorial Lecture. *Australian Stage*, Nov 20. http://www.australianstage.com.au/200911223015/news/industry-news/2009-philip-parsons-memorial-lecture.html?directory=3. Accessed 5 Jan 2015.

Bailey, John. 2009. A Dramatic Imbalance. *The Age*, Oct 18. http://www.theage.com.au/news/entertainment/arts/a-dramatic-imbalance/2009/10/17/1255624775745.html. Accessed 9 Jan 2015.

Bakshy, Eytan, Winter A. Mason, Jake M. Hofman, and Duncan J. Watts. 2011. Everyone's an Influencer: Quantifying Influence on Twitter. *WDSM* 11: 65–74.

Balme, Christoper. 2014. *The Theatrical Public Sphere*. Cambridge: Cambridge University Press.

Baym, Nancy. 2010. *Personal Connections in the Digital Age*. Cambridge: Polity.

Bell, David. 2001. *An Introduction to Cybercultures*. London: Routledge.

Bentley, Alex, Mark Earls, and Michael J. O'Brien. 2011. *I'll Have What She's Having: Mapping Social Behaviour*. Cambridge: The MIT Press.

Berger, Christopher. 2012. *The Social Media Strategists: Build a Successful Program from the Inside Out*. Boston: McGraw-Hill.

Blake, Elissa. 2010. Geeks, Tweets and Bums on Seats: How Social Media Is Shaping the Arts in Australia. *Sydney Morning Herald*, July 10. http://www.smh.com/au/entertainment/theatre/geeks-tweets-and-bums-on-seats-20100709-103g8.html. Accessed 9 Aug 2013.

Borland, Micheala. 2010. Enter Theatre Women: Stages Left, Right and Centre. *The Australian*, Oct 6. http://www.theaustralian.com.au/news/enter-theatre-women-stages-left-right-and-centre/story-e6frg6n6-1225934576279. Accessed 6 Jan 2015.

Bridgstock, Ruth S. 2011. Making It Creatively: Building Sustainable Careers in the Arts and Creative Industries. *Australian Career Practitioner Magazine* 22(2): 11–13. http://eprints.qut.edu.au/47962/4/47962.pdf. Accessed 10 Nov 2015.

Briggs, Asa, and Peter Burke. 2009. *A Social History of Media: From Gutenberg to the Internet*, 3rd ed. Cambridge: Polity.

Brogan, Chris. 2010. *Social Media 101: Tactics and Tips to Develop Your Business Online*. Hoboken: Wiley.

Cann, Alan, Konstantia Dimitriou, and Tristram Hooley. 2011. *Social Media: A Guide for Researchers*. Research Information Network. http://www.rin.ac.uk/social-media-guide. Accessed 5 Jan 2015.

Carr, Nicholas. 2010. *The Shallows: What the Internet is Doing to Our Brains*. New York: W. W. Norton and Company.

Castells, Manuel. 2001. *The Internet Galaxy: Reflections on the Internet, Business, and Society*. New York, NY: Oxford University Press.

Collins, Antoinette. 2009. Women Decry Australian Theatre as a Boy's Club. *ABC* Dec 7. http://www.abc.net.au/worldtoday/content/2009/s2763949.htm. Accessed 4 Jan 2015.

Crunch.net. 2014. The 8 Second Rule or 8 Second to Doomsday. *Crunch.net*, May 13. http://crunchnet.co.uk/blog/8-second-rule. Accessed 5 Dec 2011.

Curtin, Adrian. 2013. Recalling the Theatre Phone. In *Theatre, Performance and Analogue Technologies: Historical Interfaces and Intermedialities*, ed. Kara Reilly, 214–231. London: Palgrave.

Dowling, John. 2001. *Radical Media: Rebellious Communication and Social Movements*. Thousand Oaks: Sage.

Elkin, Ben, and Rebecca Harper-Cross. 2012. Why Our Theatre's Are Empty of Women. *Crikey*, April 27. http://www.crikey.com.au/2012/04/27/why-are-our-theatres-empty-of-women/. Accessed 10 Jan 2015.

Fiske, John. 1990. *Introduction to Communication Studies*. London: Routledge.

Frew, Wendy. 2012. Australia Council Finds Women Are Bit Players in Theatre's "Feudal System". *Sydney Morning Herald*, April 24. http://www.smh.com.au/entertainment/stage/australia-council-finds-women-are-bit-players-in-theatres-feudal-system-20120423-1xhjy.html. Accessed 5 Jan 2015.

Giannachi, Gabriella. 2004. *Virtual Theatres: An Introduction*. London: Routledge.

Goff, David H. 2013. A History of the Social Media Industries. In *the Social Media Industries*, ed. Alan B. Albarran, 16–45. London: Routledge.

Goffman, Erving. 1963. *Behaviour in Public Places: Notes on the Social Organization of Gatherings*. New York: The Free Press.

Goffman, Erving. 1973. *Presentation of the Self in Everyday Life*. Woodstock: Overlook Press.

Gramsci, Antonio. 1982. *Selections from the Prison Books*. London: Lawrence and Wishart.

Granovetter, Mark S. 1973. The Strength of Weak Ties: A Network Theory Revisited. *American Journal of Sociology* 78 (6): 1360–1380.

Gray, Jonathan. 2012. Web 2.0 and Collaborative On-Line Performance. *Text and Performance Quarterly* 32 (1): 65–72.

Habermas, Jürgen. 1962/1989. *The Structural Transformation of the Public Sphere*. London: Polity.

Hadley, Bree. 2014. *Disability, Public Space Performance and Spectatorship: Unconscious Performers*. London: Palgrave Macmillan.

Hadley, Bree. 2015. Participation, Politics and Provocations: People with Disabilities as Non-conciliatory Audiences. *Participations: Journal of Audience and Reception Studies* 12(1). http://www.participations.org/Volume%2012/Issue%201/11.pdf.

Handley, Ann, and C.C. Chapman. 2012. *Content Rules: How to Create Killer Blogs, Podcasts, Videos, eBooks, Webinars*. Hoboken: Wiley.

Henderson, Michael, Nicola F. Johnson, and Glenn Auld. 2013. Silences of Ethical Practice: Dilemmas for Researchers Using Social Media. *Educational Research and Evaluation: An International Journal on Theory and Practice* 19 (6): 546–560.

Hobson, Brenna. 2014. Has Belvoir St Theatre Turned around its Infamous "Boys Club"? *The Guardian*, Oct 2. http://www.theguardian.com/stage/australia-culture-blog/2014/oct/02/has-belvoir-st-theatre-turned-round-its-boys-club. Accessed 28 Jan 2015.

Holmes, David. 1997a. Virtual Politics – Identity and Community in Cyberspace. In *Virtual Politics: Identity & Community*, ed. David Holmes, 1–25. London: Sage.

Holmes, David. 1997b. Virtual Identity: Communities of Broadcast, Communities of Interactivity. In *Virtual Politics: Identity & Community*, ed. David Holmes, 26–45. London: Sage.

Jenkins, Henry. 2009. If It doesn't Spread It's Dead. Multipart Blog Post: 1, 2, 3, 4, 5, 6, 7, 8. http://henryjenkins.org/2009/02/if_it_doesnt_spread_its_dead_p_1.html. Accessed 19 Aug 2013.

Jenkins, Henry, Sam Ford, and Joshua Green. 2013. *Spreadable Media: Creating Value and Meaning in a Networked Culture*. New York: New York University Press.

Jordan, Tim. 1999. *Cyberpower: The Culture and Politics of Cyberspace and the Internet*. London and New York: Routledge.

Kawasaki, Guy, and Peg Fitzpatrick. 2014. *The Art of Social Media—Power Tips for Power Users*. New York, NY: Penguin Books.

Keen, Andrew. 2007. *The Cult of the Amateur: How Blogs, MySpace, YouTube, and the Rest of Today's ... Our Economy, Our Culture, and Our Values*. New York: Doubleday.

Kelly, Nicole. 2010. 4 Ways to Measure Social Media and It's Impact on Your Brand. *Social Media Examiner*. http://www.socialmediaexaminer.com/4-ways-measure-social-media-and-its-impact-on-your-brand/. Accessed 19 Dec 2011.

Kerpen, Dave. 2011. *Likeable Social Media: How to Delight Your Customers, Create an Irresistible Brand, and Be Generally Amazing on Facebook (and Other Social Networks)*. New York: McGraw-Hill.

Klout. 2012. *Types of Influencers*. https://klout.com/home. Accessed 19 Aug 2013.

Lally, Elaine, and Miller, Sarah. 2012. *Women in Theatre*. Australia Council for the Arts, Government of Australia, Australian Policy Online, 27 April 2012. http://apo.org.au/research/women-theatre. Accessed 5 Jan 2015.

Lonergan, Patrick. 2016. *Theatre & Social Media*. London: Palgrave Macmillan.

Mandell, Jonathan. 2013. Social Media On Stage: Theater Meets Twitter, Facebook, Youtube, Tumbler, Soundcloud. *New York Theater*, Jan 3. http://newyorktheater.me/2013/01/03/social-media-on-stage-theater-meets-twitterfacebookyoutube-tumbler-soundcloud/. Accessed 27 Nov 2014.

Marwick, Alice E. 2010. Status Update: Celebrity, Publicity and Self-Branding in Web 2.0. Ph.D. thesis, New York University.

Marwick, Alice and Dana Boyd.2011. I Tweet Honestly, I Tweet Passionately: Twitter Users, Context Collapse, and the Imagined Audience. *New Media and Society* 13(1):114–133.

McCarthy, Breda. 2006. Building and Sustaining Trust In Networks: Lessons from the Performing Arts. *Irish Marketing Review* 18 (1/2): 47–57.

Miller, Paige. 2013. Social Media Marketing. In *The Social Media Industries*, ed. Alan B. Albarran, 86–104. London: Routledge.

Moritz, Donna. 2013. The Shift to Visual Social Media. *Socially Sorted*. http://sociallysorted.com.au/shift-to-visual-social-media-6-tips-for-business-info-graphic/. Accessed 20 Mar 2015.

Nahon, Karine, and Jeff Hemsley. 2013. *Going Viral*. Cambridge: Polity Press.

Neutze, Benjamin. 2014c. Women in the Arts: How the Melbourne Theatre Company is Finding Female Directors. *Women's Agenda*. http://www.womensagenda.com.au/talking-about/top-stories/women-in-the-arts-how-the-melbourne-theatre-company-is-finding-female-directors/201401223472. Accessed 5 Jan 2015.

Nowak, Martin, A. 2011. *Super Cooperators: Altruism, Evolution and Why We Need Each Other to Succeed*. New York, NY: Free Press.

O'Neill, Stephen. 2014. *Shakespeare and YouTube: New Media Forms of the Bard*. London: Bloomsbury.

Page, Ruth. 2012. *Stories and Social Media: Identities and Interaction*. London: Routledge.

Parmelee, John H., and Shannon L. Bichard. 2012. *Politics and the Twitter Revolution: How Tweets Influence the Relationship Between Political Leaders and the Public*. Lanham: Lexington Books.

Pearson, Erika. 2009. All the World Wide Web's a Stage: The Performance of Identity in Online Social Networks. *First Monday: Peer-Reviewed Journal on the Internet* 14: 3.

Pérez-Latre, Francisco. 2013. The Paradoxes of Social Media: A Review of Theoretical Issues. In *The Social Media Industries*, ed. Alan B. Albarran, 46–59. London: Routledge.

Ploeger, Dani. 2013. Performance Art as Pornographic Smartphone App. *SCUDD Newslist*, Nov 1. https://vimeo.com/78257191. Accessed 19 Dec 2013.

Putnam, Robert. 1995. Turning In, Tuning Out: The Strange Disappearance of Social Capital in America. *Political Science and Politics* 28: 664–683.

Rainie, Lee, and Barry Wellman. 2012. *Networked: The New Social Operating System*. Cambridge: MIT Press.

Ries, Al, and Laura Ries. 2002. *The 22 Immutable Laws of Branding*. New York: Harper Business.

Ruben, Brent D., and Lea P. Stewart. 1998. *Communication and Human Behavior*, 4th ed. Boston: Allyn & Bacon.

Sant, Toni. 2014. Art, Performance, and Social Media. In *Routledge Handbook of Social Media*, ed. Jeremy Hunsinger, and Theresa M. Senft, 45–58. London: Routledge.

Schackman, Daniel. 2013. Social Media Content. In *The Social Media Industries*, ed. Alan B. Albarran, 105–116. London: Routledge.
Schechner, Richard. 2002. *Performance Studies: An Introduction*. London and New York: Routledge.
Shannon, Claude E. and Weaver, Warren. 1949/1989. *The Mathmatical Theory of Communication*. Chicago: Board of Trustees for the University of Illonois.
Shirky, Clay. 2008. *Here Comes Everybody: The Power of Organizing Without Organizaitons*. New York: Penguin Press.
Supple, Augusta. 2011. Merit vs Misogyny in Australian Theatre—And What We're Going to Do About It. *Augusta Supple*, Jan 17. http://augustasupple.com/2011/01/merit-vs-misogyny-in-australian-theatre-and-what-were-going-to-do-about-it/. Accessed 15 Jan 2015.
Stuart, Toby E., and Olav Sorenson. 2007. Strategic Networks and Entrepreneurial Ventures. *Strategic Entrepreneurship Journal* 1: 211–227.
The Australian. 2012. The Sound and the Fury of Australia's Women Playwrights and Theatre Directors. *The Australian*, Nov 3. http://www.theaustralian.com.au/arts/review/the-sound-and-the-fury-of-australias-women-playwrights/story-fn9n8gph-1226508371732. Accessed 5 Jan 2015.
Tönnies, Ferdinand. 1955. *Community and Association*. London: Routledge and Kegan Paul.
Trottier, Daniel. 2012. *Social Media as Surveillance: Rethinking Visibility in a Converging World*. Abingdon: Ashgate Publishing Group.
Usher, Robin. 2009a. The Age: Theatre Company is Failing Women Directors. *The Age*, Oct 2. http://www.theage.com.au/it-pro/theatre-company-is-failing-women-directors-20091002-gfh1. Accessed 15 Jan 2015.
Usher, Robin. 2009b. Theatre Company Ends "Boys' Club". *The Age*, Nov 19. http://www.theage.com.au/national/theatre-company-ends-boys-club-20091118-imkp.html. Accessed 15 Jan 2015.
Way, Geoffrey. 2011. Social Shakespeare: Romeo and Juliet, Social Media, and Performance. *Journal of Narrative Theory* 41 (3): 401–420.
Wilkinson, Chris. 2009. Australian Theatre should Get Real. *The Guardian*, Oct 14. http://www.theguardian.com/stage/theatreblog/2009/oct/14/australian-theatre. Accessed 28 Jan 2015.
Wong, Kyle. 2014. The Explosive Growth of Influencer Marketing and What It Means for You. *Forbes Online*, Sep 10. http://www.forbes.com/sites/kylewong/2014/09/10/the-explosive-growth-of-influencer-marketing-and-what-it-means-for-you/. Accessed 28 Nov 2014.
Zara, Christopher. 2012. Racially Charged Casting Controversy Rocks Historic Theater. *IB Times*, July 14, 2013. http://www.ibtimes.com/racially-charged-casting-controversy-rocks-historic-theater-723433. Accessed 22 Aug 2013. Accessed 28 Nov 2014.
Zarella, Dan. 2010. *The Social Media Marketing Book*. Sebastapol: O'Reilly Media.

# CHAPTER 3

# Social Media as Theatre Stage: Aesthetics, Affordances and Interactivities

The concept of the spectator whose collaboration in the theatre consists mainly of sitting back, watching the show and clapping, laughing or crying in the correct places has not completely gone from the theatrical landscape. Articles offering advice to spectators still often seek to maintain the atmosphere that theatre makers of the nineteenth and twentieth century's "civilizing" mainstages created, normalised and naturalised. Richard Watts (2013), for instance, advises spectators to be respectful to the show that a theatre maker has so lovingly created. This, for him, means coming prepared, and prepared to see the big picture of what a theatre maker was trying to present, beyond the issue of whether they like the content, aesthetic or meaning conveyed—coming prepared to be present in the experiential moment, where they will find themselves mentally if not physically immersed in the flow of a fictional world, forgetting where they are, who they are or what has happened before or will happen after this moment in time. The aim, it appears, is to create the experience that Mihalyi Csikszentmihalyi calls "flow", where "[c]oncentration is so intense that there is no attention left over to think about anything" (1990, 71), and time, space, place and personal concerns beyond the theatre fade away. This, for Watts (2013), means coming well rested, staying silent, and switching off devices such as iPhones, iPads and iPods that might interrupt the illusion, the momen, and the way it is meant to unfold. It is, as Caroline Heim (2015) shows, an attitude that some spectators take to heart, leaving them wary of the intrusion of new technologies into the fictive world, because they worry it will interrupt



B. Hadley, *Theatre, Social Media, and Meaning Making*,
DOI 10.1007/978-3-319-54882-1_3

the "deep sense of enjoyment that is long cherished and that becomes a landmark in memory" (1990, 3) that they associate with exciting moments of Csikszentmihalyi's flow-style engagement with theatre.

For all that this view still prevails in some quarters, the late twentieth and early twenty-first centuries have also seen many theatre makers, commentators and critics become more interested in challenging these assumptions about theatre, spectatorship and meaning making. Susan Bennett (1997), Richard Butsch (2008), Lynne Conner (2013), Christopher Balme (2014) and others have all written about the way theatre makers are working to recreate theatre, its style and its institutional structures to facilitate a more active, available and publicly visible conversation—in the auditorium, and in taking work out of the auditorium into streets, shopping malls, and other public spaces and places, including those online. Most who write about theatre audiences today acknowledge the part that social media might play in fostering new relations with spectators, society and the public sphere. Although many talk mainly about the feedback possibilities that social media presents, commentators such as Toni Sant (2008, 2009, 2013) and Patrick Lonergan (2016) also acknowledge the part it might play in theatre production as much as in theatre criticism. Indeed, for many contemporary theatre audience scholars, the two—the performance text and the paratexts around it—are inseparable parts of what Conner (2013) characterises as the overall theatre experience. Most acknowledge the way these possibilities capture the interest of theatre makers. To date, though, most have not had scope in their own studies of audience, spectators and meaning making to connect this to detailed discussion of the history, evolution or examples of theatre makers who are using social media to develop new aesthetics, new aesthetic interactivities or new dissemination and archiving possibilities, as much as new audience engagement protocols, in their work.

In this chapter I touch on precisely these aesthetic, production and dissemination possibilities by examining the way some mainstage theatre companies, as well as more innovative new independent companies, collectives and activist artists, are creating work that requires spectators to turn their iPhone, iPad or computer on, not off, to fully engage with the flow of their work. At this stage I examine these production, distribution and archiving practices without turning to whether or not spectators might choose to share the choices they make in interpreting the work with producers, fellow consumers or the public at large before, during or after the show in some form of critical commentary.

As Sant has noted, the history of theatre created or conveyed through social media type technologies is longer, deeper and more diverse than many think. As she makes clear, the history of social media theatre "goes back to the first years of text-based social networking platforms like MUD, MOO, and IRCS" (2014, 46). Accordingly, while it may be what Geoffrey Way (2011) characterises as "a fairly recent practice" when compared with those that have been around for centuries or millennia, there is already a decades long history.

The first thing that is important to understanding this terrain is that the production of theatre on, in or incorporating social media is but one small part of the broader spectrum of digital theatre. As Beryl Graham observes, the digital arts includes "any art made with, and for, digital media including the internet, digital imaging, or computer controlled installations" (2007, 93). It thus includes any work that uses digital technology, computers or Wi-Fi to incorporate text, image, sound or video projections into performance, or to allow performers, participants or audience members to improvise with these projections during a performance, as well as things such as robotic art, cybernetic art and art produced through programs, applications or algorithms. Some of this does not meet even the broadest definition of social media—as a platform, or application, that allows two-way communication, collaboration and content creation between artist and audience. So, as Sant notes, "Not all works of internet art or online performances involve social media" (2014, 46).

This chapter consider only theatre that incorporates social media, as a two-way interaction technology, to archive performances, or achieve a broader dissemination of performances, or actually create new sorts of participatory, immersive, telematic, networked or netactivist performances—theatre that takes advantage of branded platforms such as Facebook, Twitter or YouTube, or similarly two-way interactive bespoke platforms that the theatre maker sets up themselves, to connect performers and spectators, live realities and virtual realities, proximate action and remote action, in new ways. This definition is inclusive enough to capture a diversity of performance practices while bracketing off work that uses projections, animations or avatars, in combination with live actors, to create a fictional world that spectators still just watch the way they would any show on any stage, without the stage–spectator contact that characterises social media. This still includes a range of work. It includes performances stored online in archives, performances streamed online to audiences near or far, performances that offer transmedia components that the audience can use to learn more about the characters, content, plot or context of a performance, performances that incorporate voting, liking or linking to allow the audience to drive the action in some way, immersive, telematic or networked performances that use technology to allow spectators to connect with remote participants, mixed reality, augmented reality or even almost totally virtual reality, and performances that unfold fully online on the theatre maker's own websites, blogs, microblogs or other social media platforms, as "virtual theatres", inside or outside the politics of mainstage theatre venues. It potentially also includes work such as "flash mobs" or similar sorts of guerrilla theatre, which, as Jonathan Gray (2012) notes, use social media to gather participants, get them into a public space at the same time, document their actions and disseminate them as widely as possible, whether for protest, entertainment or marketing—and if it does then it potentially includes any call for collaborators, participants and audiences via local or global online networks. These performance styles and strategies can overlap with each other, with other types of participatory performance or other types of digital performance. Indeed, Gray (2012) notes, they can also overlap with the social self-performance of theatre makers and companies looking to build their brand through some of these same online platforms. They can be described in different ways by the theatre makers, who may use labels such as "immersive", "telematic", "networked" or "cyber" theatre, in ways that are not consistent with each other. The motivations for creating work that incorporates social media in the first place can also vary. For some theatre makers the motivation can come from a desire to experiment with new technology, or experiment with theatre's form via new technology, as part of an innovation agenda. For other theatre makers, the motivation can come from a desire to explore the personal, social or political issues that the new technology is raising in their community, via a content–form nexus that can become critical to the impact of the work. For still others it can come from a desire to experiment with new ways to extend the audience for theatre as competitor forms such as film, television, new media and games take over more and more of the market.

Perhaps the main reason it remains difficult to define "social media theatre" is because there is still debate about whether there is a distinctive aesthetic emerging in it. Some commentators, such as Way (2011), say that they can "already [see] certain trends in the ways productions attempt to weave social media sites into their practices" (2011). Others, such as Sant (2014), suggest that the medium is not mature enough yet to allow us to identify trends in online performance, let alone social media performance, as a specific subset of online performance. "Is the internet just a new way to perform and make art, or is this a new medium with formal and aesthetic possibilities of its own?" she asks. For Sant, "[p]articularly with social media, attempts to answer this crucial question cannot yield a satisfactory answer yet" (52). Theatre makers are, she contends, still in the equivalent of the silent film era—or, indeed, the era before the silent film era—when distinctive styles, scenographies and dramaturgies for cinema had yet to emerge.

Although diverse, new and difficult to define in terms of aesthetic trends, social media theatre is, as I noted in Chaps. 1 and 2, easy to identify by the hopes cited by artists who advocate for it. As Gray (2012) notes, the characteristics of Web 2.0 social media technologies align well with calls from performance practitioners and scholars to create more immersive, interactive, participatory, accessible or inclusive performance experiences. These technologies provide people with opportunities to see work—important for those who live outside the London and New York powerbases of the mainstage Western theatre industry—to interact with work or to actually participate in the production of work. What I would add to Gray's observation is that, though it is by no means universal, many of the most innovative uses of social media theatre also share a desire to create a situation where spectators act as co-creators but, at the same time, also reflect on their role as co-creators, and their part in making, and making meaning of, the event (Hadley 2014). Like the offline performances that inspired Bennett to write *Theatre Audiences*—and so many other authors of books on theatre audiences—these online performances "not only la[y] bare the 'rules' of viewing but ask if these rules [ar]e appropriate" (1997, vii). They try to make the spectator's part in negotiating meaning plain, by both creating and disrupting the emotionally engaged flow style experience that Watts (2013) describes. Certainly, work of the sort that he describes to does have power. It can draw spectators through from tentative intellectual engagement into fully immersed engagement with what is happening on stage. There is, though, also power in pulling spectators in and out of this fully immersed feeling or state, combining moments of intense emotional engagement, where spectators start to mistake themselves for characters they see onstage, with more reflective moments where they think about what the characters do, and what they themselves might do in the situation, make comparisons, make judgements and, potentially, have changes of perception. This is why many advocates of social media theatre emphasise, as Cat Hope andJohn Ryan (2014, 13) do, the idea that the encounters that unfold via such media are still ephemeral and fluid, not fixed. These are still live encounters, even if they are not physical face-to-face encounters. "User-generated content can unfold in real-time," Lonergan agrees, "and can thereafter be archived. So there is a distinction to be made between a 'live' digital performance and an archived version of the same event" (2016, 33). Even then, though, the event of encountering an archived version of a theatrical event is likely to be different each time, as the instructional, promotional and other content around the archived video or text changes, and as fellow users add comments and links to expand the experience in their own unique ways. This means that social media performance embodies both Peggy Phelan's (1993) claim that performance is a phenomenon that exists only in the present, and Philip Auslander's (2008) counter-claim that the live and the mediatised are not necessarily opposed to each other. Together, these aspirations for a participatory, unpredictable form of practice constitute a set of aesthetic, production, dissemination and impact priorities, and a politic, more so than an aesthetic, style per se. Indeed, the postmodern, post-media and post-metanarrative tendencies of many of the theatre makers most active on social media—at least in independent and activist theatre contexts—means that most would be content if these priorities and politics never resolved into a recognisable, canonical aesthetic.

While the potentials of this form of practice are clear, those of us who have thought about it have warned against "embrac[ing] an entirely utopian enthusiasm for this sort of work" (Gray 2012)—the need to avoid a technological determinist argument that might suggest that social media theatre is always going to play out in these ways, because of the technology, without recognising the industrial, social, commercial and economic factors that influence the evolution of the technology. Accordingly, in this Chapter I interrogate if, and if so how, the use of social media in theatre is playing a part in developing distinctive aesthetic and delivery strategies in contemporary theatre. If, and if so how, this is making theatre more relevant in the contemporary public sphere, in which participatory practices increasingly dominate in media, communication and cultural landscapes more generally. In particular, I interrogate the types of interactivity, agency and control that different uptakes of social media in the theatre foster or facilitate. These can be radically different, depending on the social media platform that a theatre maker uses—a wiki, a content sharing site or a collaborative content curation site—and what they use it for. Following Marie-Laure Ryan (2001, 211–212) in her analysis of audience interaction across new media, I avoid analysing audience access, engagement and interactivity in social media theatre via an interactive versus non-interactive binary. Instead I follow her suggestion that interactivity—the affordances that allow spectators to make choices, make comments or make things happen—can run along a spectrum from "selective" sorts of interactivity where a spectator has control over what they want to watch, when, where and even to some degree how to a more "productive" sort of interactivity where a spectator has control not just over these choices, their commentary or their meaning-making but over the actual outcomes of event. This is a spectrum that Lonergan has subsequently described (albeit in more binary terms) in terms of the "responsive" and the "creative" (2014, 49). The evidence suggests that mainstage theatres—like major galleries, museums and cultural institutions—have taken "about two decades to start warming up to this concept" (Sant 2014, 46) and therefore have tended to sit on a more selective rather than productive place along the spectrum compared with the independent artists, activists and mischief makers experimenting with it since the 1990s. After briefly considering uptake of social media as a theme, topic or stylistic stimulus, then, I look at the way mainstage companies, independent companies, activist artists and others are using social media to create theatre, concentrating on differences, plus degrees of accessibility, interactivity and agency.

## Social Media as/and Theme

As I have already noted, the multisignificatory performances by which we live our lives online are already informing the multisignificatory performances by which we represent our lives in the theatre—in content, aesthetics, style, scenography, and other areas. In this sense, one of the first uptakes of social media in the theatre has often been as a thematic, a topic or an approach to text, dramaturgy, scenography or design. Here, as Lonergan notes in his short textbook on *Theatre and Social Media*, theatre makers and companies "represent, explore and respond to social media on stage" (2016, 4), reflecting on the ways in which it is changing the world they have always sought to represent onstage. In many cases, he continues, these plays show the worst of the problems that social media platforms present for human relationships, and so, at the same time, they "demonstrate an impulse to map out the ethical dimensions of the social media space" (42). Using social media, its impact on society, or its impact on individual social status as a theme does not necessarily result in a performance that is interactive, or at least does not necessarily result in a performance that it interactivity in the sense that audiences have the ability to contribute to the characters, plot progression, or climax of the performance. However, the uptake of social media as a theme, a topic, or a textual, dramaturgical or design motif is worth considering insofar as it becomes a precursor to the uptake of the technology to create more accessible, interactive or participatory work.

The uptake of social media technology as a textual, dramaturgical or design motif is a subject that playwright Richard Jordan (2014, 37–48) has written about. He argues that although discussions of digital theatre tend to focus on form, not on content, looking at the way technology influences a playtext and its content is also important in understanding the impact that technology is having on theatre practices today. For Jordan, social media is becoming ubiquitous in our day-to-day social lives, and thus in the way we write, rehearse and read stories, right down to the language we use to describe our lives. The themes, topics and textual approaches used on social media—which, as I noted in Chap. 2, emphasise teller, tellability, status and impression management as strategies to maintain the attention of an audience on a fast-paced, participatory platform—are thus starting to inform the themes, topics and textual approaches used in artforms such as theatre, television and cinema in the twenty-first century. They are informing the way we write playtexts, construct story, narrative and plot progression, create characters, convey relationships between characters and so forth. Although playtexts that remediate social media as a textual, dramaturgical or design motif are not remediating it in the same way as works that rely on social media to allow a spectator to access the work at all, they are still remediating it, according to Jay David Bolter and Richard Grusin's definition of remediation as "representation of one medium in another" (2000, 45). They are just doing it at the level of content instead of at the level of form in the first instance.

One of the earliest examples of work that does this is Adam Cass's *I Love You, Bro* (2007). This play, based in part on an article that appeared in *Vanity Fair* in 2003, is a solo piece. It tells the story of Johnny, a teenager who becomes infatuated with another boy, MarkyMark, who mistakes Johnny for a girl when he meets him in an online chatroom.

MarkyMark is in fact a boy whom Johnny happens to know from school as well as the chat forum. "The plot unfolds", as I wrote in my review for national newspaper *The Australian*, "from this one moment of mistaken identity" (Hadley 2010). As the play progresses, Johnny creates and performs more and more characters in the chat room. There is Jess, a girl he creates to gain MarkyMark's interest sexually; Stingz, Jess's abusive ex-partner; and even a couple of secret agents who come into investigate the fictional Jess's fictional death. Johnny creates these characters, and recounts his creation of these characters, to try to spin out a story that will maintain MarkyMark's interest in the online relationship, a relationship which, Johnny acknowledges from the first, will lead to his own death. "Johnny keeps MarkyMark on tenterhooks throughout the various plot twists," as Jordan puts it. "[H]owever, what begins as a self-conscious manipulation gradually gives way to a game that Johnny feels he has no control over, as his various selves order up his own death" (2014, 46). Shifting swiftly from one strange moment in Johnny's story to the next, the play "captures something of the tenor of teenage impulsiveness, split-second decision-making and insatiable desire it must take to keep building and believing in this sort of shared fantasy" (Hadley 2010). For Jordan, the play thus "explores the moral, emotional and existential implications of a posthuman world, where the boundaries between flesh and data can no longer be determined" (2014, 39), where "human characters are equated with intelligent machines, either materially (via the body) or virtually (via consciousness)" (40), similar to the sort of human machines that Gabriella Giannachi (2004), Steve Dixon (2007) and Jennifer Parker-Starbuck (2014) see represented more literally in the technologised performances of practitioners such as Stelarc. For Jordan, *I Love You, Bro* is an example of a post-human play, evoking a post-human subjectivity, "in which the central character's sense of 'I' unravels within a cybernetic environment" (2014, 46), where the breakdown of boundaries between reality and representation, online and offline, backstage preparation and frontstage performance becomes too much to manage with coherence of the sort that characterises humanist notions of subjectivity. This, for Jordan, is what "fuels the unfolding drama" (40). It is also what makes the performance digital, in the identities it depicts and in its textualities, if not in a technologised mode of delivery to audiences. In the production I reviewed, at La Boite Theatre in Brisbane in 2010—the first professional production, three years after the premiere as part of Melbourne Fringe Festival, and before the play achieved success with productions across Australia and Europe—the director, David Berthold, used social media and other technological motifs strongly in the scenography. He placed "Johnny (Leon Cain) in a stark world, the real contours of his bedroom delineated only by angles, lines and words in a compact set" (Hadley 2010) designed to give a sense of the significance of the online world to the construction of Johnny's identity and story.

This interest in the way social media is influencing our everyday social self-performance, be it extreme in Johnny's case in *I Love You, Bro*, important or even just mundane, has also appeared in a lot of other performances, in Australia and around the world. While Cass's portrayal of Johnny emphasizes self-performance online, other portrayals emphasise, for example, self-performances in an increasingly networked society. In the year following Cass's *I Love You, Bro* in Brisbane, for instance, we also saw Liesel Zink's *A Collection of Various Selves* (2011), based on 800 people's contribution to a Facebook page associated with the project during its development. The contributed text was presented by four dancer performers in a multivocal spoken and movement piece in order to reflect on "the pressure we feel to project an illusion of happiness, independence, success, and 'togetherness' to the public eye" (2011). Here, the form of the piece, with snippets of status updates overlaying each other, again remediated the form of social media, albeit in a different way. In the USA a similarly motivated piece, *Your Life: Onstage*, was presented at La Jolla Playhouse at around the same time (Bravo 2009).

Using social media as a source of inspiration, dialogue, or stimulus for workshopping characters and scenarios, recording improvisations for future use in a show or research readily leads to using the medium in the show itself. It readily leads to interest in social media as a form for creating, presenting or disseminating work. It has, for example, become popular for use with young people, as a ubiquitous technology to get their storytelling abilities started, as well as for mainstage, contemporary and independent performance companies. According to Lonergan, "[a] strong pattern in plays about social media is that many are either about teenagers or are directed toward teenage audiences. The risks to teenage users of social media have been widely reported by the print and broadcast media—probably to an exaggerated extent" (2014, 37–38). As in the case of examples such as *I Love You, Bro*, the ubiquity of the technology in young people's lives leads to strong levels of engagement with it as a topic in dramas for them—and, eventually, by them. In the UK, theatre companies such as C&T have been set up specifically to explore these possibilities, using the new technology across aesthetic, as well as education and audience development, contexts (www.candt.com). In the USA, theatre maker Barbara Gottfried Hollander (2014) has written a book on *Participating in Plays, Skits, and Debates with Cool New Digital Tools* to encourage others to take up the approach.

A more internationally well-known US example where use of social media as content and use of social media as medium start to come together is The Builders Association's *Continuous City* (2007). The performance tells the story of a father and daughter trying to stay connected via the smartphones that the father is travelling the world to sell and, in doing so, remediates the networked relationships that characterise social media both in and around the production. In addition to being the means by which father and daughter connect—in one half of the production the father is onstage and the daughter seen only in projections of online space, in the other this reverses—and the motivator for many of the motifs, themes and stories that emerge in this story of lives lived across many locations, social media enables The Builder's Association to connect with and incorporate the real cities that the production visits. The show, the makers suggest, "reaches directly into each city the production visits through a participatory website and on-site filming to create a global and local production. *Continuous City* is about people far from home. *Continuous City* is where we live now" (The Builders Association n.d.). The performers blog, as The Builders Association's director, Marianne Weems, explains, is "about the places and people" they meet on their tours, as well as the friends, family and colleagues they are away from while they tour, "[s]o we're integrating the real cities we visit, the real people we meet in them, and the virtual cities interspersed between the real ones" (cited by Neri 2008). The boundaries between real world and represented world, offline world and online world, performers, spectators and social life start to blur.

Another internationally well-known UK example where use of social media as content and use of social media as medium start to come together is *The Radicalisation of Bradley Manning* 2012 by Tim Price and the National Theatre of Wales. The play tells the story of Bradley (now Chelsea) Manning, an US soldier and former Welsh resident, held in prison without charge of treason, waiting for military trial or court martial, for many years. Manning was imprisoned because he was accused of leaking hundreds of thousands of military documents relating to the

War on Terror in Iraq and Afghanistan to WikiLeaks. The production used internet communication technology prominently in its design and directorial realisation, and every performance in the season was broadcast over the internet, linking up the form, content and context of the play, and asking questions about contemporary issues such as the radicalisation of young people online. Several post-show discussions of these topics were also streamed on the internet. The design, according to Daniel Yates, was "surrounded by CCTV graphics which frame your viewing, quite literally, as one of voyeurism" (2012). This voyeurism did not, however, need to remain silent, solo and anonymous. "White watching," as Matt Trueman notes, "viewers c[ould] communicate with each other via a textbox onscreen" (2012), commenting on their reading of this "neatly self-aware" show.

As these examples show, the strategies that people use to negotiate issues of identity, self-performance, relationships, trust, social status and so forth provide stimulus for many contemporary performance makers. Where The Builders Association's *Continuous City* and the National Theatre of Wales' *The Radicalisation of Bradley Manning* move beyond the uptake of social media as a theme, topic or textual approach in *I Love You, Bro*, or as a verbatim text source in *Various Selves*, is that they start to bridge the gap between uptake as content and uptake as form, albeit not yet inside the show itself. Together these remediations of social media in the theatre at a thematic, textual or design level constitute an important precursor and parallel to the uptake of social media in theatre in other ways, extending its aesthetic and interaction possibilities into new terrains.

## Social Media as/and New Media Archives

Another area in which the uptake of social media has been highly evident in the first decade of its emergence as a mainstream technology is in archiving, and, in particular, the ambition of many theatre makers to find new ways to archive theatre works.

The archive, as Rebecca Schnieder argues, is "habitual to Western culture" (2012, 138). Its root, in the Greek word *archon*, meaning the head of state, acknowledges its status as an authoritative historical record. Historically, the archive, and the collection of theatrical texts and paratexts held in a library's theatre archives, constitutes the authoritative word on aesthetic quality, innovation and impact in the theatre industry.

Of course, archiving theatre's ephemeral events presents a problem, which, as Schnieder (2012), Reason (2006, 2003) and other theorists observe, is precisely why theatre historians have tried to solve the problem through textual, visual, video and other documentary items in their collections designed to shore up theatre's status in Western culture.

In the late twentieth century the archive was critiqued for its narrow, patriarchal and political decision-making process—the criteria by which archivists or the authorities that employ them determine which shows, writers or performers are important enough to be in their collection, and thus in the canon of Western theatre. Although presented as neutral histories, archives are always cultural constructs that dictate what is worth remembering. If we take the shows above as an example of the way Western theatre archives construct memory, history and authority, for instance, a successful mainstage show such as *I Love You, Bro* clearly has the most chance of making it into the archive, and the canon, as a result of reviews, critiques or documentation in academic circles. The path into the archive for an independent show such as *Various Selves* is less predictable. For young people's self-devised performances there is little chance of entering the archive, or the canon, unless the work is a collaboration with celebrated companies such as The Builders Association.

Where social media is seen as useful in this context is in reshaping the archive, and stretching it to include a more democratically determined range of works. Although search engines, metadata, tags and other means of filtering content might not initially be thought of as facilitating a two-way interactive use of a technology, they do in fact do this. In doing so, they fundamentally change the nature of the archive. An archive produced via a social media platform, such as a wiki, allows spectators, scholars, historians and interested amateurs to choose their own path through the content, based on their criteria for importance. They are no longer bound by the archives, the collections or the academic treatise that chart them. This is because a wiki, which holds content, collections and articles digitally, does not have the linear structure of a physical library catalogue, or a physical library layout, where each item has to sit on a specific shelf. It has a rhizomatic, networked structure where each item can be tagged to as many topics as might be relevant, engaged in any order, at any time and in any place. It can hold more theatre texts and paratexts. It can hold textual, visual, video and other types of theatre texts and paratexts. Moreover, many new online archives allow audiences to add content too. "The task of the archivist is to manage the public transcript," as Daniel Downes articulates it, but "[i]n the digital society we each engage in activities of selection, reproduction, and storage that were once the province of a professional elite charged with the task of creating and maintaining monopolies of knowledge" (2005, 131). Accordingly, Conner agrees, online platforms have "adjusted the nature of that power structure," at the same time as they have "increased individual access to paratextual data and as such profoundly altered the role and capacity of paratexts to facilitate the meaning-making operation" (2013, 79).

There are many examples of theatre makers, companies and communities taking advantage of Web 2.0 technologies to construct their own archives today. In some cases, these are archives of well-studied theatre makers such as William Shakespeare where people take advantage of the fact that, "[l]ike the great expositions of the past, cyberspace can become a permanent exhibition of cultural traditions in which our predecessors speak to us" (Downes 2005, 131). Many major institutions, including the British Library, the Shakespeare Birthplace Trust, the Royal Shakespeare Company (RSC) and Shakespeare's Globe, have started using the internet, and social media, to increase the accessibility, interactivity and value of their archives (Rumbold 2010). Although W.B. Worthen (2014, 165) claims that Shakespearean performance, and indeed all performance, has historically been fairly peripheral to the broader digital humanities projects, he nevertheless acknowledges an explosive expansion of Shakespeare content online in the past decade (2014, 148). This includes scholarly content, such as critical articles, clips and reviews. For instance, Worthen (48) cites the value of the Global Shakespeares online platform (http://globalshakespeares.mit.edu/#). This also includes less scholarly content. For instance, Stephen O'Neill (2014, 3) notes that of the 30 million pieces of Shakespeare content online, and the 1 million pieces on YouTube, the most popular, with 55 million views, is an MTV parody called *Dr Seuss vs Shakespeare: Epic Rap Battles of History #12*. These archives thus both confirm and challenge the weight of Shakespeare in the theatrical canon.

These sorts of archival projects are paralleled by projects attempting to add "other" theatre makers into the archives. For example, both the Brooklyn Museum in the USA and the Theatre and Performance Research Association (TAPRA) in the UK have promoted wiki-a-thon projects where people gather to add women artists into Wikipedia. These initiatives challenge the terms of the Western theatre canon by putting once marginalised practices by women, people of colour, people with disabilities and others into the canon or by creating new canons. Sometimes, these archival projects concentrate on not-so-well-studied communities of theatre makers outside the US, UK and Western European power base of the theatre industry. In the Americas, the Hemispherica Institute maintains an archive of American, and particularly Latin American, practices (www.hemisphericinstitute.org), with a clear orientation towards the collection of radical, experimental and innovative work. In Australia the AusStage database (www.ausstage.edu.au) developed by dozens of Australian theatre scholars, with the help of six cycles of Australian Research Council funding from 2000 to date, maintains an archive of Australian practitioners, productions and touring histories. Like the groups in the USA and the UK that set out to add women's voices to theatre archives, these groups set out to challenge their status as terra incognito in dominant Western ways of mapping out the world, and, by extension, the theatre world. Incorporating texts, images, videos and reviews, and even access to tours of digitally rendered examples of theatres, as well as basic data, these niche archives are often the most active and interactive in terms of allowing communities of people to comment, co-create and become part of the structure of authority of the archives. They include new features such as temporal mapping, geomapping and translation, as well as the data visualisations of the theatre venues that allow those who engage with the archive to see the relations between a constantly growing body of content in new ways.

Individual theatre makers and companies also take part in this sort of archiving. For instance, while mobilities studies scholars such as Kim Sawchuk and Arseli Dokumaci at Concordia University's Mobile Media Lab in Montreal, Canada, are starting to archive the work of disabled theatre makers, theatre makers themselves are doing this too. Katherine Araniello and Aaron Williamson of the Disabled Avant-Garde, for example, use a YouTube Channel to create a collection of work by the historically most marginal participants in theatre-making communities. The new technology enables these theatre makers to distribute their work through a new channel, to connect with spectators, and with scholars, in a way that never would have been possible while the archives remained under the guardianship of able-bodied authorities.

For individual theatre critics, social media can be similarly useful in their efforts to circulate their works. For well-known Australian theatre critic Alison Croggon, for instance, a WordPress blog may not have been necessary to make sure that her criticism makes it into the record, but it has made her contribution broader, and the connections between her contributions clearer, as part of a coherent body of work that she worked on for years under the title *Theatre Notes* (http://theatrenotes.blogspot.com.au/). It has also made the whole oeuvre open to comment and critique in a way that is not possible in a gatekept form such as a newspaper. While it has not been a necessity for a well-known critic like Croggon, this use of social media can also create employment and income in a context where stable jobs running theatre criticism columns, like those that Croggon has held, or well-known UK critics such as Lyn Gardiner have held with outlets such as *The Guardian*, are no longer so available.

For all of these theatre makers, companies, critics and communities, social media platforms allow them to add documents to the record, add annotation to those documents and, in some cases, facilitate active, participatory, performative engagement with the documents. Indeed, for some, the active, participatory, performative engagement can be pivotal, creating new performance encounters each time a new spectator visits the archival site. As part of their Anarcha project (www.liminalities.net/4-2/anarcha/) about African American history, black history, feminist history, disability history and the use of slave women as subjects in surgical experiments to develop modern gynaecological methods, for instance, the Olimpias placed documentation from participants on an online platform called an "anti-archive". This anti-archive randomly delivers content to users who decide to engage with it, creating live encounters, surprises and perhaps even surprisingly powerful new connections with and within the content, regardless of the fact that the spectator's encounter with the traces of the work is no longer a face-to-face one.

Performative in its engagement in a different way, Suzon Fuks' Waterwheel platform (www.water-wheel.net/) brings technological affordances to enable promotion, documentation, archiving and live streaming of performances through a feature called The Tap together. Built as part of an Australia Council for the Arts interarts fellowship, the Waterwheel platform allows performance makers, scientists and activists who are interested in water, the environment, ecology and sustainability around the world to connect. An active performance-dissemination platform, as well as a repository for documentation, and an archive, as well as a place where people who share mutual interests can connect (which links out to Twitter, Facebook and newslists), the

Waterwheel platform brings performance and para-performance activities together in a near unique platform. Within it, a variety of different forms of performative engagement with content and people become possible.

These new forms of archive create whatcultural historians such as Amelia Jones and Adrian Heathfield (2012), Schnieder (2012) and Reason (2003, 2006) and others characterise as participatory, performative documentation of events, where the impermanency, partiality and mutability of the documentation is of value precisely because it pushes artists and spectators to play with, discuss and debate historical accounts of theatre practices again and again. In these archives the act of engaging with the documents, and the traces, tracks and remains of the events captured in those documents, is in itself an active encounter in which the spectator has agency. Sometimes this is a selective agency, where the spectator can choose what they want to see, when, where and how, and what it means. Sometimes this is a more productive agency, where the spectator can add to what they see in the archives. For advocates of this new approach to documentation and archiving, social media platforms are rich with potential—the potential to break down the linearity of the archive via metadata, tags and search mechanisms that allow spectators to plot a much more personalised path through theatre history. The potential to break down the authority of the elite, as marginalised theatre makers, companies, critics and communities add themselves to the record, and offer alternative, popularised and politicised archives, which acknowledge their own partiality and perspectivality, The potential to break down the historicity of the archive, via the creation, presentation and dissemination of participatory documentation in which the work, and the encounter with the work, is not just captured but recreated anew as each new audience member encounters it.

This, of course, is not to say that the process of archiving is now problem free. Developing bespoke platforms, or even digitising content into branded platforms, and updating it constantly to be accurate and usable each time search engines such as Google come out with new software, takes time, energy and effort. There are relatively few funding agencies that support archiving as a priority, and, where they do, they choose based on their own mission, agenda and area of authority. This can end up reinserting a sort of elitist gatekeeping into the archiving process, as can the politics within the communities of people who take up an archiving project, some of whom may still be attached to older structures of authorship, authority and status-building. This means that seeing multiple competing archives emerge to create the story of the same content—and, indeed, witnessing those moments where so many crew members, participants and spectators pick up a camera it starts to seem as though the documenters outnumber the spectators—is becoming common. There is also the question of who, besides students, scholars and fellow community members who already know of the subject archived, might actually engage with the documents. While archives of canonical figures such as Shakespeare have an advantage when it comes to creating conversational and circulatory appeal—the fact that their already canonical status means that they are on school curriculums that force students to search them out, for instance—this is not the case for archives created by marginalised groups. In this sense, while their personal, social and professional motivations to create pages, posts and conversations about the work may be clear, they still face challenges in creating content that will have circulatory appeal. Together, these issues can influence when, where, why, how and how much the textual, visual, video and conversational content uploaded into theatre archives on social media platforms is used, and who has power on these platforms.

## Social Media as/and New Media Access

While the projects mentioned above use social media to create a historical archive, many theatre makers are also using social media to create contemporaneous documentation of their current shows. These theatre makers use social media platforms to stream shows, or snippets of shows, or snippets of rehearsal documentation, research, reviews, interviews and other paratexts designed to build an audience's interest in attending the show.

Well-subsidised companies such as the Royal Shakespeare Company, Shakespeare's Globe and the National Theatre in the UK have all been early adopters of this technology, using it to stream their productions of already-canonical Shakespeare plays, often in cinema-based evenings or events ascribed the status of people's performances. "While information about Shakespeare, his theatre, and various forms of Shakespeare's texts has been available in digital form for some time," Worthen argues, "the major innovation in online Shakespeare in the past decade has involved performance … Theatre companies now regularly post clips of productions on their websites in addition to broadcasting full pay-per-view productions to theatres" (2014, 148). According to Worthen (2014),

Stephen Purcell (2014, 213) and other commentators, the National Theatre has been a leader in tapping into the possibilities of this technology. It has been streaming its own productions of Shakespeare plays such *All's Well That Ends Well*, *Hamlet*, *The Comedy of Errors* and *Timon of Athens*, as well as co-productions of Shakespeare plays such as *Othello* with the Donmar Warehouse and *King Lear* with the Manchester International Theatre Festival, into cinemas via its NT Live programme. By presenting the streamed performances in cinemas or on computer screens at a designated day and time, rather than on DVD, the company creates a telematic event for remote spectators engaging the production in real time. As Murray Smith reminds us, "[w]atching a film in a cinema is not exactly like watching TV or reading a novel for technological, institutional and spectatorial reasons" (1995, 12). The affordances—which, as O'Neill (2014, 6) explains, in this context mean the sorts of interactivities that the screen object tends to facilitate—in a cinema are different from those for television. The new technology does increase the spectator's ability to see the show when, where and how they want to. However, streaming into a cinema at a specific day and time means that there is still some need to interact "live"—or "as live" in the case of shows streamed a few hours later to play in the evening in Australia or New Zealand—if not always face to face, with artists and fellow audiences members, in the way audiences in traditional theatres do. There is therefore still some level of event-ness, or ephemerality, in streamed performance, whether in the high-tech models offered by companies such as the National Theatre, which offer edited camera views, or low-tech models by more independent theatre companies, which offer little more than a camera set up in front of the stage from a single viewpoint.

In addition to offering live streamed shows, companies such as Shakespeare's Globe have also offered access to other programme activities, such as workshops in Shakespearean character, content and acting styles for schools groups "conducted in real time through web cameras" (Nelson 2014, 204), where exercises, Q&A and other activities could all be much more interactive than a workshop where students outside London simply followed a DVD.

Though the cost of providing bespoke workshops can be prohibitive, and in fact proved so for Shakespeare's Globe, other companies have found other ways to use social media to give audiences access to their productions and production processes. Geoffrey Way (2011), for instance, writes of how Elizabeth Hunter, director of the Sloss

Performing Arts Company in Birmingham, USA, decided to use social media sites such as Facebook, Twitter and YouTube to allow audiences access and insight into the company's 2010 production of *Romeo and Juliet*. After inviting audiences in Birmingham and beyond to take part in the experiment, Hunter and the ensemble put up Facebook profiles for the characters, run by the actors playing them, so that people who "friended" them could be privy to images, accounts of rehearsal exercises, experiments and decisions, and even provide feedback. The experiment continued into the show's season, with Hunter finding Facebook (with 700 followers) more conducive than Twitter (with 150 followers) to the experiment. With such streaming, dissemination and real-time documentation practices, social media allows these companies to create a sort of living culture of engagement with Shakespeare plays, along the lines that new performance archivists advocate, this time in relation to only their own offerings.

Other mainstage theatre companies have explored similar opportunities for presenting a living archive of their work. In my context in Brisbane, for example, although the main theatre companies in the city—the state theatre company, the Queensland Theatre Company and the other major professional theatre company, La Boite Theatre Company—have yet to experiment with live streaming, like most theatre companies today, both offer snippets of shows, interviews and reviews for spectators to engage with online before, during or after seeing the performance. In the case of the Queensland Theatre Company, the effort to enable greater engagement with its performances via social media has been supported by a "Geek in Residence Program" run by the Australia Council for the Arts. Offered to nine state and mainstage theatre and dance companies across Australia, the programme paid for a "geek" to join the company for a year, to teach them "how to update their websites and fire up their social media profile, as well as archiving digital material and learning about live and online Performance" (Plumley cited by Blake 2010).

Although these practices do offer a living archive of a company's production practices, adopting social media has not always lived up to the aspirations of a programme such as "Geek in Residence Program", which is designed to encourage mainstage companies to learn about digital theatre innovation as much as about improving websites, documentation and dissemination. As Way (2011) argues in his analysis of the Sloss Theatre experiment, for example, although it "advertised the use of social network sites as an integral part of its performance and a performance experiment in and of itself", the actors' tendency to avoid interacting as their character, and instead post as themselves, meant that the experiment became more of an audience development exercise than an aesthetic experiment. Many such experiments have been successful in audience development terms. They have provided new opportunities to access traditionally inaccessible productions, or traditionally inaccessible aspects of the production process such as the rehearsals (Holland 2009, 258), as well as new archives for later analysis of trends in the canonical theatre that mainstage companies tend to privilege. They have been useful for actors looking to document their own process, recording things they have tried, decisions they have made and sequences they have set. They have been useful for scholars in documenting this process, developing accounts of those decisions to inform their analyses of the shows. They have been useful for other artists to see how social media has been used in the production's development and/or dissemination. They have been used to make platforms available, or applications, that share everything from motivations, to training methods, to rehearsal methods, documentation of shows, programmes, reviews, paratextual material and more, simply by swiping a mobile phone against a Q-code. However, these sorts of experiment are, as Way (2011) contends, still strongly controlled and edited by the companies. In this sense, these practices constitute a living new media archive, but the level of interactivity with the work they provide is not greater than the level of interactivity with the work that post hoc historical archives provide, and, indeed, it is often lower on the spectrum. It remains, in Ryan's (2001) terms, at the selective end of the spectrum of interactivity. If there is any co-creation, it is not in the aesthetic domain but in the critical domain, where the audience has the power to determine their own perception and interpretation of the work. It raises the question of whether these real-time documentation practices are in fact becoming a way in which companies can take back authority over their place in the archive, as other archives become more ready to acknowledge their partiality, perspectivality and openness to alternative narratives.

The questions around these types of archiving practices thus both replay and differ from those raised by the changes to historical archiving practices that the uptake of social media in the theatre also allows. Many mainstage companies are in receipt of regular government and sponsor subsidies, with rules requiring that they experiment with social media engagement with their audiences. In this sense, though the time, effort and cost of creating and disseminating content through social media platforms is still an issue, it is not as much of an issue as it is for archival projects. However, their compulsion to post, their character when posting and the content can be linked to a desire to develop new audiences as much as to a desire to innovate in their work. This can create conversations with circulatory appeal, as a current show prompts spectators to click through to, like or follow posts, in a way that non-current historical archives do not. The spectators' agency in these interactions does, though, remain at the selective end of the spectrum, which may hold limited appeal, particularly if more productive participation has been held out as part of the promise. This, according to Purcell, means that many mainstage adoptions of social media for archiving, documenting and disseminating work tend "to reaffirm traditional categories of 'liveness' despite (or perhaps because of) their own implicit challenges to them" (2014, 213). As Sant argues, "[p]articipation is an essential element for the survival and growth of social media" (2014, 51). If participatory promise remains unfulfilled, these uptakes of social media may not maintain or grow spectator interest in the short, medium or long term. This may not be an issue for historical archives, where ongoing engagement over days, weeks, months and years is not necessarily part of the encounter they are looking to create with spectators, but it can be for contemporaneous archives, where ongoing engagement is often crucial to a company's sustainability.

## Social Media as/and New Media Aesthetics

When theatre makers take up social media technologies in the ways described thus far—take up wikis or YouTube channels to create, disseminate or stream archives of their work to audiences—they allow spectators increased access to a production, and to elements of a production process that they would not normally be privy to, before, during or after a show's completion. They allow spectators increased access to training, rehearsal and creative development activities taking place around a show or a season of shows. This in itself already starts to shift what spectators see, when, where and how, and thus shift the relationships between producers, performers and spectators. However, these practices are still extending the circulation of a show created on a conventional stage, rather than enacting a show on the non-conventional stage of the social media app or platform itself. In parallel with these experiments, then, some artists are also taking further imaginative leaps and actually making shows specifically for, or on, these new platforms. Although adopting social media platforms as a means of developing or disseminating work already starts to shift the producer–performer–spectator relationships that underpin it, Way argues that "[a]n even larger shift occurs when social media become the platforms for dramatic performances" (2011). In other words, it is when theatre makers start to use social media to stage work that aesthetic innovations that have even greater scope to change relationships, participation patterns and agency really start to emerge.

Even the most cursory survey of the field shows that the types of works that theatre makers are producing via social media as a platform or stage for performance are already diverse. They run the gamut from a new generation of immersive, telematic and networked performances, to a new generation of participatory performances, to a new generation of pranksterish or guerrilla performances that hijack the self-performances already present on the platform to turn them to new ends, comment on them, critique them or change them, in the process blurring the boundaries between drama and day-to-day life, by mimicking the daily forms and formats of identity performance, play and games. The motivation for theatre makers to produce these types of work also runs the gamut, from the aesthetic to the political, where the more activist theatre and performance makers re-engage, re-enact and re-envisage relations on social media platforms to try to comment on them. The works can take place in theatres, where Wi-Fi allows performers and spectators to transmit text, voice or visuals from one part of the auditorium to another, in both theatre and online spaces at once or totally in online spaces. The works can take place across many different platforms and many different timescales, from 5 min to 5 weeks, with many different types of producers, performers, spectators or members of the public involved. The choices depend on the technological possibilities that the artists see in the platforms, the social and self-performance problems that the artists see in the platforms, or a combination of the two. The works, though, are almost always spectator-oriented, focused on making remote, proxy or participatory spectatorship possible, although, as I will shortly argue, the types of participation can again vary.

## Immersive, Telematic and Networked Performance

The first main category of work making use of social media technologies to create new aesthetics, interactivities and styles of art is immersive, telematic or networked performance. Although such work has been around as long as the internet, the emergence of social media platforms makes the technologies more accessible to more artists because high levels of coding or programing skill are no longer necessary. In terms of definition, it is theoretically possible to differentiate immersive performance, telematic performance, networked performance and cyber performance. Immersive performance can be defined as work that tries to draw spectators into a fictional or fantasy world. Telematic performance can be defined as work that tries to draw two or more spectators at remote locations into the same fictional world. Networked performance brings spectators from a range of locations—often at nodes, or hubs, in particular locations—into the same fictional world. The terms "cyber performance" and "cyber theatre", which are also occasionally applied to these works, are by other artists reserved as a descriptor for work that takes place totally online, such as work that occurs in a simulated world on the Second Life platform (Chatzichristodoulou 2010; Chatzichristodoulou et al. 2009; Varley Jamieson 2008). However, as Hope and Ryan (2014) argue, in practice, theatre makers tend to deploy these features of immersive, telematic, networked or cyber performance as suits their own purposes, and they use the terms in slightly different or even contradictory ways. Whatever the technological features in focus, the work is often explicitly characterised as experimental or innovative, drawing its funding from sponsors, supporters and agencies that are interested in the digital disruption and digital innovation agenda.

Although histories can vary in terms of what they characterise as the "first" immersive, telematic or cyber performances, there are key touchstones for this type of work.

One such touchstone, discussed by Suzan Kozel (2007), Gabriella Giannachi (2004), Yoni Prior (2014) and others, is Paul Sermon's *Telematic Dreaming* (1992). In this piece, Sermon creates an online connection between two beds, in two locations, laying an image of the artist in one of the beds over an image of the spectator-become-participant in the other bed via the real-time recording and projection of the two sets of images from the two locations. Although it precedes the emergence of social media platforms as we know them today, the technology can now be replicated by remote communication platforms such as Skype. In a sense, *Telematic Dreaming* is both an immersive work (in that it invites spectators into a mixed or augmented reality) and a telematic work (in that it invites people in two different locations into the same mixed or augmented reality). The spectators are immersed in both the actual world of the real bed and the virtual world of the projected bed, and, because the artist could see both streams of video in real time, he could invite the spectator-become-participant to interact with him in real time. According to Kozel, "[t]he effect was astonishing: it was one of contact improvisation between an image and a person, between a ghost and matter" (2007, 36). Recounting the way the work unfolded, Kozel claims:

> The intimacy between the two divergent bodies was compelling. The people tended to be shy of Paul's image on the bed. It was common for them to sit upright on the edge of the bed and tentatively reach for his hands. He responded slowly, gently, making his movements match theirs. He danced with them. It became clear that the position of power was Paul's. Paradoxically, even though he appeared as a projected image he was still able to intimidate ... In his work Paul's body became virtual (i.e. a projected image), yet the rapport between image and person was very real and evoked a social and sexual dynamic familiar to us all (36).

As Kozel (2007, 36) and Giannachi (2004, 107) argue, *Telematic Dreaming* was an interactive performance, but the interaction of the piece was strongly directed by the artist, who was in control of the ways in which the contact between the two players tended to unfold. Moreover, as Prior (2014, 179) maintains, it was very clearly meant to be seen mainly by the two parties involved in the encounter—the artist, and the spectator-become-collaborating artist—not by an outside audience watching the parties interact on the actual-and-virtual bed. For Prior (179), the co-location of the two participants on the flat surface of the bed means that *Telematic Dreaming* did not face the challenge of trying to find a scenographic relationship to another audience, watching, participating or performing their role from another angle, that would retain the illusion of actual and virtual realities coming together seamlessly. It used one-to-one, [virtual]-face-to-[virtual]-face technology to facilitate one-to-one, [virtual]-face-to-[virtual]-face technology interaction, rather than to foster more multiple interactions between a range of performers, participants and spectators, where there is a need to find a way to realise what Prior (179) calls the "impossible triangle" between the three—something that Prior and others have had to wrestle with more in more recent types of immersive and telematic performance work.

A work such as *Telematic Dreaming* as a touchstone in the evolution of the use of two-way interactive media in performance provides an example of work that is primarily—or at least largely—motivated by aesthetic innovation. What Sermon seeks to do in creating the work is to bring his spectator-become-participant into a mixed, augmented or virtual reality, a fantasy world, in a way that would not be possible in day-to-day life—in this case a fantasy world in which the two are lovers, connecting intimately, physically, on a bed that becomes the entire landscape of their world. Motivated by aesthetic innovation, with experience and engagement as its defining elements, managed by means of a one-on-one encounter, and managed by means of a mainly artist-driven or artist-directed encounter, the work is about the singular perspective, of the single spectator, participating in the engaging experience of connecting with a sort of ghost lover.

Other touchstones in the uptake of two-way interactive media in performance take the technology's possibilities in different directions. The work of UK mixed reality company Blast Theory, for instance, takes much of its impetus from the affordances of role-playing games. Although Blast Theory's work has been varied—in *Kidnap* (1998) audiences volunteer to be kidnapped, in *Uncle Roy All Around You* (2003), audiences are asked to make a year-long commitment to a stranger they have tracked down via a smartphone game through a cityscape, in *Rider Spoke* (2007), audiences use instructions on a computer device to cycle around a city seeking a hiding place in which to record a message, and in *Too Much Information* (2015), the audience use smartphones to seek out intimate secrets in city streets—it is always multilayered in the types of telematic connections it creates. The work uses social and locative media to set up missions, journeys or games in which a spectator-become-player interacts with a real world with virtual overlays, but the real world with overlays is a more complex urban space, and the connections with other characters, scenarios, settings, and realities within the space are more complex than those created in earlier works, such as *Telematic Dreaming*. In the interactive installation, performance and game piece *Desert Rain* (1999–2003), for instance, a group of players are given a photo of a person, then tasked to find them by moving through a mixed reality space in which they are confronted with highly mediatised images of war, referencing the highly mediated images of war that became the hallmark of most people's experience of the First Gulf War. As Giannachi (2004, 115–122) observes, the spectators-become-players enter this highly mediatised world via their own avatars, in the way they might enter the mixed, augmented or virtual reality of a game via an avatar. "The participants were taken through a journey, from the real to the virtual then back again," she recalls, "only to find out that what appeared as virtual could in fact be real and hence also leave a real trace (of sand) in the viewer's lives" (119). In *Desert Rain*, then, Blast Theory uses two-way interactive, immersive and telematic technology to make spectators reflect on the illusions that such technologies can create, in which the real and the fictional start to blur, and in which a sense of responsibility to others within this reality can start to falter—to bring spectators into the flow of the experience, feeling it, forgetting the real world outside the fiction, but then bring them out of the flow of the experience, to reflect on it, and think about it. The work is still artist facilitated, and to some degree artist directed, but the one-to-one relationship is placed in a wider context, a more public context and a more metareflexive context, where the spectator is asked to take more responsibility for the actions, interactions and attitudes they choose to display during the encounter. In this sense, this type of work is a more meaningful or relevant precursor to the modern uptake of social media in theatre because it raises the issues of human identity, relationships and responsibilities in a technologised world in the way that later works also often aim to.

A body of work such as Blast Theory's, as a touchstone in the evolution of the use of two-way interactive social media in performance, provides an example of work that is primarily—or at least largely—motivated by the politics of participation, collaboration, choices and reflection on choices. While the work often uses game structures, where it differs from games and gamified everyday encounters is in the sort of metalevel reflection it tries to create. Comparing Blast Theory's work to more entertainment-driven work highlights this. For instance, in Deb Poulson's *Scoot* (2004–2009, www.scootagency.com), a real-time interactive game popular at festivals with family audiences, young spectators-become-players are tasked to act as a SCOOT agent called a S'Avatar, reporting information gathered back to the agency, creating teams and competing with others while moving through public space, such as the Southbank parklands when it was presented during the Brisbane

Riverfestival in 2007. *Scoot* uses social and locative media to mediate, replay and reposition relationships within a real life environment, to blend the real life and represented environments into a mixed reality. The technology is a precursor to now increasingly popular augmented reality games, such as that offered via the Pokemon GO app. In selecting characters to engage with, paths and encounters, the players are selecting their own experience. However, they are not necessarily called on to think about these things at a metalevel. In the work of companies such as Blast Theory, by contrast, the interactions are designed to prompt reflection on action, interaction and choices. They blur the boundary between drama and daily life by mimicking day-to-day forms, such as smartphone games, but they are distinguished from games by the fact that capturing and reflecting on the spectators' choices is often central to the aesthetics, poetics, politics and impact of the work.

## Virtual Performance

The term "virtual performance" is occasionally applied to these immersive, telematic and networked performances, where audiences are drawn into a mixed or augmented reality, which references games, play and identify performance in contemporary culture, and asks both artist and audience to take part in the flow and unfolding of the action. For some artists, though, the terms "virtual theatre" or "cyber theatre" are more rightly reserved for another category of work that takes place almost totally online—almost totally in the sense that the participants are always going to have some grounding in the real world where they work with their computer to enter the virtual world.

The touchstone for this type of performance is the MOO and MUD theatre that began almost as soon as these types of platform became available to communities online (Giannachi 2004, 89–94). "As creative people [begin to] inhabit virtual worlds," Stephen Schrumm observes, "they bring their ideas for art and performance with them into these brave new worlds" (2009). As Purcell notes, for instance, it was not long after Second Life (a simulated reality platform set up as an other life, with an other society, economy and system) was set up that groups such as the SL Shakespeare Company emerged. As a Second Life theatre company, the SL Shakespeare Company allowed avatar citizens of an avatar world to watch other avatars perform inside a visualisation of the Globe Theatre in Second Life (2014, 221). In other words, in what

Iryna Kuksa and Mark Childs (2014), Stephen Schrumm (1999) and Randal Walser (1991) have called a virtual or cyber playhouse. In such work, each participant performs their role as actor or as audience member by means of an avatar—what Schrumm (2009) has likened to a mask but, in this case, the masks are multiplied as a person takes on a Second Life avatar, which in turn takes on a character avatar, in the theatre. Though such avatars may be more or less realistic, these virtual theatres move beyond mixed or augmented reality into a virtual world. Here, one participant is not projected into another participant's reality, or remote reality; all participants are projected into a cyberspace that has no location in the physical world. Perhaps paradoxically, though such online theatres and theatre-making practices are less reminiscent of real life, in the sense that they leave the real world behind, they are also more reminiscent of real life in the sense that they frequently replicate a lot of "the outward trappings of theatre" (2009) in the virtual world they create. Stage, stalls, auditorium and foyers—not present in most of the mixed reality immersive and telematic work described above—are often present in these virtual theatres. Textual, visual and, later, video clues and cues remediate more realistic representations of the theatre, stage, actors and auditorium than in most immersive or telematic performances, where the work unfolds from a bed, bedroom, hotel room or warzone. Naturally, this is not universal practice. Ian Upton, for example, found it easier to engage spectators when he moved beyond real world theatre models in works such as *Ritual Circle* in Second Life, basing them on non-theatre places, which can call on and create new emotional resonance as readily as replicas of famous theatres such as the Globe. For him,

> Second Life is primarily a 3D social networking site, and people within it have formed communities and are subverting the space for their own ends, whether they are going to dance clubs, playing role-play games, creating galleries or doing theatre. Fundamentally, if the communities weren't there it would be irrelevant whether a building was there or not; whereas in the real world the buildings don't need the people to exist, they would still be there and have their own meanings and history (Upton 2014, 133)

Though remediating real theatres remain important to many makers of virtual visualisations of theatres—to perform in them, or even just to tour them—others have experimented with alternative approaches. In the *Machinima Futurista* experiment at the Georgia Institution of

Technology, for example (Bolter et al. 2013), Jay David Bolter, Blair MacIntyre, Michael Nitsche and Kathryn Farley took the opposite approach, taking avatars from Second Life and placing them in the real world, in videos of real world settings, which have a greater likeness to life than the digital theatres, so it made it seem as if the avatars were entering the real world. For advocates, the blurring of avatars and real-life actors and settings in work such as Upton's, or Bolter, MacIntyre, Nitsche and Farley's, allows it to move beyond old-fashioned debates about liveness, presence or the diminishment of it in a digital world and to explore new alternatives.

A more recent incarnation of cyber theatre where replicating real life theatres becomes far less important is Helen Varley Jamieson's Upstage (www.upstage.org.nz/), a purpose-created platform where artists, activists and other participants use avatars to perform plays, performances and post-show talks on a social media-style platform. This bespoke platform allows participants to log in from anywhere in the world, at allocated performance times, and take part in performances. In operation since 2003, the Upstage platform has already had a long life, and a varied one, as a stage for what Varley Jamieson calls "cyberformances" (2008). This includes presenting regular "festivals" celebrating landmarks in the platform's life with a varied set of cyberformances. In the 08082008 Upstage Festival I reviewed for *Australian Theatre Online* (Hadley 2008a), for instance, the programme curated by Varley Jamieson, Vicki Smith and Dan Agnihotri-Clark featured a dozen performances from new media artists in New Zealand, Australia, the USA, Canada, Europe and the Middle East. Spectators connected either from their home computers or at "nodes" in their country to watch a set of works thematised around presence, absence, emplacement, ecology, connections, identity, power and storytelling in cyberspace. In *RxEgo-Go* by Tara Rebele (USA), Miljana Peric (Serbia) and Suzon Fuks (Australia/Belgium), a woman takes a pill and, with a hallucinogenic whirl of sound and colour, collapses into UpStage as an avatar, then considers how to get out, while a teleprompt robot tries to cure her of the aesthetic interdisciplinary that's causing her ills via a digital lobotomy. In *Noir Night* by Kristin Carlson and Sheila Page (USA), audiences are asked to think about their connection to their body image as two dresses ("Frump" who feels ugly compared with the gorgeous "Red Dress"), search for a missing self, chased by a Mr Big character with gangster costume and guns. In *Amazigh Storyteller* by Nadia Oufrid (Lebanon), the artist's struggle to reconcile her Amazigh (Berber) and Arab identities is told against a slide show of her land and people. In *Merznet* by Ben Unterman, Daniel Silverman, Maya Jarvis and Inouk Touzin (Canada), text from Kurt Switters' poems is used to share the story of an ever-growing group confronted by a stranger who will not speak to them until sirens and shots ring out and a riot begins. In Noxitera by Antoinette LaFarge (USA) and Marlena Corcoran (USA/Munich/Seoul), a biome built from global warming data becomes a slide show of a green-blue world, blended with a poetic stream of text about beginnings and endings that becomes a visual poem. In *Workshop Zoo*, by Katarina Djordjevic Urosevic with Matija, Kaja, Isidora, Luka and Sofia (Belgrade), children from Serbia ask where animals live, and what associations animals hold, while images of animals play across images of the planet and the ocean. The aesthetic is diverse, and the avatar characters are depicted through figures, line drawings, colours, sounds and other symbols in all sorts of imagined spaces and places, few of which bear any resemblance to human players in a conventional theatre. During each of the Upstage performances, a chat panel to the side of the cyberstage allows spectators to share questions, asides, interpretations and revelations—the whispered conversations that go unseen in a conventional theatre—including critique of other cultural phenomena playing out elsewhere on the web (e.g. the Beijing Olympics Opening Ceremony). This feature of the platform creates connections and a sense of collective creativity among the global spectators-become-participants. In a platform like UpStage, participation, as well as meta-level reflection on participation, and on larger global politics, facilitated through chat mechanisms similar to those seen in *The Radicalisation of Bradley Manning* site, again becomes a feature that the use of social media technology in online performance foregrounds. The affordances of the platform facilitate new blurrings or combinations of performance and para-performance.

## Mainstage Participatory Social Media Performances

The next major category of work making use of social media is a new generation of participatory performance which takes place via these platforms. The main difference between these next examples of participatory performance and the immersive, telematic or cyber performance work is the fact that these works are not trying to create a visual of a new mixed, augmented or virtual reality into which the spectator can step. They are, rather, about using social media platforms to play out adaptations of old performance pieces, or purpose written new pieces, using the affordances of Twitter, Facebook or other platforms as the stage for the work.

As with the archiving and streaming of theatre work online, Shakespearean theatre provides some of the major touchstones for this uptake of social media in the theatre. There is a long history of Shakespeare on the internet. Toni Sant (2014, 45) writes, for example, of Stuart Harris and the Hamnet Players presenting *Hamlet* via internet relay chat as far back as the early 1990s. In April 2010, almost two decades later, the RSC, under the artistic direction of Michael Boyd, and in collaboration with multiplatform company Mudlark, deployed 4000 posts over 5 weeks to present Tim Wright and Bethan Marlow's modern retelling of *Romeo and Juliet* called *Such Tweet Sorrow* on Twitter and other internet platforms (2010, www.wearemudlark.com/projects/such-tweet-sorrow/)—an experiment that has, in the years since, become among the most commonly discussed examples of social media theatre.

In promotional material, *Such Tweet Sorrow* was cast "as a dramatic performance on Twitter, instead of a dramatic performance adapted to Twitter" (Purcell 2014; Sant 2014; Way 2011). Though based on mediated , recordable, repeatable tweets, it was characterised as a real-time performance event rather than a remediation of a past performance event on an alternative platform. In this sense, the ambition from the start was to produce a work that would retain the ephemerality, unpredictability and power of the live human-to-human encounter that Way (2011), Hope and Ryan (2014) and others argue can be as present in online theatre encounters as in offline theatre encounters, even if this encounter unfolds in a virtual-face-to-virtual-face rather than physical-face-to-physical-face form. A cast of six actors—James Barrett and Charlotte Wakefield in the title roles of Romeo and Juliet, with others in the roles of Mercutio, Nurse, Juliet's sister Jess, Juliet's brother Tybalt, and Friar Laurence—were given daily instructions to guide their telling of their character's story on Twitter. Use of a story grid instead of a complete script allowed the actors to share supposedly real-time events and relationships, and share these in their own words rather than in Shakespearean language. The characters' self-performances on Twitter constantly tried to reflect emerging conventions of self-performance in social media in the brevity versus depth, importance versus mundanity, frequency, diversity and appeal of their posts—or, when they did not reflect those conventions, draw attention to that non-conformance by declaring that the character was still learning to use the platform. The main plot-based posts were interspersed with posts about work from Jess or about big nights out from Mercutio, embodying the collapse of personal, social and professional life that is characteristic of relationships on these platforms. The fictional world was given an extra dimension with links to photos, videos and music videos of the characters created for the purpose, such as a YouTube channel set up to give insight into Juliet, embodying the multimedia characteristics of communication on these platforms. Throughout the month, social media users were invited to interact with or offer advice to the characters, either on main plot points or on more mundane and peripheral points, or both. As Purcell (2014, 221) notes, while actors were given instructions, they were also asked to interact and improvise with audiences and with actual things happening in the world at the time. This meant that the audience could, at least in theory, become active participants in the performance through the conventions of Twitter conversations—and thus, in theory, highlights the way in which this form of performance remains live, ephemeral and unpredictable.

According to some commentators, the creators' clear familiarity with and choice to adopt the conversational conventions of Twitter as outlined in Chap. 2 allowed *Such Tweet Sorrow* to overcome difficulties that Dixon (2007) and others had identified with past digital performance practices. These, according to Way (2011), included the fact that it can be hard to get all audience members to join an online platform at the same time, or use the platform in the same way, and this can make it challenging for theatre makers to successfully address the style, substance and frequency of a remote audience's interaction with their work. The fact that Twitter is set up on the premise that people will not see every single tweet, will drop in and out, will scroll back a little but not days, weeks, months or years, taking part in both synchronous and asynchronous communication—together with a timeline that the producers offered for latecomers to catch up—allowed *Such Tweet Sorrow* to overcome issues with who joined the platform, when and how. It also allowed *Such Tweet Sorrow* to overcome difficulties that other scholars have identified with Shakespearean performance in that it allowed audience members to engage via a modern platform and modern self-performance conventions with which they were already familiar.

According to other commentators, though, the attempt—though admirable—was not altogether successful. For Purcell, for example, there were "formal and stylistic problems" (2014, 221) with an "uneasy" mixture of Shakespearean, modern and internet language, which could not altogether be overcome by the fictional convention that some of the characters were still attempting to learn the Twitter form. Lonergan agrees, noting the ways in which the combination of historical and contemporary language, improvised and predetermined plot, jarred with audience attempts at more productive intervention in the plot such as a blog post on "10 Reasons Why Mercutio Must Live", and thus produced problems and paradoxes in the experiment (2016, 48). What their comments point to is the fact that the metareflection on the conventions of communicating via social media—a factor in the success of some of the immersive social media performances discussed earlier—was a factor that had the potential to cause failure with this more mainstage company's efforts to engage the new technology to create new work—a result, perhaps, of the differences in the sort of flow experience that an experimental company versus a mainstage company typically tries to create for their audiences. As Lonergan observes, "the plot of *Such Tweet Sorrow* had been predetermined by the existence of the original *Romeo and Juliet*" (47–48). More precisely, the plot had been predetermined by the RSC's desire to follow the original *Romeo and Juliet* plot points. Accordingly, attempts by audience members to use the affordances of social media technology to critique, challenge or change the plot by exercising the full scope of the productive, not just selective, co-creativity that these platforms allow brought a sense of failure rather than a sense of freedom in this case.

Whether read as a success or an experiment with some stylistic failures, the project worked well enough for the RSC to produce a follow-up, *Midsummer Night's Dreaming*, in 2013, with support from Google Creative Lab (https://www.thinkwithgoogle.com/campaigns/midsummer-nights-dreaming.html), in which live performance and interactive internet updates retold the story of *A Midsummer Night's Dream* over the midsummer weekend in real time (Purcell 2014, 221). This said, the RSC's subsequent work in this and other social, locative and mobile media experiments still tends to be among the most experimental of its endeavours, and to be co-created with other companies, advertised as a value add to the seasons rather than a central part of the company's core seasons.

Though among the best known, *Such Tweet Sorrow* is by no means the only project to attempt to present a modern retelling of a Shakespeare play, or of another conventional play, via a social media platform. Though acknowledging that the most talked about uptake of social media in theatre thus far has been as a marketing tool, scholars such as Sant (2014), Worthen (2014) and Purcell (2014), as well as theatre critics such as Cathy Westbrook (2014) in the UK and Viviana Vargas (2014), Alex Ates (2014) and Jonathan Mandell (2013) in the US, have all written about what Mandell characterises as a "small but growing" (2013) set of companies using social media for performance itself. Sant (2014, 45) cites Sarah Schmelling and Angela Liao's *Hamlet* (*Facebook News Feed Edition*) (2008), which presents the main plot points as though Shakespeare were posting to the site. Worthen (2014, 148–149) cities Elliott Visconsi and Katherine Rowe's iPage app presenting *The Tempest*, as well as the Explore Shakespeare app produced by Cambridge University Press. Purcell (2014, 220–221) cites UK company Punchdrunk's site-adapted, interactive adaptations of *A Midsummer Night's Dream* (2002), *The Tempest* (2003), *Romeo and Juliet* (*The Firebird Ball*, 2005) and *Macbeth* (*Sleep No More*, 2003, 2010), in which the audience move through multimedia installations in public spaces and places, encountering actors and actions, via devices like customized headsets. Mandell (2013) cites Whit MacLaughlin's Macbeth-based *Fatebook: Avoiding Catastrophe One Party at a Time* (2009) for UK company New Paradise Laboratories, in which audiences connect with a cast of 13 actors' characters via Facebook, Twitter and YouTube profiles, posts, conversations and conflicts, along with a Fatebook website, characters who eventually invite them to a party in a warehouse where they encounter characters on a maze of screens and in person in a cyclical event, eventually culminating in an "accidental" killing of a character. Casting themselves as an internet-based theatre company, New Paradise Laboratories is also building a bespoke online performance platform called FRAME to further their work (www.newparadiselaboratories.org), bridging the territory between social media site-based performance and two-way interactive performance on purpose-built platforms such as UpStage. Mandell (2013) also cites the work of US "neo-futurist" Jeffrey Cranor, who each week since 2010 has been asking followers to write plays on Twitter, plays that adapt other plays, or that feature a psychic, or some other subject, resulting in works such as the Henrik Ibsen *Hedda Gabler*-inspired "JORGEN: Sorry darling, life doesn't seem to be turning out as we planned. HEDDA: Whatevs (Hedda walks offstage and shoots herself)" (cited by Mandell 2013). Cathy Westbrook (2014) cites other efforts to foster co-creative communities in the Theatre in the Cloud project by UK company Futuredream, and the Storylines project by the UK's Pilot Theatre, which encourage spectators-become-co-creators to collaborate in the development of work online. Other attempts at creating co-creative communities have moved from plays into production seasons. In the UK, for example, My Fierce Festival has invited a co-creating community of spectators and other stakeholders to vote on which shows should be included in a given year, and thus to become co-curators.

In each of these examples, publicity, promotional material and press position work as "experiments" which have the potential to popularise theatre in a digital age by exploring new aesthetic possibilities, and new interactive possibilities, which allow audiences to feel more ownership of, and thus investment in, a work or a festival of works. "Theatre-makers have never been restricted by space," says Cathy Westbrook, and these experiments represent efforts to start finding "the right style for the web" (2014). While the work of smaller companies may not be as prominent as that of the major companies in pieces such as the RSC's *Such Tweet Sorrow*, it is necessary to address questions of access and appeal for new generations of audiences. It is important precisely because of its differences from some of the more mainstage work—in particular, the fact that the mainstage experiments do not display or display pleasure in the meta-level reflection seen in the immersive, telematic and networked performances by companies popular on the international festival circuit, such as Blast Theory, Rimini Protokoll or The Builder's Association, or companies working on cyberformances platforms, such as Upstage; plus, of course, the fact that mainstage experiments tend to sit alongside core seasons rather than become central to them, and to the whole mission of the company, also distinguishes them from the work of companies such as New Paradise Laboratories or Futuredream.

## Prankish, Activist and Political Participatory Social Media Performances

As these experiments in social media theatre have unfolded in mainstream and more independent theatre contexts over nearly a decade now, there have also been experiments by more prankish, activist and political artists in this area. While the aesthetics of this last category of work are diverse, they often turn on the potential new media holds not only to encourage spectators to make choices—productive, not just selective, interactivity—but also to reflect on their choices. The artists use Facebook, Twitter or other social media platforms as the stage on which they play out a purpose-written, provocative and often quite politicised work, the performance unfolding in the liminal online world, a real world rather than an artificially constructed mixed, augmented or virtual reality. The works are prankish, or guerrilla, because they are designed to play out a social reality but, at the same time, turn it, critique it or comment on it. In this sense, blurring the boundaries between daily self-performance on social media platforms, dramatic performance on social media platforms, and performances in other public spaces is central to the aesthetics and politics of the work.

The historical touchstone for this type of work is the early *Ethno-Cyberpunk Trading Post* (1995) project of Guillermo Gómez-Peña's La Pocha Nostra performance group. In this work, Gómez-Peña, James Luna and Roberto Sifuentes broadcast images of themselves performing stereotypes of Latin American identity—from Zorro, to gang members, assassins and transvestites—informed by the views of synchronous and asynchronous audiences encouraged to "send in images, sounds, and texts about how [they felt] Mexicans, Chicanos and Native Americans should look, behave, and perform in the 1990s" (Gómez-Peña 1999, 57). According to Giannachi (2004, 144), this and other "techno-diorama projects" received more than 20,000 hits over three years and formed the basis for later work, such as *Mexterminator* (1998) and *Museum of Fetishized Identities* (2000). The work provided audiences with the opportunity to anonymously reperform their worst prejudices and, perhaps, in seeing these responded to and replayed in such over-the-top ways by Gómez-Peña and his collaborators, reflect on their worst prejudices. "With this," Giannachi argues, "Gómez-Peña draws attention to one of the fundamental characteristics of the Web: although it feels like a secure and enclosed environment, probably because of its friending interface, it is in fact a very public arena" (2004, 145). When spectators choose to co-create online performances, their insights, stereotypes and prejudices—in this case their prejudices about Latin Americans—are placed on the spot and in the spotlight in a public forum populated by potentially thousands of people in and beyond their own personal, social and professional networks. Their beliefs, attitudes and behaviours become exemplars for fellow spectators and society at large to judge, to critique and, potentially, to challenge too. This, for artists like Gómez-Peña, productively raises the stakes of the performance for their co-creating spectators, and thus the potential ethical and political efficacy of the performance.

A more recent work that puts spectators on the spot and in the spotlight in an effort to make them think about their attitude towards Others is *Domestic Tension* (2007) by Iraqi American performance artist Wafaa Bilal. In this installation, Bilal invited spectators to use a webcam in a chat room on his website (www.wafaabilal.com) to target him with paintballs while he was in residence in a living room set up in a gallery for a week in Chicago in the USA. With the artist in this living room all day every day for a month, spectators-become-co-creators could target and trigger the paintball gun to pelt him with colours remotely at any time. "Once logged into the site," Lara Stevens explains, "spectators could participate in the work by manoeuvring and/or firing the gun in the gallery and/or communicating with the artist and other participants in the artwork through online instant messaging—a format typically of massive multiplayer online gaming" (Stevens 2014, 79)—except that in this online game, remote targeting of an Iraqi in his living room led to real consequences, in a two-way interactive online performance that tried to prompt spectators-become-co-creators not just to choose their own course of action but to contemplate it, compare it with other spectator-become-co-creators' course of action and, in doing so, become exemplars for society at large to judge. At a time when other Iraqis were regularly being targeted for bombing by US drone strikes as part of the so-called War on Terror by the Bush administration, these questions were particularly fraught and politicised. "Throughout the month," Stevens notes, "the paintball gun was shot 65,000 times from online users in 136 countries" (2014, 79), splattering Bilal and his surrounds. This resulted in the artist "experiencing a relapse of post-traumatic stress disorder (PTSD) from which he had suffered as a persecuted Shia under Saddam Hussein's Ba'athist Party rule [in Iraq]" (80)—a real consequence, and thus a real chance for spectators-become-co-creators to reflect on the consequences of their remote, game-like, war-like relationship with an Other when encountering them online versus offline.

In a later participatory social media performance, starting in 2011 and running for several years, UK/US artist Brian Lobel invited audiences to become co-creators of a work with equally real—if not necessarily equally traumatic, or at least not necessarily equally physically traumatic—consequences for the artist. In *Purge*, Lobel invites audiences to gather in a live art space or auditorium, comment on and contribute to the construction of his network of friends by going through his Facebook friends with them. Lobel told stories about who the friends are, how he met them and how he maintained contact with them, and then invites the audience to vote to defriend or not defriend them. In putting his own relationships in the spotlight, he also put his spectators-become-co-performers' choices about his relationships in the spotlight. Elements of the performance, including the audience's decisions with regard to which of his Facebook friends he would keep, became visible not just in the face-to-face performance in the theatre but in the online performance of posts or people being added or removed from his network. This strategy of putting spectators' choices on the spot and in the spotlight so that they become fodder for fellow spectators and society to judge is, as I have argued elsewhere, a common strategy in participatory performance art (Hadley 2014). In Lobel's *Purge*, as in Bilal's *Domestic Tension*, the spectatorial performances become exemplars for the public's scrutiny, albeit in distinctly different ways. In *Purge* it is Lobel's friendships with a diverse range of fellow artists, activists and scholars, who form the digital tracings of the events in his life that have made him who he is, that are at stake. In *Domestic Tension* it is Bilal in his visibly Iraqi body who is at stake. In both cases, though, using social media technology to interact with real people, in real time with real consequences for both sides becomes a prompt for spectators to reflect on the way their use of digital technology to manage more or less remote relationships with more or less different others might have real consequences for those others.

While Lobel's participatory social media performance positions him as the present party, and his Facebook friends as the absent co-performing parties who may or may not remain part of his networks depending on how votes flow, other artists' participatory social media performances have turned this logic, using the technology to position themselves as the absent party impacted by other more present people's choices. In *Reach Out Touch Faith* presented by Sarah Rodigari with Joshua Sofaer and a goat as part of the Going Nowhere programme at the Arts House, Melbourne, in 2012, Rodigari delegated her own role in her own work to another person, Emma Hall, to facilitate a performance focused on her absence as much as her presence in her own artistic, social and self-performances online. Addressing the ongoing reality of life as an international travelling artist, the ongoing reality of the tyranny of distance in the digital age (particularly in Australia) and the aesthetics of what Claire Bishop calls "delegated performance" (2012a) by untrained performers, as well as questions about authenticity, aura and whether the presence of the artist's body, face to face with the audience, is critical to performance, the piece "performs the possibility of making a live performance in another city without physically being present" (Rodigari 2012) via two-way interactive media. It comments on whether technology is in fact producing the changes in labour and production relationships that make the live, local and unique irrelevant in a global digital age, changes that are sometimes claimed as potential consequences of its increased intrusion in our lives and our art.

Bilal's, Lobel's and Rodigari's performances are solo—or at least solo with co-creating spectators of tens, hundreds or thousands online. However, other participatory social media performances by activist theatre, performance and mixed-media collectives are less artist-led in nature. For example, founded by An Xiao in 2009, the @Platea performance group consists of a committee of eight core cross-media artists, together with a larger contributing network of artists, who come together via a Facebook page and a collaborative blog to come up with ideas for social media performances. The group's name, according to Gray (2012), references the idea of theatre as a public space, stage or platform on which all sorts of ideas can be played out, negotiated, contested or changed. As with most of the more participatory social media performances described above, @Platea uses a score or a set of rules rather than a script as the starting point for a performance, and it invites players to improvise with this core in their own ways. "During the event," Gray explains, "participants follow their own interpretation of the protocol" (2010), an improvisation, interpretation and the relationships between the prompts, the performances and their impact can become the subject of later debriefs on the collective's blog. In *Co-Modify*, the first piece that Gray participated in with the collective, the players picked a company to become an imaginary sponsor of them on their Facebook, Twitter or blog page for a week in 2009 "to see if the performers could catch the attention of their sponsorship company such that actual advertisements for the company might show up on Facebook or other pages" (Gray 2012; cf. Murnane 2009a, b). Targetting well-known US companies such as Adobe, Sharpie or Target, the participatory online performance score commented on what a social media platform's algorithms allow companies to pick up about people's self-performances on these platforms. It prompted a debrief discussion about the topic, in which some participants expressed concerns about "being made the non-consensual participants in a social experiment" (Gray 2012), or, more simply, "an uncritical celebration of advertising". While Bilal's, Lobel's and Rodigari's performances were framed as social media performances, where spectators might have had some awareness that their choices were becoming exemplars for fellow spectators and society to judge, here there was no such awareness or consent, making both the artists and their audiences more vulnerable in the encounter. "The irresolvable outcome of this discussion is less important", Gray argues, "than that it occurred at all and was part of the performance" (2012), a notion I return to in Chaps. 4 and 5 where I look at engaging audiences in debate about performance online.

While Bilal's, Lobel's, Rodigari's and @Platea's performances are specific scored, if not fully scripted, events, there are also a number of well-known artists who take social media performance further by performing their entire life online for weeks, months or even years. Among the best known is Chinese activist artist Ai Wei Wei, who is well known for broadcasting his life online—including broadcasting his life via four webcams while under house arrest for dissidence in his native China—as a sort of social-cum-aesthetic performance in which people can follow his every move. At the same time, other artists use the data generated by their day-to-day interaction with social media technology to make their work. In doing so they are connecting themselves with the so-called "quantified self" movement in which participants use apps to track any and every aspect of their lives—their body, their physical activities (e.g. sleeping, eating and exercise), their social activities and so on—by turning visualisations of such data into sculptures, installations or performance pieces. In the *Tracing Mobility* project curated by Elly Clarke at Galerie Suvi Lehtinen in Berlin in 2011, for instance, art collective Plan B turned GPS data tracking of movements around the city into a performative project, documenting it, tracing it on walks, and asking participants and spectators to talk about it. The patterns produced by the maps and the tracings of movements tracked by digital and social media became the material for the art and its reflection on life. In a similar work called *Quotidian Record* in 2012, Brian House put a year's worth of location tracking data onto an EP for people to listen to for the Eyebeam

Gallery in New York. In these works, records of the performative interactions with people, situations, environments and institutions are collected, and are represented in digital or non-digital artworks that audiences are encouraged to engage with, to reflect on how technology is influencing their day-to-day lives.

The work of these live and activist artists is diverse, reflecting on a range of contemporary social concerns, from remote warfare, to how relationships persist when lives are lived through digital technology rather than face to face, to how living lives in this way leaves us open to our personal data being collected and used against us by corporations, governments or other agencies. The work asks its audiences-become-co-creators to make choices that have real impacts on the real lives of the artist in one way or another, and potentially to present their choices as cases for fellow spectators and society to scrutinise. The work is open to criticism from a range of angles—from other followers, friends and connections upset at being drawn into participatory online performance, From spectators-become-co-creators upset that the choices they have made have been perceived as prejudiced, racist or capitalist. From commentators who are upset that the work comes too close to reconfirming the negative aspects of internet-based relationships that it sets out to critique. This may, though, be the very thing that moves the work from the selective to the productive end of the interactivity spectrum, allowing audiences to self-consciously reflect on, and in some cases intervene in, the internet-based relationships presented. What the works seem to share, with all their differences, is game-like structures to activate spectators, and allow spectators to have an actual impact on the way the work unfolds in online and offline worlds through their attitudes, actions and choices. They can actually injure Bilal's body, interrupt Lobel's relations with his friends or interject in Rodigari's performance, and they can also actually see other spectators-become-co-creators choosing to do this, sometimes in online space, sometimes in offline space and sometimes in both spaces at once. Although the artists still provide structure—which puts limits on what Gareth White (2013) calls the "horizon" of the spectator's possible participation in the performance—the structure is simpler, and thus more open to the spectator interacting with it productively. The engagement is not just experiential and meaningful but effects the progress of a performance that will not necessarily continue to a predetermined point regardless of what they do. It is also visible to fellow spectators and society. The stakes of the work are, as a result, higher than they would be if a spectator were engaging with a closed fictive world, anonymously, in the dark. The spectators' responses are visible and trackable on social media platforms—which, for all their fast-paced ephemerality and their private feel, do retain data indefinitely into the future, unless a user takes advantage of the "right to be forgotten" legislation starting to emerge in European jurisdictions. The spectator is thus more likely to feel awkward or embarrassed, creating a moment of uncertainty in which they can at least potentially start to think about their choices and decisions. This, for the artists, particularly for political artists such as Bilal or Gómez-Peña, is what gives social media performance the power they are looking for. The two-way interactive technology, and the artist's use of it in these more prankish, guerrilla and political works, can at least potentially make spectators more self-conscious of their attitudes, action, and choices in the moment, and, potentially, when they encounter similar moments—the issue of drone war, or of presence, absence, authenticity and relationships that live, grow, decline and die entirely online, or the way corporations are making use of the data we share when we live our lives online—in future.

What is interesting about these more prankish, guerrilla and political social media performances is the fact that, though they clearly acknowledge the power, agency and authority of the spectator in making, and making meaning of, a performance, they also acknowledge the twin-edged sword that this power puts into spectators' hands. In these works, participating in a collaborative, co-creative encounter online, in which the spectator has the power to make their own voice heard, can result in displeasure, antagonism, anger and feelings of alienation as readily as in a utopian feeling of engaging in a democratic community of equals. The aesthetics, affordances and interactivities of the work are more productive, though not necessarily more positive or celebratory. Though the tenor of participation can be fun in work like Lobel's or Rodigari's, as much as it can be morbid in work like Bilal's, all of the works at some level engage with power, powerlessness, marginalisation and the problems of exclusion in the digitally driven environments that have become our everyday environments. As Gray (2012) notes, for many, engaging in debate about these issues (offline, or via the metalevel reflection on practices on the online platforms themselves) is itself an integral part of the performance, its flow and its impacts.

## Social Media, Aesthetics and Interactivities

Adopting social media in what Bennett (1997) would call the "inner frame" of theatrical production, to develop new aesthetics, new presentation methods and new dissemination methods, based on the new and more interactive affordances of these media, has the potential to impact on many aspects of a theatre maker's work. As the examples in this chapter show, social media can be deployed as topic, as stimulus for text, dramaturgy or scenographic style, as archiving technology, as live streaming technology, as well as a stage for collaborative creation, presentation and reception of performance works. The two-way interaction in social media theatre performance can be more or less like standard artist audience interactions in the theatre, on the one hand, and more or less like standard poster–poster interactions in performing day-to-day life, relationships, games and politics on social media platforms, on the other hand. These interactions can be accessible or alienating, pleasurable or problematic, or both by turn as the event flows and unfolds.

The examples in this chapter show that these technologies do allow those who cannot see certain theatre work (whether because of geographic location, lack of funds, disability or other factors) access. They can see an NT Live show, or at least a version of it, streamed live or in the archives at some later point. They can make synchronous or asynchronous contributions to the feel, flow and, in some cases, content of an RSC work presented via platforms such as Twitter or Facebook. They can make and share meanings before, during or after seeing the work, with the artist, arts organisation and other authorities less able to gatekeep the flow of information than they were in the past—a possibility which, though barely flagged here, is discussed in Chaps. 4 and 5. In this sense, the affordances of social media platforms do have potential to give spectators more access to participate in theatre and theatrical meaning making. They do have potential to generate at least some shifts in the theatrical ecosystem, and the relations between artists, arts organisations, venues and audiences that are no longer the passive, well-prepared and attentive masses letting artists make all of the choices that Watt (2013) was looking for.

What the examples in this chapter also show, though, is that it is too early to make definitive claims about a distinctive aesthetics of social media theatre. In Sant's words, "[a]lthough media theorists like Lev Manovich (2001, 2012) have attempted to identify what aesthetic elements are unique/indigenous to the internet and the digital technologies associated with it, the medium is arguably not mature enough to enable the full identification of the essential qualities that make remarkable online performance/art different from works in other media" (2014, 52). The content, creator motivations, context, funding available, appeal, and factors determining success and failure vary as much as the style of the work. Clearly, social media archives, streaming activities, adaptations and interactions all still try to engage with a notion of event-ness—an event-ness that hinges on a spectator engaging with the app or platform that the artists use, in a specific way, at a specific time, to engender a specific sort of experience, rather than being present face to face with the artists as they produce the work. It may be engagement over about the same time period as a standard theatre show, as in streamed performances of *Hamlet*, *Othello* or *Timon of Athens*, or such as *The Radicalisation of Bradley Manning*. It may be engagement over hours, days or weeks in works like those on Upstage or Waterwheel, or *Such Tweet Sorrow* or *Ethno-Cyberpunk Trading Post* or Ai Wei Wei's streaming of his day-to-day life. It may be an engagement of moments in the case of *Telematic Dreaming*, *Domestic Tension* or Jeffrey Cranor's tweet plays. Or it may be engagement before, during and after engagement with live performance, as in *Desert Rain*, *Call Cutta in a Box*, *The Attendants*, the RSC's *A Midsummer Night's Dream*, *Sleep No More*, *Fatebook: Avoiding Catastrophe One Party At A Time*, *Purge* or *Reach Out Touch Faith*. Alternatively, it may involve engagement with work as it is made, as in *Various Selves* or Sloss Theatre's *Romeo and Juliet*, as it is presented, as in *Continuous City*, or after it is made, as with the Anarcha anti-archive. In some cases, engagement may turn more on reflecting on a work that spectators were not really aware they were a part of until after, as in *Co-Modify*. This engagement with event-ness is, as Purcell (2014, 212) notes, at odds with some older discourses that suggest that online theatre is more about catching up with work that a spectator could not be present for than a present meaning-making moment in and of itself. The argument, as Christie Carson and Peter Kirwan articulate it, is that "the digital audience member is required to engage with the form as well as the content, losing her/himself in it until the 'layers' of meaning become apparent" (Carson and Kirwan 2014, 239), just as they do in any theatre. Certainly, mainstage streaming uses cinematic camera techniques to direct attention, much more than other social media theatre. As Viviana Vargas (2014) notes, some streaming is so basic that it recalls "the first films of our time and just setting a camera in front of a stage". However, given that realist theatre has always directed audience attention to characters, scenarios and story points more heavily than what Hans Theis Lehmann (2006) calls post-dramatic theatre, this may be more about the aesthetics of the mainstage than the medium per se. Indeed, if we take mainstage streaming out of the equation, much social media performance tends to display the aesthetic fragmentation, multiperspectivality, intertextuality and other features that Lehmann (2006) characterises as post-dramatic. As Prior (2014, 171) and others note, the constraints and challenges of working with digital technology—the flatness of screens, and of actors and audiences on them, the fraughtness of trying to direct sightlines of two- or three- or four-way interaction between actor, screens and audiences, focus issues, pixelations, connection drop-outs, delays, and miscommunications—often become part of the aesthetic of the work, and become symbolic, metaphorical or metonymic of the technology's role in human relationships. A do-it-yourself aesthetic, in which production processes are simple, manual and visible to spectators, can also be part of some work. Perhaps most importantly, in social media theatre, as in much post-dramatic theatre, the separation between the factual and the fictional world is not as stable as it is in dramatic theatre, and there is far more acknowledgement of the way meaning is made in the liminal space between stage, spectator and society.

As Sant argues, though, these sorts of observation about the post-dramatic aesthetics of much social media theatre only tend to affirm that the jury is still out on whether it is emerging as "a new medium with formal and aesthetic possibilities of its own" or "just a new way to perform and make art" (2014, 52). For all their potential, the works produced to date have not always pushed the boundaries of the traditional theatre ecosystem. For example, a number of theatre critics and scholars have lamented the fact that as interesting as experiments to date might be, they have all too rarely been repeated, or become a regular part of a mainstage theatre company's work (Carson 2014; Sant 2013; Westbrook 2014; Worthen 2014). The exception might be streaming but, of course, commentators like Carson (2014) see this as little more than a modern version of mainstage companies' relations with broadcasters such as the British Broadcasting Corporation that do not impact much on their main mission or programming. Clearly, some of the more independent and experimental companies do consistently produce work that engages these technologies. For example, Blast Theory in the UK have a mission to create mixed reality theatre, and New Paradise Laboratories in the USA does have a mission to create internet theatre. However, Westbrook (2014) also laments the fact that, while mainstage companies' experiments with things like streaming might be very visible, smaller companies' and artists' work can still be invisible, lost among the masses looking to attract a global audience online. Whether she means the work of companies as well known on the international festival circuit as Blast Theory, Rimini Protokoll or The Builders Association, or equally well-known individual activist artists such as Wafaa Bilal, Brian Lobel or Sarah Rodigari, is less clear—all would seem to be visible in some ways in some communities. What is clear is that, for some commentators, the critical mass of energy and enthusiasm for the uptake of these new technologies early on in the five years from 2007 to 2012 has not translated to as much activity as they might have expected, especially on mainstages.

The factors limiting the uptake of social media in theatrical production, distribution and reception are complex, variable and different for independent versus mainstream companies. For independent companies and practitioners, the fact that most take a post-media approach to their work, and this means they are always switching media to suit each new work's premise, aesthetics and politics, is a factor. For mainstream companies, the fact that expectations about the medium, and how to aesthetically engage audiences via the medium, are yet to fully emerge is factor. As Carson (2014, 228) contends, the fact that Shakespeare has so often been used to test the waters with these new technologies, to get subscriber audiences familiar with the tools, without straying too far from the safe centre of the mainstream, is not that surprising. It is in itself a sign of fears about what the digital, economic and other disruptions of this period might mean for mainstream theatre makers—a known strategy for testing new types of work, as a gimmick, a value add or a collaboration with an independent company, without alienating audiences or risking revenue streams. There are, however, a host of other issues that also arise and attract attention when it comes to aesthetic uses of social media in the theatre.

Certainly, funding is an issue. As Ryan Nelson (2014, 204) notes, making, maintaining and building on social media theatre initiatives might be cheaper in the twenty-first century than it was in the twentieth. However, as soon as we move beyond individual artists doing work they believe in on their own time, it still requires a cast, creatives, equipment, support and the ability to meet expectations in terms of quality, personalisation and appeal, which companies large or small may not be able to live up to. This, for Nelson (2014), is why some experiments, such as the Globe experiments with offering remote Shakespeare workshops, have been withdrawn rather than extended.

The fear that social media performance is simply a way of commodifying, commercialising and distributing both company- and fan-produced content to the masses to make money is also an issue. "[C]entral to this discussion", according to Lonergan, "is the issue of labour: of how the work we do online generates money" (2016, 65). The National Theatre, The Globe and other mainstage theatres present their efforts to stream their work, share their work and showcase audiences' responses to their work—critiques, parodies and self-produced versions where they present their own take on characters, scenes or songs to the public—as efforts to make their work more accessible. As Purcell (2014, 215) notes, however, their efforts have been subject to criticism—in particular, to suggestions that they are using these technologies to turn theatre into cinema for mass audiences just to make money, or taking advantage of fan-contributed content to make money. These practices thus raise questions about whether the mainstage companies that make use of them are actually "democratising creativity", as Lonergan puts it, or simply "us[ing] their fans' labour as a form of highly effective free marketing" (2016, 4). If theatre makers and companies do not manage these relationships carefully, he warns, "individual theatre-goers are likely to become increasingly aware that theatre's are deliberately staging online interactions with us not because of a desire for closeness and intimacy but to sell more tickets" (66), undermining the discourse about accessibility that underpins so much of their uptake of social media.

The related fear that social media performance is not enough like live performance to have any real value in itself apparently remains an issue for some commentators too. As Nelson puts it,

> The biggest challenge digital media poses for a performing arts venue, more than any other type of cultural institution, is the presentation or evocation of the live experience. Unlike museums, galleries or libraries where real-world content can often be adapted more congruously for online life, the nature of live performance appears to demand the real-time presence of the individual (2014, 204).

Nelson (2014), Purcell (2014), Way (2011) and others agree that the use of social media in theatre, to present performance texts themselves, not just para-performance texts such as cast lists, programmes, photos, video clips, interviews and reviews, forces spectators to stretch the boundaries of their definition of the term. This stretching of boundaries still leads detractors to suggest that, in losing something of the live, face-to-face characteristics of conventional theatre, social media theatre loses something of its value. The RSC's production of *A Midsummer Night's Dream*, for example, was subject to criticism on the basis that it "failed to transmit a version of the live performance in Stratford" (Carson and Kirwan 2014, 240). Similarly, the National Theatre's production of *Coriolanus* was subject to criticism that it failed to transmit the most engaging elements of the live performance to its online spectators(Arroyo 2014). Although Jose Arroyo did see the show at Cineworld (because he could not get a ticket to a sold-out screening at The Electic in Birmingham) on a designated day, at a designated time, so he was seeing a live stream rather than a DVD, he felt that the camera angles, cuts and close-ups were random and poorly realized on screen. He felt that the scale of the show was also poorly translated to the screen. Moreover, without the ability to direct his own attention, he was "constantly aware that actually being there would be that bit better" (2014). Though accepting (somewhat condescendingly for those in remote countries colonised by the British) that it is nice that these streaming exercises extend the privilege of seeing the performances to remote audiences, Arroyo and those who share his views do not like them. This criticism is, as Nelson (2014) rightly asserts, serious for subsidised mainstage theatres that see themselves as custodians of a theatre form. On the one hand, as O'Neill notes, "social media has become a way for these cultural institutions not only to engage with audiences—videos from both the RSC and the Globe feature vox pops from audience members—but also to construct and disseminate their own cultural value, and indeed Shakespeare's too" (2014, 37). On the other hand, however, it also offers a channel for other producers, spectators and members of the public to contest or critique their construction of themselves as custodians of the form now and into the future if they do not like their efforts, experiments or innovations in this area. A risk which, as Purcell (2014, 215) notes, leads companies like the National Theatre and the Globe to cast their streamed shows as secondary value-add offerings not meant to be of the same priority as the live, real-time, unrepeatable performances in the theatre when judging their custodianship of the form.

Predictably, these criticisms lead to a fear that social media theatre is simply an adaptation or a substandard derivative of an original. Interestingly, this is a critique that has been applied both to more independent work and to mainstage work. Gray (2012), for instance, notes that this happened when An Xiao asked the @Platea collective to reperform Vito Acconci's *Following Piece* (1968), where he picked random passersby in New York and followed them. *Following Piece 2.0* online was critiqued not just for being too close to stalking but for being too close to the original, and thus for being derivative. "A contributor to the blog claimed that what we were doing was nothing like Acconci's performance," Gray recalls, "and that social media was no place to be doing performance work and comparing it to artists like Acconci" (2012). Similar critiques are levelled at modern remediations of Shakespeare online by traditionalists who do not see the remediation as anything more than a lesser replica of the original performance in the original medium.

Looking at these criticisms, it is clear that some theatre makers—mainstage theatre makers more than independent theatre makers—are caught between faith to form and faith to perceived modern funder and/or market demands to make more use of social media. These dilemmas have, for example, been embodied in the Australia Council for the Arts' Geek in Residence Program, where the remit was for the geeks to assist across the aesthetic, critical and audience development domains of the chosen company's work, but the reality was often only small one-off experiments in the aesthetic domain, with more attention being paid to the criticism and audience development domains overall. These dilemmas see many mainstage theatre makers using social media mainly for one-off aesthetic experiments which have a special status alongside, and thus outside, their main programmes, for streaming, or for non-aesthetic functions, rather than as an exciting aesthetic possibility that they are keen to continue building on. This is not to say that streaming a Shakespeare play, or tweeting a modern retelling of a Shakespeare play, is not an innovation. Nor is it to say that other work that has been pursued by the RSC since the *Such Tweet Sorrow* experiment—for example, tagging locations along a road in London so that people can use their smartphone to hear local history before, during or after a promenade performance based on a Shakespeare play *Adelaide Road* (2011a)—is not an innovation. It is simply to note that the interactivity sought in such work may be at one end of the spectrum and, moreover, that the work in itself may have special status as a value add rather than as primary programming. These value adds, like the valueadds of cast lists, programmes, photos, video clips, interviews and reviews available around a show, are valuable, particularly if they improve access or appeal to particular sets of audiences. However, the emphasis on them does mean that some mainstage companies use social media theatre projects such as the RSC's *Such Tweet Sorrow* or *Adelaide Road* more as experiential marketing designed to encourage non-adopting spectators to consider coming to the main shows than as a means to innovate in those shows. "[I]n this formation," Trueman has claimed, social media experiments alongside mainstage shows sometimes "merely function as gateways, attempts to seduce new audiences into theatres, rather than things that have intrinsic artistic merit" (2012).

In a mainstage context, then, these activities can be more about what is today called "transmedia marketing" than about the future of the theatre form itself. Transmedia, as defined by Henry Jenkins (2003, 2006), is a form of storytelling in which characters, scenarios and plots connected to a particular storyworld, play out across multiple media platforms, each providing a different window onto a different facet of the storyworld in which different scenarios unfold. Although the components of transmedia stories connect with each other, they also expand, extend and reimagine each other as a story moves across platforms. In this way they eventually result in what Jenkins characterises as "a narrative so large that it cannot be contained within a single medium" (2006, 95). Transmedia storytelling is popular with fans of particular storyworlds—for instance,*Dr Who*, certain anime cartoons or Shakespeare. It is, as Sant (2014), O'Neill (2014) and Lonergan (2016) have noted, a popular practice with fans, activists and those who spend a lot of their leisure time on social media platforms. It is also increasingly popular with marketers looking to engage with fans. Accordingly, while the term "transmedia storytelling" relates to fan communities where people pick up stories and play them out further for the amusement of themselves and their friends, the term "transmedia marketing" has also emerged as a way to describe what Elizabeth Evans calls "practices such as franchising, merchandising, adaptations, spin-offs, sequels and marketing" (2011, 2), where companies create platforms to allow fans to indulge in these pleasures, or to acquire new fans. The power and popularity of transmedia practice is located in its ability to give audiences, as co-creators, a chance to create texts, change texts, change the meanings associated with texts and challenge authority (61). For advocates, this is not a threat to the original texts. It is a way to increase audiences, increase demand among audiences, and help ensure the sustainability and success of the film, television or literature product that they function alongside.

The term "transmedia marketing" has not been translated from the screen industries to the theatre industries as yet. The use of social media theatre as a value-add experiment by mainstage theatre companies does nonetheless fit the definition of transmedia marketing because it allows audiences to engage with characters, content and plot in a spin-off performance online, without necessarily impacting on the main performance. Indeed, it may help to sustain the main performance that the spin-off is based on. As Jenkins (2003, 2006), Evans (2011) and others have argued, transmedia has its own aesthetic merits. It extends stories across platforms, episodes and experiences, and allows audiences opportunities for co-creative, collaborative and community building engagement, because the affordances of the platforms it plays out on are geared to co-production, participation, convergence of multiple media and constant circulation of ideas. As Kathleen Sweeney puts it,

> transmedia [i]s a multiplatform approach to storytelling that mirrors how we consume stories as an interweave of texting, screen capture, remix dialogues, and theatrical and television viewing. Since the digital revolution, myriad content producers actively upload media files via YouTube, Vimeo, blogs, and websites, and the influence offan culture on consumer interactivity has shifted the role of viewer to one of active collaborator. (2010)

Transmedia is particularly prevalent in film culture, as well as in television and literature, and much has been written about the way it is prompting aesthetic, technological and industrial convergences in these contexts. There is, though, surprisingly little written about how it is being deployed in theatre practice. There is an article by Patrick Colm Hogan in Marie-Laure Ryan and Jan Noel Thon's collection on transmedia across disciplines, but it is actually more about what is chosen/not chosen in *Hamlet*, and what would be equivalent in other media, than examples of transmedia *Hamlets* (Hogan 2014; Ryan and Thon 2014, 6). There is a strong argument to be made that when mainstage theatre makers use social media, they are often using it as transmedia marketing, taking advantage not only of the opportunities it offers to create new content, with new partners, but to connect with audiences who are happy to move across media, choosing more based on the story or on the experience of the story than on the form (Jenkins 2006, 2). This transmedia practice clearly has aesthetic merits but, by and large, its artistic merit and mission is different from that of the mainstage company's central programming.

It is difficult to say why mainstage theatre makers so often take a transmedia marketing approach to social media theatre. The issues identified here undoubtedly all play a part. However, the issue of liveness, originality and traditionality may be more a problem for specific audiences—such as subscriber audiences—than for theatre makers themselves. As Conner observes,

> [r]ed-level anxiety over this shift[ing boundary between the live and the digital] is evidenced in a range of books, articles and editorial, from Andrew Keen's *The Cult of the Amateur: How Today's Internet Is Killing Our Culture and Assaulting Our Economy* to every third op-ed piece in *The New York Times* and *Wall Street Journal.* (2013, 9)

These sensationalised discourses inform some of the statements set out by detractors above. They also underpin other reactions, such as the reaction to critic Daniel Yates (2012) reviewing *The Radicalisation of Bradley Manning* by the National Theatre of Wales after watching it online, not in the theatre. For Yates, this was not an issue because watching online was always already a viewing position provided in the work. "To demand that theatre back out of all this in the name of being present to protect some notion of pure experience is by now nothing more than puritanism perversity", he wrote, because, in reality, most theatre makers are "starting to think of us as an audience online as well as offline" (Yates cited by Trueman 2012). For others, though, this was an issue, and Yates was taken to task the way other critics or scholars have sometimes been for commenting on work they have not seen live. The presence of these discourses in the public sphere notwithstanding, though, there are likely deeper issues beneath this liveness debate for theatre makers' decisions about adopting social media in theatre themselves, as distinctive from other stakeholders.

For most artists and academics, the live versus mediatised debate does not hold much appeal anymore. As demonstrated in Chap. 2, debate about whether online media can create real connections between real people in real time is largely over. As Schrumm confirms, "studies have shown that computer-mediated communication can be as real as face-to-face communication" (2009). In drama, theatre and performance scholarship, debate about whether online media is fundamentally ontologically distinct from live media is also, following Auslander (2008), a debate that has largely been had. Most today accept Auslander's argument that "the historical relationship of liveness and mediatisation must be seen as a relation of dependence and imbrication rather than opposition" (53). Though the use of social media platforms as a stage means that the work is recordable and repeatable, it is still real-time interaction in a way that a pre-recorded film, television show or book is not. This being the case, it is difficult to believe that concerns about liveness are the main reason that mainstage theatre makers are using social media more in value-add events and experiences than in mainstage shows. It seems more likely that theatre makers are using social media in this transmedia marketing style to avoid the risks associated with adopting new forms when they are not yet sure whether or not they will allow them to maintain connection to their mission and current markets.

Using social media is a risk precisely because it puts theatre spectators' participation on the spot and in the spotlight. This means that if traditional spectators do not like it when smartphones come out in the theatre, the new technology puts their displeasure on display to a wider public than would have been possible in the past. While presenting this sort of spectatorial displeasure suits the aesthetic, social or political agendas of a more independent company, an independent artist or an activist artist, who may well be hoping to co-opt displeasure, prejudice or other spectatorial displays to make their point from the start, it is less likely to serve the interests of mainstage theatre makers. With their remit as custodians of the form, and their reliance on taxpayer subsidy that they receive only as long as they maintain that custodianship, authority and status, staging spectatorial displeasure may not be in their interests at all. As Worthen notes, "[t]he contemporary intermediation of "Shakespeare" is pervasive, remaking how we read, research, write about, see, and perform Shakespearean drama" (2014, 148). This is already happening on open access platforms, where anyone can share their thoughts. Academic, professional, amateur, artful and pranksterish posts sit alongside posts that are totally unrelated to the topic. Real, scholarly, committed comments and critiques are all too easily lost in the mass, or stolen, transformed and turned against original meanings for play or for political purposes (Carson and Kirwan 2014, 249). "The fact that these conversations are visible at all is", as Carson and Kirwan claim, "the main shift inaugurated by digital platforms" (249). They cite the example of "the hijacking of comment threads (for example in Saul Frampton's *Guardian* article 'Who Edited Shakespeare?' (2013), where the 262 comments beneath the article are dominated by discussion of Shakespeare's 'true' identity)" (Carson and Kirwan 2014, 249). This sort of co-option of the channel, conflict or commentary is par for the course for platforms where relations between posters, posts, texts and topics are "mutable and dialogic" (O'Neill 2014, 5). The results of these conflicts, commentaries and co-options are uncertain and uncontrollable, but very trackable by means of searches and software. "The digital world", as Carson contends, "takes content out of context and therefore disengages it from its original meaning-making structures. New meaning-making structures are developing but these are fluid and without solid underpinning, making it almost impossible to predict which structures will stand and which will fall" (Carson 2014, 226–227). For activist performers, co-option of their social media stages in unpredictable ways may help to make some of their points. For mainstage companies, however, there is a risk that unpredictable co-option of their social media stages may lead subsidisers, sponsors, subscriber audiences and others that they rely on for their funding to rethink their custodianship over a theatrical legacy. "If content is no longer king, and Web 2.0 is all about community," Nelson contends, then questions can arise such as "what role does an arts organisation have in encouraging debate at the same time as retaining a role as an authoritative creator of cultural meaning?" (2014, 202)—a question that becomes especially thorny if funders, sponsors and other stakeholder see displeasure at a mainstage company's offerings online.

To suggest that mainstage theatre makers may be using social media theatre projects mainly as transmedia marketing projects is not necessarily a criticism. Innovation can take place in para-performance texts and activities as much as in mainstage performance activities. Innovation in special social media projects or experiments alongside mainstage programming allows theatre makers to take risks. It allows them to assess the content, quality and appeal of the interactivity such innovation offers to audiences. There is good transmedia theatre and there is bad transmedia theatre, and if special social media projects are seen to be of dubious quality—for example, seen to offer only the dubious pleasure or displeasure of what Graham (1997, 163–164, 171) calls "token" control over the encounter—audiences will say so. Their action, interaction, and reaction will still be less certain, less likely to follow traditional critical trends, and available to anyone who happens to see or to search out the traces of their encounters online. It will still have the potential to become part of the "big data" set that stakeholders can search out to assess the quality of the company's work. Critically, though, it will not matter as much to the main thrust of the company's work. In a climate of social, technological uncertainty and austerity, it makes sense. "The survival of theatre is economically tied to a willing audience," as Bennett suggests, "not only those people paying to sit and watch a performance but increasingly those who approve a government, corporate or other subsidy" (1997, 4). It is, though, an interesting observation about the way-policy, industry and production prerogatives influence aesthetic practices within different sectors of the theatre industry, and limit or liberate the potential for those sectors to push the boundaries of theatrical form via their uptake of social media technologies.

## References


Arroyo, Jose. 2014. Screening Shakespeare: Coriolanus Doesn't Captivate at the Multiplex. *The Conversation*, 5 Dec 2014. http://theconversation.com/screening-shakespeare-coriolanus-doesnt-captivate-at-the-multiplex-22682. Accessed 5 Jan 2015.

Ates, Alex. 2014. The World Wide Theater at Our Fingertips. HowlRound, 27 Aug 2014. http://howlround.com/the-world-wide-theater-at-our-fingertips. Accessed 9 Jan 2015.

Auslander, Philip. 2008. *Liveness: Performance in a Mediatized Culture*, 2nd ed. New York: Routledge.

Balme, Christoper. 2014. *The Theatrical Public Sphere*. Cambridge: Cambridge University Press.

Bennett, Susan. 1997. *Theatre Audiences: A Theory of Production an Reception*, 2nd ed. London: Routledge.

Bolter, Jay David, Blair MacIntyre, Michael Nitsche, and Kathryn Farley. 2013. Liveness, Presence, and Performance in Contemporary Digital Media. In *Thorughout: Art and Culture Emerging with Ubiuqitous Computing*, ed. Ulrike Ekman, 323–336. Cambridge: MIT Press.

Bravo, Britt. 2009. 5 Ways Theatres Can Use Social Media. *Cultural Entrepreneurship Blog*. Global Centre for Cultural Entrepreneurship, 10 Aug 2009. http://culturalentrepreneur.org/blog/5-ways-theatres-can-use-social-media. Accessed 5 Aug 2013.

Blake, Elissa. 2010. Geeks, Tweets and Bums on Seats: How Social Media Is Shaping the Arts in Australia. Sydney Morning Herald. 10 July 2010. http://

www.smh.com/au/entertainment/theatre/geeks-tweets-and-bums-on-seats-20100709-103g8.html. Accessed 9 Aug 2013.

Butsch, Richard. 2008. *The Citizen Audience: Crowds, Publics and Individuals.* London: Routledge.

Carson, Christie. 2014. Creating a Model for the Twenty-First Century. In *Shakespeare and the Digital World: Redefining Scholarship and Practice*, ed. Christie Carson, and Peter Kirwan, 226–237. Cambridge: Cambridge University Press.

Carson, Christie, and Peter Kirwan. 2014. *Shakespeare and the Digital World: Redefining Scholarship and Practice.* Cambridge: Cambridge University Press.

Chatzichristodoulou, Maria 2010. *Cybertheatres: Emergent Networked Performance Practices.* PhD thesis, Goldsmiths, University of London.

Chatzichristodoulou, Maria, Janis Jeffries, and Rachel Zerihan. 2009. *Interfaces of Performance.* Farnham: Ashgate.

Conner, Lynne. 2013. *Audience Engagement and the Role of Arts Talk in the Digital Era.* London: Palgrave Macmillan.

Dixon, Steve. 2007. *Digital Performance: A History of New Media in Theater, Dance, Performance Art, and Installation.* Cambridge and London: MIT Press.

Downes, Daniel. 2005. *Interactive Realism: The Poetics of Cyberspace.* Montreal: McGill-Queens University Press.

Evans, Elizabeth. 2011. *Transmedia Television: Audiences, New Media and Daily Life.* London: Routledge.

Giannachi, Gabriella. 2004. *Virtual Theatres: An Introduction.* London: Routledge.

Graham, Beryl. 1997. *A Study of Audience Relationships with Interactive Computer-Based Visual Artworks in Gallery Settings, through Observation, Art Practice, and Curation*, PhD thesis, University of Sunderland, UK.

Gray, Jonathan. 2012. Web 2.0 and Collaborative On-Line Performance. *Text and Performance Quarterly* 32 (1): 65–72.

Hadley, Bree. 2014. *Disability, Public Space Performance and Spectatorship: Unconscious Performers.* London: Palgrave Macmillan.

Hadley, Bree. 2008a. 080808 UpStage Festival. *Australian Stage Online* Sunday 10 Aug 2008. http://www.australianstage.com.au/reviews/international/080808-upstage-festival-1745.html.

Hadley, Bree. 2010. Teenage Loner in a Chat Room Tangled up in Guile and Gullibility. *The Australian* July 26 2010. http://www.theaustralian.com.au/news/arts/teenage-loner-in-a-chat-room-tangled-up-in... 8 Aug 2010.

Heim, Caroline. 2015. *Audience as Performer: The Changing Role of Theatre Audiences in the Twenty-First Century.* London: Routledge.

Hogan, Patrick Colm. 2014. Emplotting a Storyworld in Drama: Selection, Time, and Construal in the Discourse of Hamlet. In *Storyworlds Across Media: Towards a Media-Conscious Narratorology*, ed. Marie-Laure Ryan, and Jan-Noel Thon, 50–66. Lincoln: University of Nebraska.

Holland, Peter. 2009. Performing Shakespeare for the Web Community. In *Shakespeare in Hollywood, Asia. and Cyberspace*, ed. Alexander C.Y. Huang, and Charles S. Ross, 252–262. West Lafayette: Purdue University Press.
Hollander, Barbara Gottfried. 2014. *Participating in Plays, Skits, and Debates with Cool New Digital Tools*. New York: The Rosen Publishing Group.
Hope, Cat, and John Ryan. 2014. *Digital Arts: An Introduction to New Media*. New York: Bloomsbury.
Jenkins, Henry. 2006. *Convergence Culture: Where Old and New Media Collide*. New York: New York University Press.
Jenkins, Henry. 2003. Transmedia Storytelling. *Technology Review*, 15 January 2003. Cambridge: MIT Press.
Jones, Amelia, and Adrian Healthfield. 2012. *Perform, Repeat, Record: Live Art in History*. Bristol and Chicago: Intellect.
Jordan, Richard. 2014. Digital Alchemy: The Posthuman Drama of Adam J.A. Cass's *I Love You Bro*. In Digital Performance Futures in Australasia, ed. Glenn D'Cruz and Gorkem Acaroglu. *Australasian Drama Studies* 65: 37–52.
Kozel, Susan. 2007. *Closer: Performances, Technologies, Phenomenology*. Cambridge: MIT Press.
Kuksa, Iryna, and Mark Childs. 2014. *Making Sense of Space: The Design and Experience of Virtual Spaces as a Tool for Communication*. London: Elsevier.
Lehmann, Hans Thies. 2006. *Postdramatic Theatre*. London: Routledge.
Lonergan, Patrick. 2016. *Theatre & Social Media*. London: Palgrave Macmillan.
Mandell, Jonathan. 2013. Social Media On Stage: Theater Meets Twitter, Facebook, Youtube, Tumbler, Soundcloud. *New York Theater*, 3 Jan 2013. http://newyorktheater.me/2013/01/03/social-media-on-stage-theater-meets-twitterfacebookyoutube-tumbler-soundcloud/. Accessed 27 Nov 2014.
Murnane, Ingrid. 2009a. Co-Modify: Were You Hoodwinked? *@Platea: A Global Online Public Art Collective*, Blogger 13 May 2009. Accessed 19 Aug 2013.
Murnane, Ingrid. 2009b. Some More Co-Modify Performance Highlights. *@ Platea: A Global Online Public Art Collective*, Blogger 6 May 2009. Accessed 19 Aug 2013.
Nelson, Ryan. 2014. Developing a Digital Straetgy: Engaging Audiences at Shakespeare's Globe. In *Shakespeare and the Digital World: Redefining Scholarship and Practice*, ed. Christie Carson, and Peter Kirwan, 202–211. Cambridge: Cambridge University Press.
Neri, Louise. 2008. Culture: The Builders Association. Interview 27 November 2008. http://www.interviewmagazine.com/culture/theatre-the-builders-association#_. Accessed 18 Aug 2013.
O'Neill, Stephen. 2014. *Shakespeare and YouTube: New Media Forms of the Bard*. London: Bloomsbury.
Parker-Starbuck, Jennifer. 2014. *Cyborg Theatre: Corporeal/Technological Intersections in Multimedia Performance*. London: Palgrave Macmillan.
Phelan, Peggy. 1993. *Unmarked: The Politics of Performance*. London: Routledge.

Price, Tim. 2012. The Radicalisation of Bradley Manning. The National Theatre of Wales. https://www.nationaltheatrewales.org/bradleymanning.

Prior, Yoni. 2014. Impossible Triangles: Flat Actors in Telematic Theatre. *Australasian Drama Studies* 65: 168–190.

Purcell, Stephen. 2014. The Impact of New Forms of Public Performance. In *Shakespeare and the Digital World: Redefining Scholarship and Practice*, ed. Christie Carson, and Peter Kirwan, 212–225. Cambridge: Cambridge University Press.

Reason, Matthew. 2003. Archive or Memory? The Detritus of Live Performance. *New Theatre Quarterly* 19 (1): 82–89.

Reason, Matthew. 2006. *Documentation, Disappearance and the Representation of Live Performance*. London: Palgrave Macmillan.

Rodigari, Sarah, with Sofaer, Joshua. 2012. *Reach Out Touch Faith*, Going Nowhere [Festival], Arts House Melbourne Australia. Available online http://goingnowhere.net.au/program/reach-out/.

Rumbold, Kate. 2010. From "Access" to "Creativity": Shakespeare Institutions, New Media, and the Language of Cultural Value. *Shakespeare Quarterly* 61.3: 313–336. http://muse.jhu.edu/journals/shq/summary/v061/61.3.rumbold.html. Accessed 22 Aug 2013.

Ryan, Marie-Laure. 2001. *Narrative as Virtual Reality: Immersion and Interactivity in Literature and Electronic Media*. Baltimore: Johns Hopkins University Press.

Ryan, Marie-Laure and Thon, Jan-Noel, ed. 2014. *Storyworlds Across Media: Towards a Media-Conscious Narratorology*. Lincoln: University of Nebraska.

Sant, Toni. 2008. A Second Life for Online Performance: Understanding Present Developments through an Historical Context. *International Journal of Performance Arts and Digital Media* 4 (1): 69–79.

Sant, Toni. 2009. Performance in Second Life: Some Possibilities for Learning and Teaching. In *Learning and Teaching in the Virtual World of Second Life*, ed. Judith Molka-Sanielsen, and Mats Deutschmann, 145–166. Trondheim: Tapir Academic Press.

Sant, Toni. 2013. Theatrical Performance on the Internet: How Far Have We Come Since Hamnet? *International Journal of Performance Arts and Digital Media* 9 (2): 247–259.

Sant, Toni. 2014. Art, Performance, and Social Media. In *Routledge Handbook of Social Media*, ed. Jeremy Hunsinger, and Theresa M. Senft, 45–58. London: Routledge.

Schnieder, Rebecca. 2012. Performance Remains. In *Perform, Repeat, Record: Live Art in History*, ed. Amelia Jones and Adrian Healthfield, 137–150. Bristol and Chicago: Intellect. http://www.trincoll.edu/Academics/centers/TIIS/Documents/Schneider-Oct.%203.pdf. Accessed 22 Aug 2013.

Schrumm, Stephen A. (ed.). 1999. *Theatre in Cyberspace: Issues of Teaching, Acting and Directing*. New York: Peter Lang.

Schrumm, Stephen. 2009. Theatre in Second Life® Holds the VR Mirror up to Nature. In *Handbook of Research on Computational Arts and Creative Informatics*, ed. James Braman, Giovanni Vincenti, and Goran Trajkovski, 376–395. Hershey: IGA Global.
Stevens, Lara. 2014. Alienation in the Information Age: Wafaa Bilal's *Domestic Tension*. *Australasian Drama Studies* 65: 77–98.
Trueman, Matt. 2012. Noises Off: Will Social Media Change the Face of Theatre. Theatre Blog. The Guardian 26 April 2012. http://www.guardian.co.uk/stage/theatreblog/2012/apr/26/noises-off-social-media-theatre. Accessed 27 Nov 2014.
Upton, Ian. 2014. Creating Experiences for Virtual Spaces. In *Making Sense of Space: The Design and Experience of Virtual Spaces as a Tool for Communication*, ed. Iryna Kuksa, and Mark Childs, 128–133. London: Elsevier.
Vargas, Vivianna. 2014. The Big Merge: Internet and Theatre. *HowlRound* 14 September 2014. Accessed 28 Nov 2014.
Varley Jamieson, Helen. 2008. *Adventures in Cyberformance: Experiments at the Interface of Theatre and the Internet*. MA thesis, Queensland University of Technology. http://eprints.qut.edu.au/28544/1/Helen_Jamieson_Thesis.pdf.
Walser, Randal. 1991. Elements of a Cyberspace Playhouse. In *Virtual Reality: Theory, Practice, and Promise*, ed. Sandra K. Helsel, and Judith P. Roth, 51–64. Westport: Meckler.
Watts, Richard. 2013. How to Be a Good Audience. ArtsHub 11 Nov 2013. http://www.artshub.com.au/news-article/features/performing-arts/how-to-be-a-good-audience-193438. Accessed 27 Nov 2014.
Way, Geoffrey. 2011. Social Shakespeare: Romeo and Juliet, Social Media, and Performance. *Journal of Narrative Theory* 41 (3): 401–420.
Westbrook, Cathy. 2014. How to stage theatre's online future, *The Guardian* Theatre blog with Lyn Gardiner, Monday 14 April 2014. Available online http://www.theguardian.com/stage/theatreblog/2014/apr/14/stage-theatre-online-future.
White, Gareth. 2013. Audience Participation in Theatre: Aesthetics of the Invitation. London: Palgrave Macmillan.
Worthen, William B. 2014. *Shakespeare Performance Studies*. Cambridge: Cambridge University Press.

CHAPTER 4

# Social Media as Critical Stage: Controversy, Debate and Democracy

Theatre, as a live art form, lives and dies in the moment when stage and spectator meet. As a result it is dependent on documentation, commentary and word of mouth—the posters, programmes and previews that circulate before the show, and the reviews that circulate in the weeks, months and years after the show—to have a legacy in the public sphere. This means that performance texts are always are intimately connected with these para-performance texts that circulate in the foyer, in post-show talks or in the press. In the eighteenth, nineteenth and twentieth centuries, published reviews came to play an increasingly critical role in framing these connections between what happens on stage, what is said about what happens on stage and, therefore, what happens on stage the next time. As spectators' representatives, reviewers describe, document and report on a show. They are the "influencers" who guide spectators, and give them a sense of what to expect and what to make of the experience. In the twenty-first century, social media, and the new sorts of personal, social and professional communication it makes possible, is having a significant influence on this tradition of review, comment and critique. It is making new modes of commentary, which give spectators more say over where, when and how their interpretations of a performance are represented, and thus more say in the debates that drive dominant ideologies, possible. This transfer or translation of critique, commentary and word of mouth onto social media platforms, and the way it changes the negotiation of meaning in theatre, is the topic of this chapter.



B. Hadley, *Theatre, Social Media, and Meaning Making*,
DOI 10.1007/978-3-319-54882-1_4

## Theatre, Meaning Making and Traditional Media

To examine the effect of social media on theatrical meaning making, it is useful to look to the past before turning to look towards present or future possibilities—to look, in particular, at the role of the critic as an influencer in theatrical meaning making.

The role of the critic, as it is understood at the start of the twenty-first century, is a result of enlightenment thinking about citizens and citizenship in a democratic society. In a technological sense, the critic's role only became possible with the advent of technologies such as the printing press. In an ideological sense, the critic's role only became possible in the context of enlightenment philosophy, and enlightenment thinking about how theatre can play a role in cultivating good citizens who can perform a productive function in society. As Richard Butsch (2008, 4) explains, post-enlightenment philosophers and policy makers distinguished between a public of citizens concerned with rational ideas and a crowd of individuals who—whether cast as rowdy or just as passive—need the right ideas prescribed to them to become better citizens. In this paradigm, a proper audience is defined by policy makers, theatre producers and thus, ultimately, by fellow theatregoers too as a public, a set of political actors, who contribute to rational debate in the public sphere (2). Theatre—and other media, communication and cultural performance practices—becomes a forum for contributing to this debate (12). Theatrical performances, and para-theatrical performances such as review, commentary and criticism, become part of the "conversation, information spread from person to person" in an agora-style public sphere that "produc[es] public opinion" (13).

By the close of the twentieth century, Butsch (3) argues, the concept of the audience as a public had been co-opted by radical media, communication and cultural performance practices and practitioners. The concept of the audience, as a group of political agents, was co-opted by activists who wanted to see the rights of citizenship become available to all—not just to the able, white, heterosexual men from wealthy backgrounds many enlightenment thinkers had in mind when thinking of citizens (7)—so that all could be part of the conversations that shape society.

Before the twentieth century, though, the concept of the audience as a public to be cultivated was used by the elite—the established social authorities—to argue the need to tame theatre audiences. As Lynne

Conner puts it, "[i]n sociological terms, *the* audience is sometimes a 'crowd' and sometimes a 'public,'" and, when conceived as a crowd, "*the* audience has often been constructed as dangerous: feared for its ability to incite civil disobedience, to become violent, and to spread prurience and disease" (2013, 7, original emphasis). Accordingly, Susan Bennett (1997, 2–3) argues, in the eighteenth, nineteenth and early twentieth centuries the social elite set out to ensure that theatre attendance brought social benefit to citizens rather than encouraging riots among unruly crowds that would be difficult to control (cf. Butsch 2008, 24–37, 64–68). They took it upon themselves to ensure that spectators could become a public, not a noisy, unruly or riotous crowd "susceptible to making the 'wrong' choices about what constitutes 'good' art" (Conner 2013, 7).

To do this, the social elite needed to drive both the aesthetics of plays on stage, and the review, commentary and critical reception of these performances, censoring any that might cause problems for susceptible individuals. "These critics considered theatre to have a public duty not only to cultivate," Butsch notes, "but also to socialize people, and, by extension, to prevent social disorder" (2008, 68). They thought that, for democracy to work, they had to channel information to make the "right" choices clear to the confused masses (55). The new role of the critic, and the commentary they provided, was part of that channelling. "[A]round the turn of the century," Butsch says, these "gentlemen took upon themselves the tasks of criticism and censure by establishing and contributing their observations to the first theatrical publications" (24)—with telling titles such as *The Theatrical Censor* and *The Mirror of Taste*. By the mid- to late nineteenth century, the review became a common feature of the by then nearly 150-year-old US and UK newspapers. Famous critics emerged, such as William Winter (*New York Tribune*, 1865–1919) and John Ranken Towse (*New York Evening Post*, 1974–1927). In the early years there was often an almost romantic emphasis on celebrated actors. By the twentieth century, rational and at times brutal analysis of the plays and actorly performances became the norm for a new generation of critics, such as Kenneth Tynan in the UK, Richard Palmer in the USA and Leonard Radic in Australia.

Throughout this period, the critic came to take on the role of the "representative" spectator. Representative spectators, as Conner's (2013) italicisation in talking about *the* audience suggests, were typically seen as a homogenous set of white, middle-classed, heterosexual, able men.

The critic, as the spectators' representative, had the right to dictate the reading of plays and performances, to help the masses react properly. Indeed, they had the responsibility to do so. "Since it is the young, the idea, the thoughtless, and the ignorant, on who the drama can be supposed to operate as a lesion for conduct, an aid to experience and a guide through life," *Mirror* editor Stephen Cullen Carter explained in 1920, "it becomes a matter of great importance to the commonwealth that this very powerful engine ... should be kept under the control of a systematic, a vigilant, a severe, but a just criticism" (cited by Butsch 2008, 24). In this paradigm, Butsch observes,

> Professional drama critics were the primary spokesmen for this new [theatre cultivating citizens], guiding laymen and women in their search for cultivation and the theatre, and elevating art of commercialism and entertainment. Instead of the traditional puff pieces they wrote critical reviews, set standards of dramatic taste, and expected audiences to practice cultivation. (68)

Traditional dramatic theories became the basis of their judgements. The professional critics tended, as long-time critic Palmer explains, to base "judgements on commonly accepted standards or briefly explain any special criteria used in assessing a performance" (1988, 8). For, of course, traditional theories—such as the Aristotelian three unities—could still present problems in reviewing non-traditional or alternate-traditional plays such as those of Shakespeare.

Though theatre always counted critique, commentary and word of mouth as central to its production, distribution, reception and consumption, the emergence of the paid professional critic was as much of a "game changer" as anything else in the industry before or after. The near contemporaneousness comments of one person—typically, a white, middle- or upper-class, heterosexual, able man—that might once have been gossip, based on that person's perception, interpretation and prejudices, passed on to a few friends or colleagues in their own community, became something much more influential to the industry and audiences. The new paid, professional critics took advantage of the then still newish technology of the printing press to write, print and publish their word not just for a more literate mass audience but for the purpose of producing the historical record. The critic took control of word of mouth, commentary and meaning making, on the premise that he—then later in the twentieth century she—had the right, and the responsibility, to make, manage and manipulate common people's reactions to shows for the good of society. The critic became the primary spectator, the spokesperson who sought to typify the view that spectators had, or should have had, of a show—a situation that persisted for over a century. As Palmer explains it,

> A reviewer looks at a theatrical production from the point of view of the audience. Live or "legitimate theatre" in particular depends on the chemistry of an audience's presence. All of the effort of playwrights, actors, directors, and designers aims ultimately at eliciting a response from the audience. Theatre goers play roles as important as the actors. Those who complain about the critic often grumble, in the same breath, about audience inadequacies: impatience, limited sensibilities, and jaded tastes. To the extent that the reviewer serves as a spokesman [sic] for the audience, with the ability to articulate or exemplify its reactions, contempt for audience and critic alike shows a failure to recognize audience tastes as a necessary ingredient in any formula for theatrical success. (1–2)

The critic's authority to speak for spectators was based on their presence at the show, their expertise, their explanatory power and their eloquence. "While responding to a play like the rest of the audience," Palmer puts it, "a reviewer must also articulate reasons for a specific evaluation of the performance. Ideally, any audience member needs a reviewer's knowledge, perceptiveness, and ability to respond fully to a production" (102). Palmer acknowledges that these guiding principles do not necessarily mean that a specific critic's comments are guaranteed to be accurate, authentic and unbiased. Nonetheless, their expertise does give confidence that they can offer the viewer the advice they need to "fully" respond to a performance. In his summary of the critic's primary roles, Palmer (5) casts them as paid professionals who can document the show, determine its success, deliver background, assist theatre-goers in choosing and interpreting shows, provide entertaining accounts of shows, or advocate for shows, as well as provide a historical record. Moreover, they can do this under editorial time pressure—though, in his account, Palmer (1) does distinguish between the reviewer, who writes in a contemporaneous, journalistic mode and timeframe, and the critic, who writes in a less contemporaneous, academic mode and timeframe (cf. K Wilkinson 2009).

What Palmer overlooks throughout his account of his time as a theatre critic, of course, is the critic's power to create, not just capture or convey, spectators' tastes—to present a reading that the common masses are meant to consciously or unconsciously interpellate into their own reading, and their own representation of that reading to family, friends and fellow theatre-goers. The critic's role is productive, performative and world-making. The critic's response is not just a memory of a performance, or a remediation of a performance, but is, in many ways, their own performance of their own agenda. It can, as the show fades into memory, readily overtake the material reality in public debate about what a theatre piece means. That, of course, is why the original critics' and censors' role was so clearly connected to the power to create the public sphere. It is a power of which other critics of the time clearly were aware. As George Bernard Shaw said, for instance,

> Some day they will represent my articles, and then what will all your puffs and long runs and photographs and papered houses and cheap successes avail you, O lovely leading ladies and well-tailored actor-managers? The twentieth century, if it concerns itself about either of us, will see you as I see you. Therefore study my tastes, flatter me, bribe me, and see that your acting-managers are conscious of my existence and impressed with my importance. (cited by Lutz 1974, 190–110).

Those who act as paid, professional critics in the later part of the twentieth century and early part of the twenty-first century are more ready to acknowledge the power they hold than their predecessors. However, their work, like that of their predecessors, has been highly gatekept. This means that even if they wanted to acknowledge their own identity position as a factor that helps or hinders their influence, the form itself made this impossible. In their historical form, press reports of spectators' responses were always gatekept, noise free, negotiation free forms of communication. One person, in the role of the expert, sent a message about a show's meaning and impact to another, in the role of the audience—a simple, straightforward, linear communication model, with none of the complexities seen in contemporary social media communication technologies cited in Chaps. 2 and 3. The critic, and their editor, determined the register, discourse and ideology in the message. There was little room for noise, feedback or other personal, aesthetic or political factors to find their way into the exchange. There were letters to the critic or the editor, but in print forms those too were gatekept to control or conceal competing views.

Before the advent of technologies such as photography and videography, the critic's record became the main record of a show. To this day, reviews constitute "a major portion of the holdings of libraries with theatre archives" (Palmer 1988, 7). Which, in the historical record, can tend to make spectators' responses seem more unified than they may in fact have been. A phenomenon that filtered from review and critique into academic commentary on performance, at least in a traditional 'theatre studies' mode, until the advent of more 'performance studies' modes which acknowledge spectatorial diversity in the late 1980s and early 1990s. Authors talked about spectators as single block who were supposed to have some sort of common response to a show.

Over the years, artists and audiences have struggled with the question of how to speak back to a review that risks harming their reputation in this historical record. The typical advice is that it is best not to respond to a bad review because it risks the artist being seen as biased, expressing sour grapes or having a tendency to take themselves too seriously. Successful rebuttals are rare, so the advice tends to be that if an artist has to respond, they should not do so in the heat of the moment. "I think the internet makes all that [heated] stuff easy to go off half cocked, be really angry, then repent at leisure," Alison Croggon claims. "So, yes, don't write angry" (cited by Watts 2012) .

As noted in Chap. 3, many artists, audiences and academics today have started looking to social media for ways to speak back to the myth of singular meanings. Initiatives such as the AusStage database, the Hemispherica database and others make an effort to acknowledge, archive, review and advocate for a diversity of practices and also a diversity of audience responses to those practices. Many mainstage theatre companies, as well as many independent theatre companies, activist artists and press outlets, have also started asking spectators to turn their phone on, post, tweet or otherwise share their thoughts on a show with producers, fellow spectators and the public at large before, during or after the show, or sometimes without even having seen it.

## Theatre, Meaning Making and Social Media

The discourse above notwithstanding, the critic's desire to drive perception, interpretation and taste has not been proved to be a causal agent in producing influential theatre. As Wesley Schrum puts it, "[t]hat critics mediate the relationship between artworks and publics has often been suggested but never adequately tested" (1991). While there are a few studies of commercial entertainment where critics' opinions have been shown to influence consumption, the evidence, in the case of theatre, is less clear. For all their claims, Schrum suggests, "[c]ritics do not have the power to 'make or break' shows" (1991). Or, as Miranda Boorsma and Hans van Maanen more accurately put it, though critics make or break the readings that dominate the historical records, they do not necessarily make or break ticket sales, trends or public uptake of ideas presented. This, Butsch (2008, 47) contends, is because spectators are in fact thoughtful and competent, and aware that what is a flop for one critic might be a success for another. They also know that critics have been known to change their reading of a show over time—for example, celebrated critic Michael Billingham was notoriously unimpressed with now-renowned playwright Sarah Kane's work when he first saw it but, over time, and in light of others' comments, came to change his view (Stephens 2010).

This, for Christopher Balme (2014), means that the influence that theatre and theatre criticism have on the public sphere today is limited. Theatre's influence on the public sphere should be threefold, based first on the play's efforts to engage, enact or challenge cultural norms, then the theatre institution's efforts to do this, and finally the theatre industry's efforts to do this via debates that play out in the media. Unfortunately, nineteenth- and twentieth-century traditions of production, criticism and reception reduced the theatrical public sphere to what Balme characterises as a "closed circuit of subscriber audiences, professional reviewers and theatrical unions" (ix). These artists, critics and audiences talk to each other in private venues, or poorly read arts sections of newspapers, but have little influence on broader public debate. Theatre is no longer censored, Balme claims, precisely because it has so little potential to make an impact in the public sphere (16–17). Theatre is reduced to an immersive emotional experience in a black box, which takes spectators out of the flow of everyday life. It can be personally affecting, prompting spectators to think, and critics can tell us whether it did this well in terms of its theatrical, textual and technical conventions, but the experience still remains private rather than public. This, for Balme (15, 17), means that it is not surprising that it is only on rare occasions that this emotional intensity spills out into scandals, controversies or protests in the public sphere.

In the twenty-first century, Balme contends, theatre needs to "reconnect with the 'public sphere'" (4) to prove its relevance in an age of information accessibility, accountability and austerity, where social, economic, technological and environmental problems prompt people to question its value as a taxpayer subsidised practice. This, for Balme (2–3), needs to happen not just via the aesthetic interventions in the auditorium that Jean-Luc Nancy, Jacques Ranciere and Alain Badiou theorise as critical to this reconnection to political public spheres, and not just via the aesthetic interventions outside the auditorium that Claire Bishop or Nicholas Bourriad theorise as critical to reconnection to the political public spheres, but via theatre makers, institutions and industries' efforts to engage a much broader cross-section of society in their work. The power of the professional critic to have the sole say on the influence of a show is, as Eleanor Collins (2010) explains, at odds with the collaborative contribution of so many people to a show. It is also at odds with the aspiration to participatory interaction in much contemporary culture today. Now, many theatregoers want to be part of a conversation, a dialogue, by which dominant ideas can be defined or redefined (Butsch 2008, 12–13; Connor 2013, 2). They want to be creators of meaning and value. Acknowledging the appeal of this status, it is not just activists or authorities but mainstage entertainment agencies that have begun advocating—at least in their public discourse—for the power of the active citizen consumer co-creating events and experiences, and interpretations of them.

Butsch (2008), Conner (2013), Balme (2014) and others see social media as having the potential to help to reconnect theatre with the public sphere. They see social media as a platform with rich potential to give more than just middle-age, middle-class, white, straight, able men a voice in public discussion and debate. Social media platforms allow anyone to become a commentator, sharing their views with anyone with an internet connection. Unlike traditional critics, today's social media critics can also talk about performance texts and para-performance texts interchangeably. This, Conner (2013, 5) argues, is appropriate because both influence spectators' experience of theatre, how it flows, how it feels and how it effects them, before, during and after the moment of encounter. Both are an integral part of theatrical performance, and an integral part of theatrical performance's capacity to spark public as much as private conversations. Though many different media have been used to manage theatre's relation to its public over the centuries, social media is thus seen to have unique potential to redefine stage–spectator–society relationships—which, for Balme (Balme 2014, 18–19), means that it has the unique potential to redefine both the way theatre is talked about, discussed and debated, and the way these debates link what he calls "previously separate contexts' (79) to produce new conversations.

A decade and a half into the twenty-first century, the transition from print platforms with paid critics to online platforms which are open to all is already well under way. There is a clear cultural push to make more use of social media—from Twitter and Facebook, to comments boxes and apps at the conclusion of online theatre reviews by paid critics—to share messages about a show. Mainstage theatre companies, contemporary theatre companies and the press outlets that make their living by documenting them are all asking audiences to share their thoughts about a show with artists, critics, fellow audience members and the public at large. Terms such as "tweet us", "tweet seats" and "comments are open" are finding their way into the industry's day-to-day vocabulary. Theatre makers and their audiences say they are excited about social media's potential, particularly to connect with and build communities. Hannah Suaraz, a blogger asked to tweet her responses while watching a production of *King Lear* by Bell Shakespeare, thought the show might be "dry" but discovered that it wasn't, so she wanted to use Twitter to share this with her friends to encourage them to have the same experience. "You tweet because you're excited to be seeing something live after hearing so much about it," she told others in the industry. "It's about sharing your emotions and your experience of the show. You might have a favourite scene or a line that you love and you want to share it instantly" (cited by Blake 2010). Nathalie Vallejo, Company B at Belvoir Street Theatre in Sydney's Marketing Manager agrees that this "instant feedback can be valuable" because "[i]t gets people talking about artforms and it builds creative communities" (cited by Blake 2010).

As these comments show, these new platforms are said to democratise, diversify and redefine the artist–audience relationships at the heart of the theatre. As Jill Calvin, Marketing Manager for Sydney Festival, tells Elissa Blake, "[i]t's a democratisation of art" (cited by Blake 2010). To take part in a blog, microblog or social networking site debate about a show, a season of shows or an industry issue does not demand special skills. Even if a webmaster can remove content that a theatre company or a newspaper deems too controversial from their site, a person's own social media pages can still carry and circulate that content. In this context, producers', distributors' and critics' control over what a show means start to disintegrate as multiple sorts of commentary, across multiple channels, start to connect, cross over, conflict and collapse into each other. The shift to these platforms is therefore being seen, at least on the surface, as a shift in the power relations between producers, critics and consumers.

As noted in Chaps. 2 and 3, though, new platforms do not automatically lead to new forms of practice, new ecologies or the new 'creative communities' that Vallejo speaks of. For all their potential, social media platforms are not necessarily more reliable mechanisms for theatre review, critique, commentary and debate than their predecessors. The communities that come together on them include vocal minorities, mischief makers and trolls, people who comment via pseudonymised handles, and a host of other players intent on pushing or pulling discussion in particular directions to suit their own aesthetic and political agendas. "It can get narky and unpleasant in the Twittersphere", as Blake (2010) puts it, as rumours, innuendo and powerplays sit next to congratulations and celebrations. The performances of social media users, like the performances of their eighteenth-, nineteenth-, and twentieth-century critic predecessors, can be less a remediation of the piece they are commenting on and more their own self- or social-performance in service of their own acknowledged or unacknowledged agenda. These performances are, like all performances, open to noise, feedback, conflicts of interest and other factors driving response in unexpected directions, as a community of voices competes for the role of universal spectator or spokesperson whose words will ripple out into the public sphere as the authoritative voice. It is these sometimes conflicted conversations and the strategies that lay spectators use to try to claim authority in them that I analyse here. In many of the examples I consider, it is a controversial staging of race, gender, sexuality or disability that prompts these lay spectators to participate in the conversation. Their self- and social-performance is as a result often far more emotive—or, perhaps more accurately, far more personally emotive and meaningful—than some of the generalised commentary about theatre shows and the theatre industry that I consider in Chaps. 2, 3 and 5. This being the case, I have followed Ruth Page (2012) in anonymising the potentially "off the cuff" comments about a controversial issue of any poster who could potentially be posting under their own name. In doing this, I do not intend to deny these lay spectators authorship of their comments, or their strategies for convincing others of the veracity of their comments, and I do not wish to suggest that they were not conscious of the fact that they were posting to a public webpage that would be available in perpetuity. I intend, rather, to accord them the slightly more anonymous status of the lay spectator within a larger audience group, who would not necessarily expect their statements to be subject to review, or linked to other things they have said in such a review, in the way that an artist would.

## Theatre, Social Media and the "Death" of the Critic

Not surprisingly, those with the most to say about these transitions at the turn of the twenty-first century are those who make a living as paid theatre critics. Among the more vocal is Ismene Brown, a critic with the online comment site The Arts Desk in the UK. According to Brown, "[t]he picking off of critics, who national newspapers no longer employ on full-time contracts but phone up for £60 a pop, has been going on for years" (2013) in the USA, the UK and Europe. Brown is not alone in expressing this concern. Jasmine Dotiwala (2013), producer of the Art360 programme in the UK, has argued that "[w]ithout properly trained and passionate art journalists today, we lose good coverage of, and access to, the art of tomorrow". The fear, which Sharon O'Dair also raises in a recent study of Shakespeare review, commentary and criticism, is that "all contemporary publications [will] tend towards the format of the blog at the expense of artful writing crafted over time" (cited by Carson and Kirwan 2014a, b, 248). The lack of work for professional critics means that without programmes such as Dotiwala's, which provide opportunities for young people to report on the art scene—a role that Brown sees The Art Desk playing too—they will not see this as a career prospect. The quality of commentary on theatre culture in the public sphere will decline.

For theatre critics, as for theatre artists, it is difficult to provide evidence of the value of what they do. Accordingly, Brown argues, it is difficult to "persuade the digital user to pay for expert reportage and judgement" (2013). Amateur commentary is starting to overtake professional commentary, which in turn means that "[p]rofessional journalists who cost money to employ are being smothered by amateurs who are already employed gainfully elsewhere and will chat about what they saw for nothing" (2013). For Brown and those who share her view, the fact that artists as much as policy makers fail to fight for the critics and the vital role they play in assessing shows, advocating for shows, and vitalising the sector is a problem (2013).

Interestingly, the comment function at the close of the article where Brown (2013) presented this point of view in *The Guardian* itself became full of conflict about the role of theatre critics. While she lamented the lack of support, and did find some to sympathise, she was at the same time challenged by others. The heated debate developed into a clear set of arguments for and against. Some suggested that the worth of a critic's opinions comes from decades of study, and cannot be compared to that of family, friends or colleagues. They shared the concern that losing this source of distinct, different and informed opinion would lead to a dumbing down of culture (PIB20131, via Brown 2013). Others, however, dismissed this as leftist critics struggling to maintain their own power and status by suggesting that "amateurs aren't knowledgeable" (PIB20132, via Brown 2013). There were concerns about perceived hypocrisy, as people asked if Brown actually paid contributors to The Arts Desk, along with suggestions that "[i]f you people were worth saving you would not be appealing to 'the artists' to save you and would be insisting on the artistic status of the work you do yourselves as critics" (PIB20133, via Brown 2013). For many participants the fact that no formal qualification is required to become a critic meant that their work is no better or worse than that of a blogger. As one poster said,

> While I am always pleased to read intelligent, informed criticisms of the arts, I am not sure there is much of a distinction between the professional arts critic and the enthusiastic and amateur, save that one is lucky enough to get paid. There is no specific professional exam, nor any set professional standards set out for a person to be a genuine arts critic (PIB20134, via Brown 2013)

For these posters, critics need to be able to write well, and understand the creative process and the context of the work, but professionals do not necessarily do this better than amateurs (fairisfoul, PIB20133 and PIB20135, via Brown 2013). Accordingly, they are not necessary, unless they use their power to promote the emerging artists who need the press much more than established mainstage artists (fairisfoul, via Brown 2013). At least a few posters suggested this is not happening at present, primarily because mainstage theatre makers and mainstream theatre critics are in each other's pockets (PIB20139 and PIB20131, via Brown 2013), in the sense that they are in the same networks, if not literally being sponsored or spoonfed content by theatre makers within their networks. For these posters, this means that paid professional critics can dumb down debate rather than develop a true critical culture as readily as any amateur. "[T]hey all give their mates good reviews," as one poster put it, "and ri[d]e the gravy train, its been a disgrace for years" (PIB20137, via Brown 2013). "Prostitute yourselves out to the big money and then cry because you have no credibility and no-one wants you," another put it (PIB20138, via Brown 2013).

The participants in this debate are not the first to point out a perceived conflict of interest between mainstage theatre makers and mainstream theatre critics. In the USA, the UK, Europe, Australasia and elsewhere, accounts of conflict are common. In one recent case, for example, Lyndon Terracini, Artistic Director of Opera Australia, reportedly had critics Harriet Cunningham (*Sydney Morning Herald*) and Diana Simmonds (*Stage Noise*) removed from complimentary ticket lists after they were critical of the company's shows and, in Cunningham's case, also the company's choices for their 2015 season (Cunningham 2014; Maeres 2015; Simmonds 2015). The critics, and their publication outlets, were not pleased. Simmonds said: "You take the rough with the smooth—or you get off the pot and take nothing at all" (2015), casting the director's actions as "childish" (cited by Maeres 2015). Though the opera company claimed it offered the publication outlets the opportunity to send other critics to review their shows, the outlets declined because that would just give credence to the notion that critics are in cahoots with performing arts companies. Cunningham's publisher, for instance, said: "*The Herald's* position is that the paper will not have our critics chosen for us by companies" (Maeres 2015), and suggested that the newspaper would buy the tickets to get Cunningham there to review the company's upcoming *Faust*. Terracini chose not to provide comment for their articles on these issues, either on the issue that market prerogatives might be leading the company to choose "safe" shows, or that the company might be banning critics who took issue with their shows or seasons.

These claims typify the concerns that make many in the industry and in the community more generally suspicious of mainstream reviews and interested in what independent bloggers have to say. In Australia, outlets for independent blogging that have become more popular in the first part of the twenty-first century include Alison Croggon's *Theatre Notes* and Jana Perkovic's *Guerrilla Semiotics* (Melbourne), Jane Simmons's *Shit On Your Play*, Kevin Jackson's *Theatre Diary*, Bob Ellis's *Table Talk*, Diana Simmonds's *Stage Noise*and James Waites and Augusta Supple's self-titled blog (Sydney). Although these reviewers also write for mainstream newspapers, their own sites are assumed to give them the ability to "tell theatre lovers what they really think of the latest plays", as Stephen Crittenden articulates it (Crittenden 2012). In his own new article on the issue, Crittenden evidences the problem with mainstage reviews and the potential of social media review sites by quoting an anonymous mainstage reviewer:

> The pressure is on reviewers to be polite ... Editors are far less likely to run a bad review for fear of a breakdown in the relationship in the fight for advertising dollars. They won't say this publicly, but reviewers 'disappear' because they're too harsh (cited by Crittenden 2012)

In the current wave of theatre blogs, different voices, preferences and prejudices are certainly starting to come through. Croggon, for instance, uses her *Theatre Notes* blog to argue that while there is no innate problem with the post-dramatic deconstruction of classics by young male wunderkind directors, she does wonder why they get all the work in mainstage Australian theatre, particularly when the would-be Barry Kosky's of contemporary Australian theatre such as Benedict Andrews do not always do it well. Simmonds uses her *Stage Noise* blog to say that she sympathises with audiences who simply do not get this work (cited by Crittenden 2012). Here, the critics are freer to be blunt, and also freer to pick and choose what they comment on, why, when and how based on their personal aesthetic prerogatives—a phenomenon that Kevin Jackson says is also happening with theatre audiences, flagged by the fact that "theatregoers he knows are no longer choosing to buy full-season subscriptions" (cited by Crittenden 2012). This shift away from predictable criticism, of predictable play seasons following predictable conventions of engagement is also tied up with open access agendas—for example, making academic accounts of shows, seasons and the theatre industry in journals open to the public who pay for the academies (Carson and Kirwan 2014a, b, 248).

Predictably, Crittenden's more measured article drew less heated responses than did Brown's from posters looking to join fellow artists, critics and audiences in co-creating the narrative about the role of critics. The tenor of the comments, however, was the same. "The position of the 'official reviewer' has always been so problematic—the blog-o-forum is surely the way forward" (PSC20121, via Crittenden 2012), one poster said. "Honestly, I don't know why when ANY critic publishes a review—they don't also include various punters' comments," another said. "Usually, an audience is divided—and that is the problem of any review. Personally I wish everyone could vote and make a one sentence comment at the end of a show—then you might actually be able to gauge whether you'll like it" (PSC20122, via Crittenden 2012). The criticism, in this case, came only from a poster calling for more recognition of "the diversity of arts review blogging" (PSC20123, via Crittenden 2012) in an article where Crittenden did not really raise the issue of gender, race, ethnicity, class and ability differences in criticism and blogging, or his choices to profile some contemporary theatre bloggers over others any more than Brown did.

## Social Media, Affordances, Interactivities and Arguments

The emergence of social media theatre commentary options, including blogs and comment boxes at the close of online news articles presented online, allows anyone to try to become an influencer. The way audiences use rating, review and commentary functions to try to exercise this influence, and the way they are succeeding or failing in their efforts to exercise this influence, is still to be examined in any depth. Similarly, the degree to which these practices have impact in the public sphere is still to be examined in any depth. As Christie Carson and Peter Kirwan remind us in their discussion of Shakespeare review, commentary and critique online, "[a]ccessibility is not impact" (2014, 248). The mere fact that more people can access these platforms does not mean that more people are having an influence or an impact, so "it is important not to conflate these two" (248). It is timely, therefore, to test some of these assumptions: to look at how commentary is actually playing out online, before, during, after and around a performance, that purports to have something to say about identity, relationships, history or politics; to look at distinctive dramaturgies of discussion, debate and argument in these spectatorial self-performances on online platforms; to look at whether influence on these platforms is still based on theatrical expertise, eloquence, passion or on other factors; to look at whether influence is shared out into new networks and new communities, be these closely related, centralised communities of family, friends and colleagues, or loosely related, decentralised communities of theatregoers in general; and, most critically, to look at whether these new opportunities for commentary are creating new roles, relations and communication exchanges, remediating old forms or simply using the new opportunities to speak that these platforms provide to find new opportunities to silence others on these platforms.

I do this here by looking at examples of theatrical performances that have created controversy, where marginalised communities have taken to commenting online to try to influence the public's perception, interpretation and attitude towards these performances—*Exhibit B* by Brett Bailey and Third World Bunfight at the Barbican in the UK, *Ugly Mugs* by Peta Brady at the Griffin Theatre and the Malthouse Theatre in Australia, and *Involuntary Dances* by Rita Marcalo at the Bradford Playhouse in the UK. As Balme (2014, 15) notes, scandal does not automatically equate to activation of the public sphere. However, these cases do provide examples of individuals, communities and their allies attempting to use scandal, controversy and online staging of it in and around press previews and reviews of the shows to have influence in the public sphere.

## Exhibit B

If there has been a show in the early part of the twenty-first century that has demonstrated that theatrical performance still has the capacity to cause debate in the public sphere—and, indeed, shown some of the ways in which social media commentary might contribute to that debate—it is *Exhibit B* by white South African director Brett Bailey and his company Third World Bunfight.

In *Exhibit B*, Bailey presents black performers as exhibits on plinths in a human zoo.

This installation-style performance is a modern remobilisation of the nineteenth-century phenomenon of the human zoo, seen in fairs, sideshows and freakshows, albeit for a different purpose. In historical freakshows, African people were presented—alongside fat ladies, bearded ladies, gimps, cripples and other people with other cognitive or corporeal differences—as an exotic, titillating form of "educational" entertainment. The end goal, though, was to enforce notions of "normal" bodies by confronting spectators with images of what was "not normal" (cf. Hadley 2008b, 2014). In *Exhibit B*, modern-day spectators come face to face with some confronting scenes in the 12 tableaus they pass through. There are those entitled "Missing Link", "Civilizing the Natives" and "Origin of the Species", all inhabited by living, breathing black bodies, a silhouette of the "Hottentot Venus", Sara Baartman, rotating on a stage, a slave woman chained to the bed of colonial military officers, a set of severed heads singing, alongside asylum-seekers in today's contemporary detention centres staged as so-called "Found Objects" (*The Guardian* 2014; O'Mahony 2014). After the performance, spectators are invited to record their response to the "exhibit", and read cards where the performers have recorded some of their experiences of more everyday forms of racism that persist even today in the twenty-first century.

The aim of the installation-style performance, according to the producers and some of the participating performers, is educative, but in a more ethical way than historical human zoos. As performer Tamara Nvirenda puts it, "*Exhibit B* is making people aware of what happened [in the colonial era] and how even today asylum seekers are treated" (*The Guardian* 2014). "[It] was not made to make anyone feel guilty but to teach them" (2014), fellow performer Rania Modi argues. "I feel blessed to have been in a position where I was able to tell a story of the injustice of past and present so that the future doesn't have to be the same" (2014), another performer, Anna Modi, agrees.

Certainly, this is not a new format for artists looking to engage the ethical sensibilities of their spectators. Many women, artists of colour, and artists with disabilities have re-engaged and re-enacted historical performance styles such as the freakshow to confront their spectators with the role they have historically played in staging specific bodies as objects of scorn. As one contributor commenting on *The Guardian*'s website notes, for instance,

> [t]his reminds me of the work of Coco Fusco, particularly her "Two Undiscovered Amerindians" performance [in which she and Guillermo Gómez-Peña place themselves in a cage in front of cultural institutions in the early 1990s]. The reaction of the audience and those who haven't visited on principle could be considered part of the performance. (PTG20141, via *The Guardian* 2014)

This phenomenon has also been seen in the performance of disabled artists such as Mat Fraser, when he restaged the historical performances of

Stanley Berent (known as Sealo the Sealboy), who shared his corporeal characteristic of foreshortened arms, to confront modern-day spectators with historical ways of seeing the disabled body (Hadley 2008b, 2014).

According to the producers, and at least some of the performers, the format of the performance—the presence of living, breathing bodies who share the corporeal characteristics of their historical counterparts, in confronting, discomforting and sometimes outright distressing scenes—is critical to *Exhibit B*'s capacity to make a comment on racism. The Edinburgh cast, for example, felt that the format enabled them to enact the horrors of the past but, at the same time, stare back at the spectators and so take back agency, and the ability to ask modern-day spectators to think about their attitudes. The eye-to-eye interaction is essential, performer Shingiriai Musunhe explains, because it enables a visceral engagement with a "horror" and a historical "trauma" that "no words can describe" (*The Guardian* 2014). As this cast put it in a joint statement to *The Guardian*, "[i]n that moment when our eyes meet, we cease to be objectified and become human. Some people literally jump back. Some break into tears; others look away. Others still gaze deeper as their eyes well up" (2014). It is this visceral reaction, and the spectators' reflection on it, that—according to the producers and performers—gives *Exhibit B* its power to prompt change. The eye-to-eye engagement takes the environment of the piece "from a purely confrontational space to a conversational one, where each spectator is challenged to think of what part they play in the system, be it oppressed or oppressor" (2014). For this reason, the performers said they were proud to be part of an exhibition where Bailey—acknowledging his complicity in a racist system in South Africa—provided them with a platform to do this. "Reading the pages and pages of comments from the audience left at the end of the exhibit attests to this," the performers argue, "but we don't need to read that. We see it in their eyes" (2014). They do, however, acknowledge that people have to be part of the audience to understand how *Exhibit B* achieves this ethical encounter in which spectators become vulnerable, and responsible, to their other. "You have to be an audience in the show to fully grasp its effect" (Jay C cited by *The Guardian* 2014).

This said, there have been other cast members who have had more mixed feelings about the format, and the format's capacity to engage the ethical sensibilities of spectators. "How do you know we are not entertaining people the same way the human zoos did?" one performer asks commentator John O'Mahony writing for *The Guardian*, for example (O'Mahony 2014).

In *Exhibit B*, as in all participatory performances, the meaning of the piece emerges during the encounter with the spectators each night. Indeed, as O'Mahony notes, "the labels on each work even mention 'spectator/s' as one of their 'materials'" (2014). This means that the meaning of the work, the impact of the work, remains uncertain until this moment of encounter. On the one hand, spectators might (mis)read the piece as part of the 'human zoo' phenomenon it sets out to challenge. On the other hand, they might start to reflect on the phenomenon, together with their complicity in historical and contemporary race relations, and thus come to a change in understanding. As Berthe Njole, who played the part of Sara Baartman, tells O'Mahony,

> [w]e were playing a festival in Poland. A bunch of guys came in. They were laughing and making comments about my boobs and my body. They didn't realise I was a human being. They thought I was a statue. Later, they returned and each one apologised to me in turn. (2014)

The politics of the work is based on this often unpredictable change in individual perceptions—a fact which leads commentators such as Claire Bishop (2012b) to wonder how useful these provocative, participatory performances actually are when it comes to pushing for large-scale political change in society,

Accordingly, the format necessarily brings risks, a set of risks that Bailey has acknowledged, as have many others who have worked in the form historically and today. "For all I know, I could look back at *Exhibit B* in 10 years and say, 'Oh my God, I am doing exactly what they are accusing me of.' But that's the risk you take. It comes with the territory" (Bailey cited by O'Mahony 2014).

Although the participatory practices of political artists have always run this risk, it is amplified in a context where social media has started to shift spectators' agency, and their ability to make comment, without the intervention of gatekeepers—or, indeed, even having time to think through what they are putting out into the public sphere in their off-the-cuff comments and responses.

As a result of these issues, and the risk of (mis)reading that comes with such confrontational performance strategies, *Exhibit B* has become a controversial piece. Although it travelled to cities in European countries such as Germany and France for several years, bringing only "small demonstrations" (Carvajal 2014), when it went to the UK in the middle of 2014, it became the focus of intense interest, emotion and protest. Although the production in Edinburgh in August of 2014 was well received by critics, such as *The Guardian*'s Lyn Gardner (2014), when word got out that the Barbican was planning to present the piece in London that September, it was targeted by protestors. Activist Sara Myers set up a petition on Change.org (Myers 2014a), together with a Facebook page (Myers 2014b) and a website (boycotthumanzoouk.com) to drive a public campaign to get the Barbican's Nicholas Kenyon to cancel the performance. The petition drew hundreds of supporters, all sharing Myers' desire to shut the show down. According to their comments giving their reason for signing the Change.org petition, Myers' supporters saw *Exhibit B* as a shocking, insulting piece, insensitive in its trivialisation of suffering, and offensive "[b]ecause it is a manifestation of the very racism it claims to be critiquing" (PSM2014a1, via Myers 2014a). Supporters said that *Exhibit B* "should not b[e] given media sp[a]ce" (PSM2014a2, via Myers 2014a). The nature of this petition-based social media platform meant that Myers was able to gain a lot of supporters, mainly from the UK, though there were also a few signatories from the USA, and a few references to the recent#BlackLivesMatter social media campaign coming out of the US response to police violence against black men. All signatories reiterated her ideas again, and again, and again. There were no contrary points of view on the Change.org platform because, whether people happen upon it via a post on Facebook or Twitter, or via direct email from a friend, they do have to sign in, and thus increase the changes that the petition will succeed in what it sets out to do, before they can make their comment. All stayed on point in the sense that, while posts varied from a line or two to a paragraph or two, they all called for a boycott or a ban of the show, with few references to other racist incidents or issues. For the signatories, *Exhibit B* was not educating, enlightening or ethical, so it was not the right way to remember a past which should be forgotten, or "noted, but not in this way" (PSM2014a3, via Myers 2014a). It was clear that signatories had not seen the show. They knew no more of the piece than what Myers wrote in her protest letter, and the various platforms and posts leading to the protest letter, so signatories were noting that they would not want to have it seen for the reasons given above, rather than commenting on the show itself. Equally, though, it was clear that they were coming out in large numbers to support Myers' protest, online and, in some cases, in live protests in front of the Barbican as the scheduled performances drew nearer throughout September.

The campaign resulted in news articles in *The Guardian*, *The Telegraph* and beyond, as well as likes, links and shares on popular social media platforms such as Facebook, and thus in turn in new rounds of commentary circulating out onto new online platforms. Clearly the content had the appeal required to go viral, get wide circulation in the public sphere and get the attention of the Barbican. The protests at the Barbican became large—though, by most accounts, not violent. Accordingly, after weeks of coverage and more than 15,000 signatures to the circulating petition, the Barbican eventually let spectators know that

> [d]ue to the extreme nature of the protest outside the Vaults, regrettably we have cancelled this evening's performance of Exhibit B as we could not guarantee the safety of performers, audiences and staff. We respect people's right to protest but are disappointed that this was not done in a peaceful way as had been previously promised by campaigners (Barbican cited by Muir 2014a).

In this sense the Barbican was forced to deal with the social media commentary and controversy—not by means of the audience engagement strategies that I discuss in Chap. 5 but by cancelling the show. The Barbican was blunt in its statements about this, saying: "We find it profoundly troubling that such methods have been used to silence artists and performers and that audiences have been denied the opportunity to see this important work" (Barbican cited by Muir 2014b). The director, Bailey, was also blunt in articulating his disappointment, saying:

> I stand against any action that calls for the censoring of creative work or the silencing of divergent views, except those where hatred is the intention. The intention of EXHIBIT B is never hatred, never fear, never prejudice. It has not been my intention to alienate people with this work. To challenge perceptions and histories, yes. Explicitly to offend: no. Do any of us really want to live in a society in which expression is suppressed, banned, silenced, denied a platform? My work has been shut down today, whose will be closed down tomorrow? (cited by Muir 2014b)

As the events unfolded, new articles coming out in *The Guardian*—and, to a lesser degree, other papers such as *The Telegraph*, and other online commentary and communication platforms—drew thousands of comments from the public. The content was shared to social media sites such as Facebook and Twitter thousands of times. Over the course of a few weeks, a host of new people became spectators—or players—in the performance of public sphere debate about a theatrical performance on social media platforms. Again, most spectators-become-performers in the debate had not actually been spectators at the show in the more traditional sense of the term.

Analysis of the online performance of protest on social media applications, such as the interactive comment box at the bottom of *The Guardian*'s theatre blog, and similar functions on other news sites and other social media platforms, shows that the comments were both similar to and slightly different from those on the original Change.org petition. On the one hand, posters largely dealt with the same core issues coming up on Change.org. On the other hand, though, posters did now show two distinct for and against viewpoints in what they posted, and performed, for each other.

There was a clear dramaturgical structure to the debate. The spectators had an unspoken, culturally constructed sense of how to participate in this performance of protest, debate and dissent, to try to get their point across and give themselves authority to speak. Indeed, several showed a sense of self-awareness of this sort of debate having, if not a standard or scripted dramaturgical structure then at least a recognisable and often replicated one. At the bottom of *The Guardian*'s article announcing that the Barbican had cancelled the show (an article that drew more than 800 responses in 24 h), the first few posts included comments such as "Oh good, comments are open. This can only end well" (PHM2014b1, via Muir 2014b), "The mod's are in for a long shift..." (PHM2014b2, via Muir 2014b) and "Sit back, feet up—just going to watch the carnage..." (PHM2014b3, via Muir 2014b). These players were clearly already anticipating that this platform for audience engagement, and ostensibly democratic engagement (if *The Guardian*'s "comment is free" tagline is taken into account), might prove to be anything but a model of consensus.

The debates tended to begin with the same concerns about the "art" status of *Exhibit B* seen on the Change.org site. There, many had suggested that "This is not art" (PSM2014a3, via Myers 2014a), "This is NOT entertainment" (PSM2014a4, via Myers 2014a) and "It is a[n] ill-constructed idea that has no value whatsoever except in the attention-seeking mind of the so-called 'artist'" (PSM2014a5, via Myers 2014a). Similarly, on other sites, such as *The Guardian*, *The Independent* and *The Telegraph*'s sites, many suggested that *Exhibit B* was "degradation masquerading as art" (PTG20143, via *The Guardian* 2014) and an example of a style of art that can "come across as voyeuristic and indulgent and are not quite the bringers of social change that their creators would like or claim them to be" (PTG20143, via *The Guardian* 2014). It was therefore "self-indulgent nonsense" (PTG20144, via *The Guardian* 2014), "a vanity project" (PTG20145, via *The Guardian* 2014) and "Voyeurism. 'Art.' Ugly" (PTG20146, via *The Guardian* 2014). A few characterised it as "a self indulgent arts-farts love fest" (PHM2014b4, via Muir 2014a) designed to do more for the artist's status than anything else. "Profile raised, job done" (PHM2014b5, via Muir 2014b) one eventually put it.

The format of the piece was the problem for many detractors across all the conversations playing out on the news and social sites. Here, as one of the original Change.org signatories said, "there is no difference in concept from the original human zoos to this piece other than the fact that you are paying people to take part in this travesty" (PSM2014a12, via Myers 2014a). A few later contributors suggested, often in response to posts noting graphic representations of slavery in films such as *12 Years A Slave*, that while "[a] movie got a narrative and a reason to show you what you see on screen" (PHM2014a2, via Muir 2014a), *Exhibit B*-style installations do not. There is therefore no way of knowing "the real motive of this artist (shock value, fame)" (PHM2014a2, via Muir 2014a) without a story-based frame around the visceral encounters. Even if there is a point, or a critique or a sense of irony, these posters said, there is too great a risk that spectators will miss it and see the living, breathing bodies in the tableaus in *Exhibit B* as part of the phenomenon they challenge.

For these posters a staged performance like *Exhibit B* is just too similar to the social performances that it sets out to challenge. "It could easily be seen as simply putting Black people on show" (PTG20147, via *The Guardian* 2014), one poster argued, and so part of a long tradition of enslavement and objectification for the purpose of entertainment. Accordingly, as another contributor noted, this portrayal of black people as powerless victims "in itself means the show propagates the same power dynamic that it purports to challenge" (PTG20148, via *The Guardian* 2014). This, another claimed, citing Myers' protest campaign material, means that "[i]f Brett Bailey is trying to make a point about slavery this is not the way to do it. The irony gets lost and it's not long before the people behind the cage begin to feel like animals trapped in a zoo" (PTG20149, via *The Guardian* 2014).

For many proponents of this point of view on Change.org, and other social and news media sites, comments on their own embodied experience of what it was like to live with the legacy of slavery was the means of asserting their authority to speak. One poster, who had raised concerns about the show's earlier season in their city of Edinburgh, felt that their comments were "largely ignored because in Scotland there are hardly any black/minority theatremakers/artists" (PTG201410, *The Guardian* 2014) who share their embodied experience of the events the show portrays. The frustration, another agreed, thus came from the fact that so many of the people making comment had "no real understanding of the effects of slavery" (PHM2014b6, via Muir 2014b). For such posters, the fact that non-black people do not live with racism is what gives them the luxury to see the show as art rather than reality, a luxury that black people do not have. "Well of course if you are not the victim of the racism why would [you] take any note. But imagine you were the victim... imagine you are black and still get treated differently because you are black. How would you feel then?" (PTG201411, via *The Guardian* 2014), at least one poster put it.

For those calling for or later celebrating the closure of the show, comparison to presenting women as sex slaves, domestic violence victims being beaten, jews in a concentration camp or disabled people in an institution was seen as the best way to make this point (PSM2014a6, via Myers 2014a; PHM2014b6 and PHM2014b7, via Muir 2014b; PTG20147 and PTG201413, via *The Guardian* 2014; PTB20141, via Todd and Boitiaux 2014). Most felt it was obvious that society would not stand for this and therefore should not stand for *Exhibit B*, suggesting that a lot of posters were lay public who did not know the work of Coco Fusco, Annie Sprinkle, Mat Fraser or other performance makers who have done this in their work. Indeed, some took the point up in their own articles, casting the show as a racist work (Andrews 2014) produced without proper consultation with the lay public who were likely to be most affected by it (Malik 2014). Kehinde Andrews, for instance, said:

> [T]his exhibition is akin to a German organising a piece of "art" featuring Jewish people dressed in prison garb, numbers tattooed on their arms, locked in a contrived concentration camp.
>
> Such a piece is unimaginable and would be censored without a second thought.

> The distress at the heart of this episode is that no one organising this exhibition sees this obvious parallel because of the devaluation of black life, suffering and experiences. (2014)

These new articles provided further platforms for these debates to play out, proliferate and circulate into new networks. For those on this side of the debate, the suggestion that seeing such things could prompt a previously prejudiced person to consider their behaviour—go "hmmm that does look pretty awful" (PTG201413, via *The Guardian* 2014), as one put it—was silly. "Is anyone actually intending to go to the show thinking 'OO hang on I think I will have to go and see black people tied up and caged to convince me that actually it's horrid'?" (PTG20146, via *The Guardian* 2014), they asked.

A number suggested that while acknowledging that this history was important, there were better ways to do it. "Yes, there is the one-to-one power of such a piece but there are also wider issues at play," as one put it, particularly the issue of "whether this is the way we ought to be educated on these issues" (PTG20147, via *The Guardian* 2014). "If you want to learn about human zoo's read a history book" (PTG20144, via *The Guardian* 2014), another said. Others agreed, naming appropriate books (PTG201415, via *The Guardian* 2014). Some went so far as to suggest: "If you need an exhibition on Human Zoos to be able to empathise then you are a fucking sociopath" (PTG201413, via *The Guardian* 2014). "There are so many ways to educate yourself about the racist white-hegemonic power-structure," another agreed, "there's really no excuse to put this piece of shit together at all" (PKA20141, via Andrews 2014). Moreover, posters of colour argued: "Most Black people are aware of racism on a daily basis, so we don't need 'educating' or being pushed into a 'reaction'" (PTG20148, via *The Guardian* 2014).

The fact that the work was produced by Bailey, a white South African director, was a problem for many participants in the debate, in the initial petition and in the subsequent discussions online. This, for posters, means that it "represents black issues from a white perspective" (PSM2014a7, via Myers 2014a), failing to understand what it means for those who experience the legacy of slavery firsthand. As a result, it is just a "display of white privilege to use the pain and suffering of another race as entertainment" (PSM2014a8, via Myers 2014a). It "fail[s] to recognise how vile it is to hold an exhibition that dehumanises African people for money and entertainment" (PSM2014a5, via Myers 2014a). A lot of posters argued that it would be better to leave it to African people to tell their own stories. "[R]egardless of his intentions or beliefs it is not his story to tell or his conversation to instigate" (PHM2014b8, via Muir 2014b), one said. "Allow African people [and] the African diaspora to tell their stories," another said, "and then actually listen" (PSM2014a8, via Myers 2014a). "Only we have the right to display, depict &/or dramatise our plight" (PSM2014a9, via Myers 2014a), another agreed. To allow white people who have never lived this reality to lead the conversation is not edgy, experimental, or valid artistic expression (PJO20142, and PJO20142, via O'Mahony 2014; PTG20147, and PTG201416, via *The Guardian* 2014) but insulting (PJO20143, via O'Mahony 2014), disgusting (PKA20142, via Andrews 2014), and morally despicable (PJO20144, via O'Mahony 2014; PKA20141, via Andrews 2014). To fund, present or promote this sort of work, especially at the expense of worthier work—including work by black artists themselves—is therefore wrong (PSM2014a10, via Myers 2014a; PKA20143, via Andrews 2014).

Others countered this view, arguing that art is meant to be provocative, challenging and sometimes uncomfortable, and this is how it makes its point in the public sphere. "Art =/= Reality" (PTG201417, via *The Guardian* 2014), as one said. Society will never see any interesting art at all "if we are to equate the artistic representation of something with its actuality" (PHM2014b9, via Muir 2014b), another agreed. Accordingly, while prejudice may be "best defined by those who are directly subject to it" (PKA20144, via Andrews 2014), this does not mean that others cannot make a visceral, valid or interesting comment (PKA20144, and PKA20145, via Andrews 2014; PTG201418, via *The Guardian* 2014). Artists have to have the freedom to make their comments, others agreed, "and anybody who tells you otherwise is less evolved mentally" (PHM2014b10, via Muir 2014b). They are "completely unable to see the distinction between depicting something and endorsing it" (PHM2014b11, via Muir 2014b). In many cases, these posters did not see the fact that the creator was white as a problem. "Since when do you have to be black to be qualified to do what he is doing?" (PJO20145, via O'Mahony 2014), some asked, noting that many people experience prejudice—women, queer people and disabled people, as well as black people—and that anything drawing the audience's attention to the problem of lack of empathy for the other was worthwhile. "I suspect that if the artist behind it had been black you would see this as brave and challenging" (PKA20145, via Andrews

2014), one said. A number noted that the performers who had participated in the show were entitled to their view, and the protest leader should not speak for them or for other black people (PTG20149, via *The Guardian* 2014; PHM2014b12, PHM2014b13 and PHM2014b6, via Muir 2014b; PKA20146, via Andrews 2014; PBB20141, via Bailey 2014). The performers made this same point. "This petition assumes we can't think for ourselves," one said. "None of us have been forced to do this, and all of us can leave at any time. No one brainwashed us into taking part, and the more we do, the more proud we become of our performances" (Avril Nuuyoma, cited by *The Guardian* 2014). These participants against the protests and the calls to boycott or ban *Exhibit B* thought it unlikely that people would mistake the critique in the work for the phenomenon that it set out to challenge—it was, after all, playing in a theatre where paid ticket purchase was required to attend (PTG201419, via *The Guardian* 2014) . To condemn the audience as an ignorant, uncultured, uncivilised mass that needs to be told what to think is therefore unnecessary (PTG201420 and PTG201421, via *The Guardian* 2014). One put it, "Don't presume that I will 'get the wrong message'. How patronising is that?" (PHM2014b14, via Muir 2014b). They noted that most of those wanting the show shut down had not seen it, and so could not really know if the eye-to-eye engagement might make spectators aware of the critique or not (PTG201422, PTG201423 and PTG201424, via *The Guardian* 2014; PHM2014b15 and PHM2014b16, via Muir 2014b). "At least SEE what you are criticizing before you take action" (PHM2014b17, via Muir 2014b), they said. "The real elephant in the room is whether this really is 'good art'," they said. "It's not the first of its kind, for one thing" (PHM2014b18, via Muir 2014b).

These arguments meant little to the detractors, who, equally, pointed out that many of those defending the work—or, if not the work, the artist's right to create such work—had not seen the show. "The reality is this isn't even good art. It"s race bait 101 and I'll wager virtually none of the people here complaining about its cancellation have or would have paid to see it" (PHM2014b19, via Muir 2014b; cf. PKA20146, via Andrews 2014). The show, they noted, was being staged in a mainstream white cultural institution where it would be difficult for those who were not part of the elite to get their shows on, and, worse, difficult for those who were not part of the elite to afford the ticket price, one reason they might have to critique the work without seeing it (PHM2014b19, via Muir 2014b; PTG20148, via *The Guardian* 2014). They also complained about the lack of consultation about what the producers knew could be an upsetting show (Sara Myers, cited by Andrews 2014). The argument that black performers had agreed to participate in the show (PTG201417, via *The Guardian* 2014)—and even that performers in historical "human zoo"-style shows had also participated voluntarily (PTG20147, via *The Guardian* 2014)—also meant little. The actors, no matter what they said, were still being exploited in the name of a white man's art at best or a white man's aggrandisement at worst. "You are exploiting the actors as you know it's hard for them to find work" (PSM2014a11, via Myers 2014a), one of the original signatories to the petition said. "These 'performers' are validating this exhibition because it is part of the terms of their engagement," an online commentator argued. "If they did not agree to give these validations, they would not be engaged in this project" (PTG201410, via *The Guardian* 2014). "Personally, I would never expect the performers to speak against the piece in the news," another agreed, because "my money says if they had, they would end up unemployed" (PTG201424, via *The Guardian* 2014). Indeed, some detractors took *The Guardian* to task for presenting quotes from the performers, as though their comments could outweigh those without career or economic interest in the show (PTG201411, via *The Guardian* 2014). They said it was all a cheap trick to court controversy, and publicity, by using "Black people as props for the furtherance of a white man's fortune" (PHM2014b6, Muir 2014b). Those who had become complicit should be ashamed of themselves. One said, "It felt like a cheap trick. I looked around the room at the mostly white audience and saw shame in their faces … I myself am black and felt excluded from the point of the exhibition" (PTG201425, via *The Guardian*).

Throughout these debates circulating across news and social media sites—and drawing literally thousands of comments each time a new author published an article with a comment box below—there was little recognition of people's right to disagree with each other. More than one poster had their content removed by moderators (PTG201426, PTG201427 and PTG201428, via *The Guardian* 2014; PJO20145, via O'Mahony 2014), which, of course, they tended to read as censorship of their point of view. I was "relegated for not accurately reflecting the rent-a-mob Guardian line" (PHM2014b20, via Muir 2014b), one put it. More than one poster was accused of "trying to generate click-bait"

(PTG201429, via *The Guardian* 2014) with sarcastic, controversial or crass comments, and thus of courting scandal for attention the way some said the producers and the protest leaders had done (PKA201411, via Andrews 2014). Though *The Guardian* was the outlet that had thousands of interlocutors, and some nasty content, comments became nastier on *The Independent*'s page (Gander 2014) and nastier again on *The Telegraph*'s page (Singh 2014)—on the latter there was more about "white-bashing", "black slave traders" and "political correctness gone mad", and an unquotable level of swearing descending rapidly into slander of those with different views (PAS20141, PAS20142, PAS20143 and PAS20144, via Singh 2014). On both news and social media, a number of these interlocutors were accused of making assumptions about their fellow-spectator-become-social-media-performers' race based on the views they were expressing (PKA20148, via Andrews 2014). Across all of the platforms, debate swiftly hit fixed, polarised positions that the posters could not budge each other from.

There were a few who said there was power in simply getting people to talk about these issues. They typically articulated this in terms of the idea that *Exhibit B* was a work about the performance of the spectators, not of the performers, and the online and offline protesters were therefore as much a part of the work and the debates that it prompted as those walking through the installation. "[I]t's the viewers who are really what the piece is about" (PJO20146, via O'Mahony 2014), one argued. Accordingly, another said: "[T]he only thing making it different [from historical human zoos] is us. [T]he public" (PJO20147, via O'Mahony 2014). If so, another proposed, "couldn't we consider this pressure being put by external actors who find this offensive as part of the dialogue' that the artists want to provoke" (PKA20149, via Andrews 2014). "The protesters seem to not realise they were part of the art" (PAS20145, via Singh 2014), still another said. Together, these posters thought, the offline spectators, online spectators and protestors were all part of the tensions between different perspectives that the work sought to play out. More cheekily, one poster suggested: "Maybe the Barbican, when applying for its next Arts Council grant, can add the crowd of protestors … and look very impressive indeed in terms of community engagement" (PTG201430, via *The Guardian* 2014). In suggesting that the protest, debate and dialogue was part of the performance, they echoed Jonathan Gray's (2012) sentiments about @Platea's online activist performances cited in Chap. 3 the suggestion that having the debate is more important, impactful or productive than resolving the debate in these new forms of practice.

Unfolding in this way, though, the debate did loop through the same plot points, phases or stages again and again—the same arguments, and the same sets of assumptions about the authenticity, agency, authority and parts that others were playing, without necessarily moving forward to unpredictable new ideas, up until the point where the Barbican withdrew *Exhibit B* from its programme. The debate, at that point, became about democracy and censorship. Some, defining democracy as dialogue between viewpoints, suggested that a performance of democracy had been happening in the online debates and, later, the live protests, until the show was withdrawn. Withdrawing the show therefore put a stop to a democratic debate and "only history will tell if it has a positive or negative effect in respect of reducing racism" (PKA201410, via Andrews 2014). "Social change takes decades," this poster said. "At this stage, how can we know?" (PKA201410, via Andrews 2014). Such posters tended to think that banning shows that some did not like would never result in true democracy, equality or heathy social relationships (PKA201412, and PKA201413, via Andrews 2014). To shut a show down was a sign of social media mob rule. "We are supposed to be a democratic nation," one said, "yet mob censorship for a particular point of view is holding sway, unchallenged here" (PHM2014a3, via Muir 2014a) . It was "a victory for censorship and mob rule! (PHM2014b38, via Muir 2014b), another agreed. It was a case, yet another said, where "the abhorrent is normalised and justified through consensus" (PHM2014b21, via Muir 2014b), or, perhaps, where "the museum gave into the optics" (PBB20142, via Bailey 2014). The decision was seen as censorship and thus as undemocratic by many posters (PHM2014b22, and PHM2014b23, via Muir 2014a; PHM2014b24, PHM2014b25, PHM2014b26, PHM2014b27, PHM2014b28, PHM2014b29, PHM2014b30 and PHM2014b31, via Muir 2014b; PBB20143, PBB20144 and PBB20145, via Bailey 2014; PAS20146, PAS20147 and PAS20148, via Singh 2014). "Goddammit," one said. "Do we live in a democracy and have free speech or not. Show the damn play Barbican. Signed—A black person" (PHM2014b32, via Muir 2014b). "We need dialogue, we need art, we need a free for all, we need a space to meet and ask the uncomfortable questions," another poster said. "Censorship is never the answer" (PHM2014b33, via Muir 2014b). Another still saw it as "a sad day for activism" and suggested that the protestors "should be arrested for harassment before being forced to go to a university to attend lectures entitled: Stupidity and Protest in the Internet Age" (PHM2014b13, via Muir 2014b). Some concluded with the idea that, although the damage was done with the withdrawing of the show, they did hope that the dialogue would continue. "Hopefully with compassion and wisdom a new path will be struck by the two sides" (PHM2014a1, via Muir 2014a), one put it. Others, of course, read democracy as decision making based on majority views and, as a result, saw democracy as what happened when the show was withdrawn (PHM2014b34, PHM2014b35, PHM2014b36, PTG20147 and PHM2014b20, via Muir 2014b). "All this nonsense about censorship and mob rule highlights to me how poor a grasp British society has of democracy and what it entails, what it embodies," one of these posters said. "It's quite simple really, it's the will of the majority of people that has led to the cancellation of this piece" (PHM2014b37, via Muir 2014b)—a will of the majority subsequently effective in other cases too—for instance, in spite of a police presence, 100 demonstrators protesting at a later performance of *Exhibit B* in Paris, again stopping the performance (Radio France Internationale 2014; Hird 2014). For those outraged by the work, this was seen as a victory and a win for democracy. For those not, it was seen as a sad day and a defeat for democracy.

## Ugly Mugs

As the controversy about *Exhibit B* was playing out in Europe, another controversy, albeit on a smaller scale, was playing out on the other side of the world. Peta Brady's play *Ugly Mugs*, presented at the Griffin Theatre Sydney and the Malthouse Theatre Melbourne in 2014, drew criticism because it was based on the #UglyMugs forum that Australian sex workers contribute to in order to warn peers about problematic customers called "ugly mugs". The forum is a private platform with descriptions of rape and trauma. The playwright apparently accessed these descriptions, together with accounts of the murder of sex worker Tracy Connelly in Melbourne in 2013, and the fact that it got far less press than the murder of non-sex worker Jill Meagher in Melbourne in 2012, to write the play (Watts 2013). The playwright, director and production houses then presented *Ugly Mugs* as a "[d]aring, provocative and topical" play about attitudes towards violence against women, saying that "it asks complex questions about vulnerability and responsibility" (Griffin Theatre 2014a, b).

"Brady's characters wade through the aftermath of it," they said in promotional material, "leaving us in no doubt about the dark truths that lurk around every corner" (Malthouse Theatre 2014). Cast as an attempt to bring the "unheard voices of sex workers' onto the stage, *Ugly Mugs* was praised for "humanizing the victim" in reviews by critics such as *The Australian*'s Chris Boyd (Croggon 2014a, b). Many members of the sex worker community did not, however, see it this way. There was outcry on social media, and then on more mainstream media, prompted by Jenny Green and advocacy bodies such as Scarlett Alliance and Vixen. As Green said on her *SexLiesDuctTape* blog, and in later press interviews, "[c] onfidential accounts of rape and violence should never be entertainment" (cited by Croggon 2014a, b), and *Ugly Mugs* was guilty of doing this. As the campaign grew and "we hope our 'lives' entertained you" flyers got handed to patrons exiting the theatre to draw their attention to the sex workers' concerns, the controversy gained more and more press.

The sex workers had two problems with *Ugly Mugs*. The first was the fact that it took a private publication as a source for a public piece of entertainment. "Just wondering what part of 'Sex Worker Only Publication' did Peta Brady not understand?" (PLB20141, via Barnes 2014), said one poster contributing to the debate via comment boxes at the close of articles on *The Conversation*, *Arts Hub* and other news sites, and on social media sites. "I'd really rather someone who's never done a trick in her life not use a publication I and others have had to use to alert others about the men who've raped us as inspiration for her 'art,' and then to make such a bloody offensive hash of it" (PRW20141, via Watts 2014). Although the playwright, producers and director, Marianne Potts, began denying suggestions that the play actually used content from the publication per se, rather than content inspired by it, the notion was clearly out there in the public sphere. "Much as [director Marianne] Potts tries to downplay them, Peta Brady has two main problems," one poster put it. "[T] he play is TITLED after the booklet, it features the booklet, and in interviews elsewhere she described the stories told in the play as 'stolen' [from it]" (PRW20142, via Watts 2014). This, for many, meant "[h]er experience working with sex workers is part of the verité marketing claim made for the play" (PRW20142, via Watts 2014). The second problem, following on from the first, was that Brady's play turned the sex workers' "stolen" stories into "pity porn" which they felt "contributed to the stigma around their community" (Croggon 2014a, b; cf. Neutze 2014a, b; Northover 2014; Supple 2014; Watts 2014). As Julie Bates, co-founder of Ugly Mugs for the Prostitutes Collective of New South Wales in the mid-1980s, put it, "Brady has made a living off sex worker 'tragedy' and now she is making more money off ticket sales of her 'victim porn' play" (cited by Green 2014). The sex workers felt they were painted as figures of tragedy, as a result of unfortunate individual circumstances, abuse, alcohol, drugs or other issues, who needed to be saved from themselves and their sad and worthless lives. "*Ugly Mugs* has left audiences and reviewers with false impressions of sex workers as one-dimensional victims," protest leader Green said, "which is far from the reality of sex workers as a whole people with agency" (cited by Barnes 2014) . As another protesting sex worker demanded on Twitter, "STOP PAINTING STREET WORKERS LIKE ME AS TRAGEDIES TO BE SAVED. WE ARE PEOPLE #NOTYOURRESCUEPROJECT/#uglymugs #rightsnotrescue" (Suffragette Kitty cited by Croggon 2014a, b). For the detractors, then, the problem with *Ugly* Mugs was that it was blurring the lines between art and actually, albeit in a different fashion to the way *Exhibit B* blurred the lines between art and actuality. It did not use prostitutes as performers onstage, but it did use their stories, and thus used them to entertain the masses, educate them about the perils of life on the streets, exoticise, eroticise or otherwise stereotype life on the streets, and make money. For those who complained, this made it no better than sideshow-style pity porn—in substance, if not in the style of the performance.

The controversy around *Ugly Mugs* was only further fanned by the fact that it had received positive reviews from critics Chris Boyd (*The Australian*), Diana Simmonds (*Stage Noise*) and, to a lesser degree, Ben Neuse (*Daily Review*) and Cameron Woodhouse (*Sydney Morning Herald*), if not from Kate Herbert (*Herald Sun*), in the same way that *Exhibit B* had received positive reviews from critics such as Lyn Gardner (*The Guardian*). "All in all," Simmonds, for instance, said, "*Ugly Mugs* is a triumph for Peta Brady. She has crafted a meaningful drama that illuminates as much as it engrosses … Meanwhile, it's one of the more remarkable plays to bring the mean streets to life, not least because its authenticity is palpable and the drama as truthful as it is often shocking" (2014). This was a reading which, for sex workers worried about the way they were represented, only confirmed their suspicion that the play was pity porn made poignant by a playwright.

These debates played out in social and news media for almost a month in 2014, across the pages of *The Conversation* and *ArtsHub*, newspapers such as *Sydney Morning Herald*, blogs from Alison Croggon and

Augusta Supple, as well as the Griffin Theatre and Malthouse Theatre websites, Facebook page and Twitter pages (Barnes 2014; Croggon 2014a, b; Neutze 2014a; Northover 2014; Supple 2014; Watts 2014) . The story, and the story co-created in social and news media, was, as Croggon recalls, "full of claims and counter claims" (2014).

On the one hand the producers claimed that director Potts and playwright Brady did do research, and consultation, and therefore had the right to deal with the subject as a "womens issue" and as a "human issue" too. "As the playwright," Potts told Alison Croggon, "Peta was actively consulting with many people from the sex work community including some key organisations—she has an extensive email trail that demonstrates that her practice is sound but [it] would be breaking confidentiality to share this" (cited by Croggon 2014a, b). Moreover, Potts told Richard Watts, "This isn't just a play about the sex working community, it's a play about violence against women ... As a female I feel—and as Peta is a female as well—I feel we have every right to tell the story about violence against women" (cited by Watts 2014; cited by Croggon 2014a, b)—a "sticky question" of representational politics, as Croggon (2014a, b) said. Some of the spectators-become-fellow-social-media-performers agreed. "You don't have a monopoly over the issue," one told sex workers complaining about the play. "It is a human issue, it is an issue for all people to be made aware of" (PRW20143, via Watts 2014). As with debates staged around *Exhibit B*, posters defending the production said that it was unreasonable for Jane Green to speak for all sex workers in the same way as it was unreasonable for Sara Myers to speak for all black people, and it was neither reasonable nor democratic to withdraw artworks simply because someone was offended. "What about the sex-workers who were consulted during the development of the play? Aren't their opinions and point-of-view just as relevant?" one asked. "If art was stopped the minute 1 person (or even a few) took offense, then we would have no art" (PRW20143, via Watts 2014). At least one poster also pointed out that the playwright, director and producers had denied using the Ugly Mugs publication as a direct source in their interviews as the commentary unfolded. "[F]rankly," this poster said, "this argument was all triggered by a horrifically defamatory accusation of a breach of trust and confidentiality which seems, by all accounts, to be untrue" (PAS20141, via Supple 2014). This poster tried to turn the question of who was offending, attacking or impugning the reputation of whom on its head.

On the other hand, detractors claimed that the play usurped the space for sex workers to speak about the distinctiveness of their experiences in the diversity of their own voices. "Sex workers speak for ourselves," Green argued, "our personal stories belong to us and it is our right if, and when to tell them" (2014). Many posters took this to heart. "[T]his isn't a generalised play about domestic violence or sexual violence," as one put it. "[I]t specifically targets sex workers, and in doing so is one of the most disgusting treatments of sex workers in the name of 'art' that I've ever come across" (PRW20141, via Watts 2014). Others agreed, arguing that this was exactly what happened when Tracy Connelly was murdered, when journalists rewrote her story as simply another women's issue or another human issue. By this logic, one argued, "[y]ou can claim anything is a 'human issue' and [use that to claim space to] speak on behalf of marginalized groups—it's not right" (PRW20144, via Watts 2014). For those holding this view, "a non sex worker writing about dead hookers is whorephobic and revolting and should NEVER have been allowed to take place. To hell with the director and his [sic] 'artistic vision' or 'intention,' the real life consequences for actual sex workers are at stake here" (PGT2014b1, via Griffin Theatre 2014b). Here, the claims and counterclaims began to hinge on the "nothing about us without us" politic first highlighted by disabled people petitioning for rights in the USA three decades earlier. The slogan was adopted by sex workers and their allies who were upset that *Ugly Mugs* had indeed produced something that stole their images, stories and traumas without consulting them, let alone letting them take the lead in representing themselves. "[A]pparently," one poster said, "the opinions of sex workers when consulted was not taken at ALL—simply used to say that they have 'consulted' http://nothing-about-us-without-us.com" (PRW20144, via Watts 2014). The producer's, director's and playwright's attempts to clarify the situation did little to appease these posters' anger. "Shame on you all," one said. "This fauxpology is pathetic" (PGT2014b1, via Griffin Theatre Croggon 2014b).

As the debate continued, professional critics Croggon, Supple, Simmonds and others started to offer their own more lengthily considered perspectives on the controversy—although, unlike in the opinion pieces about *Exhibit B*, this emerged on their blogs rather than in follow-up pieces in mainstream news platforms as Andrews' (2014) and Malik's (2014) on *Exhibit B* were, and they were written by theatre workers rather than scientists or social scientists. Supple (2014) asked what playwrights were meant to be doing if it was not producing plays based on ideas, inspiration, research and other resources to contribute something to social debate. Even if it requires "an iron constitution" (2014) to do it, as well as a "moral obligation ... to make sure that the contexts in which we develop and make a work involves consultation and discussion with community" (2014). She found the Griffin Theatre Company's explanation that they presented the piece "to provoke conversations in our audience about the steps we need to take as a society to unmake traditions or patterns of violent behaviour" (Griffin Theatre 2014b cited by Supple 2014) "noble". Fellow critic Simmonds joined the conversation, saying that she disagreed with the "we as sex workers must be able to speak for ourselves" statements so strongly that "it makes my eyes water" (PAS20142, via Supple 2014), because pushed too far this would mean that people would never make art. Fellow critic Croggon joined in too, telling Simmonds that she thought that "when it comes to directly drawing on real events and the traumatic lived experience of other people as an inspiration, responsibilities kick in too" (PAS20143, via Supple 2014). From her point of view,

> to cast this as a question of 'artistic freedom' or censorship kind of misses the point by a country mile: what is at issue is who holds the power in this equation, and in this case, it's the person with the power to represent. Artists aren't used to the idea that they might have power, but we do, and we should recognise it. (PAS20143, via Supple 2014).

As the pleas, claims and counter-claims went back and forth across news and social media pages, the same old saws about whether detractors or defenders had seen the show that came out in the controversy about *Exhibit B* came out in the controversy about *Ugly Mugs* (Croggon 2014a, b). "[I]t's being argued," one poster complained, "largely, by people who haven't seen the play" (PAS20141, via Supple 2014). Interestingly, though, Croggon (2014a, b) observed, the press reports, and the public discussion within the sex worker networks, did not lead to the same level of public discussion in the theatre industry itself. "This perhaps stems," Croggon suggested, "from an understandable desire to protect the artists, and in particular Peta Brady, from attack" (2014). Croggon called attention to one of her fellow poster's warnings in this regard. "People are NOT having a mature, informed conversation about this," the poster said, "so maybe it's best that we leave this particular play be. I just think it's become too vicious and the dialogue has deteriorated. Maybe have this conversation again when people have calmed down" (PAS20141, via Supple 2014; cf. Croggon 2014a, b). Certainly, *Ugly Mugs* raised questions about representation, power, responsibility, art, who has the right to make art about marginalised communities, and how online platforms are impacting on our negotiation of these issues in the twenty-first century. Although the production was not withdrawn, boycotted or banned, the same issues about censorship, democracy and definitions of democracy that came out in the *Exhibit B* controversy began to surface in the *Ugly Mugs* controversy too. The self- and social-performance of public sphere debate in theory allowed the players with power, and those without power, to push their viewpoints. However, whether because of the issues that Croggon (2014a, b) identified, because the faux/apology from the artists played out differently, because the work itself played out differently with the performers in *Ugly Mugs* rather than prostitutes staging trauma they had been subject to, because this was about community of affinity rather than a community based on gender, race, ability or other physical attributes or because it was unfolding in a different cultural context, the *Ugly Mugs* controversy never reached the same heights as that over *Exhibit B*—not in terms of volume of content, not in terms of vitriol and not in terms of viciousness of attacks. This, in itself, raised questions about how far the controversy circulated out from sex worker networks, and theatre networks, into other networks in the wider community, which might have cared if it had been raised further in ongoing public debates.

## Involuntary Dances

The staging of controversy via online social and news media platforms that came out around *Exhibit B*, and around *Ugly Mugs*, bore some interesting similarities to another staging of controversy—in the context of another marginalised community—that I have examined in the past. In Rita Marcalo's *Involuntary Dances*, presented at the Bradford Playhouse in the UK in 2009, "Marcalo stopped taking her epilepsy medication, took stimulants such as tobacco and alcohol, and subjected herself to triggers such as strobe lighting, in an effort to induce a seizure" (Hadley 2014). In style, *Involuntary Dances* was more similar to *Exhibit B*, or to politicised performances by artists such as Guillermo Gómez-Peña, Coco Fusco, Mat Fraser and Annie Sprinkle, that provide some points of comparison to the sideshow structure of *Exhibit B*, than it was to the story-based play that became so controversial in the

*Ugly Mugs* example. It was, though, produced by Marcalo herself, and presented in a performance art, live art or installation style, without storyline per se, the tension coming from the question of whether she would or would not have a fit. Accordingly, it presented Marcalo rather than actors in the epileptic role, blurring the line between art and actuality by attempting to put an epileptic fit in an art frame to make the point the artist wanted to make.

Although my aim in analysing that work in *Disability, Public Space Performance and Spectatorship* (2014) was to learn something about how spectators respond to disabled bodies onstage, "track[ing] the way spectators' performance of meaning-making plays out in social media forums, and the way these encounters at the interstices of performance, memory, public history, private history and technology negotiate ideas about disability" (113) revealed issues with staging spectatorship on and through social media more generally too. Similar "narrative, dramaturgy, and, perhaps more importantly, negotiations" (111) of spectatorial opinion, discussion, debate and conflict played out. Structures that readily map onto online debate about *Exhibit B*, about *Ugly Mugs* and, intriguingly, even onto general debate about critics, criticism and their continued role in contemporary theatre culture follow Brown's article. Though each case showed similarities and differences—including one somewhat telling difference to be noted shortly—each moved through clear strategies, points, stages or phases—that is, through distinct manoeuvres in the spectators' performances of public sphere debate, and what spectators presumably hoped would be success in getting their views to prevail in the debate.

In the first set of manoeuvres, participants often began by claiming a position to speak from: 'I am this', or 'I have this' or 'I have experienced this.' This, according to Ruth Page (2012, 28) in her analysis of storytelling strategies on social media platforms, is the manoeuvre by which participants set up their preferred image of the self that is speaking, what sociologist Erving Goffman (1963, 1973) would call their "face" or "front". The participants were clearly self-conscious about the fact that not all posts and not all posters are equal on social media sites from the start. In these examples, though, the posters' authority, status and agency came not from their position as an established expert in the community, or even an established presence in the community, as opposed to a "newbie" poster, but from their status in terms of whether they were or were not a member of the identity group that the show (mis)represented. In online debate about Marcalo's *Involuntary Dances*, this came out in the form of claims and counter-claims about which of the posters had epilepsy, had the worst epilepsy or had a relationship with a family member who had the worst epilepsy. "It seems this young woman only has two seizures a year," one of Marcalo's critics put it, for instance. "I have already had two seizures in the past three days. I would not wish one on my worst enemy" (PJV20091, via Verrent 2009; Hadley 2014, 116). Another agreed, saying that "the idea of inducing an uncontrolled seizure in a steel basket scares me" (PJV20092, via Verrent 2009; Hadley 2014, 116), the implication being that if Marcalo really had experienced epilepsy so severely she would not want to make it into a performance that might turn sufferers into fodder for entertainment. In online debate about Bailey's *Exhibit B*, this came out in the form of claims and counter-claims about the racial identity of particular posters. Posters claiming that *Exhibit B* presented "Black people as props for the furtherance of a white man's fortune" (PHM2014b6, Muir 2014b), and that "I myself am black and felt excluded from the point of the exhibition" (PTG201425, *The Guardian*), butted up against other posters' counter-claims that "if the artist behind it had been black you would see this as brave and challenging" (PKA20145, via Andrews 2014) , and consternation from others still, saying: "Show the damn play Barbican. Signed—A black person" (PHM2014b32, via Muir 2014b). In online debate about Brady's *Ugly Mugs*, this came out in the form of claims and counter-claims about the sex worker status of particular posters. Posters claiming that this was "one of the most disgusting treatments of sex workers in the name of 'art' that I've ever come across" (PRW20141, via Watts 2014) butted up against the opinions of posters who disagreed so violently that "it makes [their] eyes water" (PAS20142, via Supple 2014). In the debate about Brown's article on theatre criticism culture, this came out in the form of posters claiming the status of a reviewer, a longtime reader of reviews or an artist who has been reviewed as a way of staking a personal or professional claim in the conversation.

In this phase of the posters's performance of public sphere debate the participants were, as Page puts it, "negotiate[ing] contracts for the rights to tell a story in the first place, rights that storytellers sometimes misappropriate" (2012, 16)—not just the right to tell the story onstage but the right to tell it on social and news media as an online stage for political and public sphere debate. Posters used statements, short narratives, short anecdotes and signatures noting their status as an epileptic, black person, sex worker or critic as a strategy to gain authority to give their opinion or their advice—personal authority which, according to Page, carries more weight than "external sources" (38) on social media platforms. The posters' face, front or identity position, performed via their back story, became a basis on which to build their own status or belittle the status of others. It became a basis on which to build "common ground" (38) with the fellow posters who they hoped would agree with their point of view—at least the fellow posters who were equally "evolved mentally" (PHM2014b10, via Muir 2014b). It was, as a result, critical to establishing the power relationships on which the rest of the performance of public sphere debate would unfold on these social or news media platforms.

In the second set of manoeuvres, participants often moved on to clarification of the status of the performance act, including clarification of whether it was authentic in what it was attempting to do. In online debate about Marcalo's *Involuntary Dances*, detractors argued: "Once one subtracts the romanticism, and the words-base of the performance, one is still left wondering if this was authentic" (PJV20093, via Verrent 2009; Hadley 2014, 117). It seemed, to detractors, to be simply a case where a woman was looking to make a name with a performance art set, via shock tactics, not an actual, authentic attempt to counter stereotypes about epilepsy in the community, and thus not real art. In online debate about Bailey's *Exhibit B*, detractors also argued that the show was about shock tactics, "an exhibition that dehumanises African people for money and entertainment" (PSM2014a5, via Myers 2014a), from a white man looking to make a name for himself, not a real contribution to racial relations, and not real art. Although black performers might have been involved, the fact that their livelihood depended on their employment in the show meant that their comments to the contrary could not be taken as authentic, any more than Bailey's comments could be taken as authentic. In online debate about Brady's *Ugly Mugs*, detractors also argued that it was shock tactics from a woman looking to "profit from violence against us" (PRW20141, via Watts 2014), not an authentic representation based on real research, consultation and community engagement, thus not real art. In online debate about Ismene Brown's article, detractors asked if she really was an authentic, paid, professional critic in her role at The Arts Desk or just trying to shore up her own already shaky job prospects by petitioning artists and audiences to value critics more.

At this point in their debate, posters asked if the artists were actually telling the full story about what they were saying, advising or advocating, or a half-truth, fiction or deceit in service of their own agendas. The posters were all too aware of the fact that non-authentic identity, and non-alignments between representation and reality, are known to be issues in the digital sphere (Page 2012, 166). They used their claims to being better positioned to understand the full, real story as a result of their identity position to support their status in the debate that they were embarking on—to reinforce their argument about the reasons why the artist they were supporting or denouncing should be subject to scrutiny, suspicion and debate about the motives, meaning and impact of their work.

In the third set of manoeuvres, related to the second, a number of posters wondered whether aestheticising these issues, topics or identity positions to frame them as art should ever be allowed at all. In the *Involuntary Dances* example, Marcalo was accused of "portray[ing] the victim-figure most of us reject" (PJV20093, via Verrent 2009; Hadley 2014, 117) , and thus doing damage to other sufferers, so it was not art, it was at best sad, at worst an awful spectacle for the art crowd. In the *Exhibit B* and *Ugly Mugs* examples, this idea that certain actualities should not be "allowed" to be made into art was even stronger. "To allow white people who have never lived this reality to lead the conversation is not edgy, experimental, or valid artistic expression" (PJO20142, via O'Mahony 2014), Bailey's detractors said, because it is not art, it is just racist. Similarly, *Ugly Mugs* "should NEVER have been allowed to take place" (PGT2014b1, via Griffin Theatre 2014b), Brady's detractors said, because it is not art, it is just whoreophobic. In the online debate about Brown's views, she was chastised for begging artists for support, and told that if she was a serious, empassioned and committed member of the artistic community she would prove this in the aesthetic quality of her reviews, not in these pleas.

Throughout the debates, the detractors again and again affirmed their belief that some things should not be made into art, or, at least, into this sort of art. They argued that only those who have lived the experience—authentically, and supported by evidence—should have the right to talk about it, in art or in online debates about the art, and the ideas and discourses that art would have society adopt. Many felt that the issues of ableism, racism or sexism that these performances were staging were simply too serious, and too emotive, to be made into art—or, at least, to be made into this specific sort of art, by these specific people, a number of whom had not had these lived experiences themselves. They claimed to know the issue in a way that the art makers and their sympathisers could not because they had not shared that experience of ableism, racism, sexism or other prejudice in a lived, embodied way and thus could not know that shock tactics that frame this actuality as art to make money were only ever going to be hurtful—that people would be shocked if other minorities were treated this way. This, interestingly, was the one point in which posters did at times reach for facts, evidence or statistics to back up the claims they were already arguing on the basis of their lived experience. Arguments based on facts rather than identity positions finally started to enter the dramaturgy of the online performances. It is a "fact" that Marcalo's epilepsy cannot be as bad as others; a "fact" that Bailey's performers cannot be relied on to speak out against their employer; a "fact" that Brady clearly did name her play after the sex workers publication; a "fact" that critics are on the gravy train, in the pocket of the mainstage companies, papers or players; or a "fact" that this person has or has not seen the show. Around this, though, much of the debate was always about asking or arguing whether someone actually can tell a story that they do not own in a lived, embodied, experiential way, in art or in online debate, with facts given only as evidence to back that up.

In the fourth set of manoeuvres, claims and counter-claims flew—those for the artists' work and those against the artists' work—using strategies outlined in stages one, two and three to press their case—to try to convince the network or community gathered on the page that they had the authenticity, authority and evidence to speak to the issue, and that their ideas should be the ones that come to dominate as a result of this public sphere debate. They extended, countered, contrasted or pointed out errors in the way that other posters told their tale and performed their role, and, in some cases, they resorted to personal insults and attacks about intelligence, intellectual capacity or morality to try to put those countering their view in their place. In some of the examples there were accusations about those putting the counterpoint of view, or those perceived as trolls, that they were posting click bait simply to heighten the conflict to a point that it became impossible to keep up with the volume of the posts flying back and forth.

In the fifth and final set of manoeuvres, at least in the response to Marcalo's *Involuntary Dances*, there were a few posters who suggested that, even if the debate was becoming irresolvable, it was good that the show at least got people talking about a topic that does not get enough coverage in the public sphere (Hadley 2014, 120). "I like to generate debate," Marcalo told reviewer Emma Tracey, "and whether people agree or not, I've seen more written about epilepsy in the last few weeks than I've ever seen before' (cited by Tracey 2009; Hadley 2014, 121), echoing Gray (2012) when he suggests that the debate is part of the performance. Interestingly, this played out differently in the *Exhibit B*, *Ugly Mugs* and Ismene Brown examples. In the *Exhibit B* debates there were a few comments along the lines that it was good that the issue was being discussed, although it was not stated in these terms, more in the posts that suggested that the spectators' online self-performance was part and parcel of the work itself and the impact Bailey wanted to have with it—and therefore that the debate itself meant that the work and the response to the work were having an impact in the public sphere. This emerged, though, only at the point where the show was withdrawn, as a means of expressing why some were so disappointed when the show's withdrawal meant that the debate had to stop. In the *Ugly Mugs* and Ismene Brown examples, though, there was not really any commentary along these lines. Instead, there were suggestions to leave the debate until a future point when feelings were less heated, not suggestions that the debate was good. That, in the end, meant leaving the debate to peter out. In this sense, whether as a consequence of the style, subject, status of the people involved or other factors, in the *Ugly Mugs* case there was less engagement with the idea that the debate itself was part of the work.

## Remediating and Remaking Artist–Audience Relationships

Those advocating for social media's capacity to overturn the power relationships that prevail in traditional criticism are clearly correct when they identify its potentials. What a survey of spectatorial performance in these examples shows, however, is that the reality is more complicated than the theory. These platforms do open up the role of the reviewer, critic or commentator in a way that traditional mainstream press could not. The similarities and differences in the way that role then functions are, though, rather complex. There is similarity in the participants' desire to determine meanings, attitudes and definitions of good citizenship, and thus play a part in shaping the public sphere. There is difference in the participants' degree of focus on aesthetics, expertise and authority based on expertise, versus their degree of focus on authenticity based on actual connection with a show's content. Social media performers focus on the latter, and thus on personal more than professional authority, as the thing that gives them the right to speak. Accordingly, staking claims in this regard takes precedence over staking claims based on expertise, eloquence, facts or evidence, which in the examples here come only after the poster has established their authority to speak based on the identity that they perform on the platforms. Many posters highlight the risk of appropriating other people's place to speak from in art, and in online discussions of art, and argue that it is unethical to speak about an issue without embodied experience of it. In this sense, when these posters claim status as the universal spectator, who has the right to say what a show means, it is not a right based on education, expertise or other supposedly "neutral" factors but, rather, on a supposedly natural right based on their own identity position.

These characteristics mean that social media commentary is not simply remediating the criticism of old. The compulsion to post content, and circulatory appeal shows similarities [with historical styles of criticism], but the style of performance when posting shows dissimilarities. Conversations carry more personal content and can sometimes be strangely divorced from discussion of aesthetic issues, except at the points where posters fight against shock tactics and in favour of story to give the issues portrayed the correct lived context that they need to be understood properly in a play. If these plurally authored conversations are remediating anything of the old theatre culture, it is the fights that break out in post-show talks or in foyers when tensions become raised, which, for Weidner (2009) , is already an innovation. "In the olden days," he believes, "people had the same opinions regarding theatre, they just didn't have the means to spread them. Or the awareness that people would care what they think" (2011). The emergence of social media has changed this. "You open your laptop, and decide the worlds needs to know how much you hated what just happened to you in the theatre" (2011). In an instant, friends, followers and fellows in the same networks know about it, and in terms blunter than they might have been when talking about this with family, friends, and perhaps the show's producers themselves, face-to-face in the foyer afterwards, assuming that the spectator-become-commentator has seen the show, rather than simply speaking about it because they feel a right or a responsibility based on personal experience. As discussed in Chap. 2, the brevity, immediacy and immediate moving on that characterises the affordances of social media communication platforms lend themselves towards this sort of content, more so than to the deep and iterative engagements with content required for aesthetic critique (on the one hand) or the critical convergences that lead to new types of commentary or critique (on the other hand). "'With great power comes great responsibility', and in this case accountability," Weidner warns (2009). The content is public, it can be seen and cited by authors like myself, and the commentators can be held accountable for it—though posting on other people's pages, or under pseudonyms, can reduce accountability for those who do not want to be exemplars for the public to judge here, in either aesthetic or critical contexts.

Though these comments suggest that online commentators' practices align with what the affordances of the platforms encourage, there are those who question whether theatre audiences have had enough time to establish a working knowledge of how to succeed on social media. According to Connor (2013), the evidence suggests

> that twenty-first-century audience members, silenced by more than a hundred years of "audience etiquette" and a surrounding culture of hierarchical interpretative gatekeeping, are decidedly unprepared to take full advantage of this potential renaissance in the meaning-making process. They lack data; they lack analytic skills; and, perhaps, most significantly, they lack the will/desire and the agency to enter the interpretative process with a level of preparedness and energy appropriate to the level of the art work itself. In short, they aren't that good at interpreting meaning and ascribing value (3)

Though Conner (2013) is correct that many theatre audiences are still learning to engage with these platforms, the examples here tend to suggest that just as many are already well aware of some of their most critical conventions, using signatures, anecdotes and self-performance styles designed to give them authority based on authenticity. They work hard to stake their claims, and struggle against misreading, misrepresentation and misappropriation of their claims. As Page argues,

> [s]taking a claim to tell or retell a story is a tricky business: it places obligations on both narrator and audience. The narrator must negotiate claims of authenticity and authority in order to tell their own or another's story: a story must be tellable but also credible. The audience must decide how to interpret the narrative. (2012, 164)

The strategies used in social media debates sparked by controversial shows give an insight into how posters do this, providing information about their identity, experience and embodied knowledge, before getting to the issues of expertise or evidence that were so important in older media, where gatekeepers gave guarantees about the authors' authority to assess the work. Posters are clearly aware of themselves, and the claims they need to negotiate to share their views, and they work very hard to do this. Whether what they are saying is real, or made up for reasons of their own, is of course a matter separate from whether they are successful.

Interestingly, these debates often—if not always—start up underneath or alongside older-style reviews, in comment box mechanisms or embedded Facebook or Twitter feeds, so there is a traditional critique at the top of the page, and collaborative commentary, conversation and conflict at the bottom. In the *Exhibit B*, *Ugly Mugs* and *Involuntary Dances* examples, this was the case, the debates going on in comments, posts and tweets alongside the articles that sparked them, with occasional cross-citations where posters connected the two. The posters cited the articles that alerted them to the show. The critics cited other articles as well as comments, posts and other public contributions, in the process increasing the cultural capital of the public commentators. In this way, two, three or four different types or traces of spectatorial response sat together, sparking each other, referencing each other, same but different, separate but together. As noted in Chap. 2, platforms such as Upstage, or chat programs on websites streaming productions such as *The Radicalisation of Bradley Manning*, also blur boundaries between performance, para-performance and metalevel reflection on the two by presenting these in tandem in this way. Though none of the *Exhibit B*, *Ugly Mugs* and *Involuntary Dances* examples went as far with integrating performance and para-performance texts as the work cited in Chap. 3, the potential to use this to prompt reflection on how we perform commentary and critique was clearly there if not fully employed yet. This potential was at least partly harnessed by the audience as much as by the artists.

This same-but-different separate-but-together status was precisely the thing that worried Brown (2013) about the increased uptake of social media commentary in the theatre industry. "The best art critics are well qualified", she argued, "by training or by practice or by a decision early on to devote their full time to studying and reviewing an art they feel passionate about" (2013). If the art critics are fired off in favour of social media commentary, which does not prioritise the aesthetic merits of the show, season or industry sector itself, functions of historical criticism such as assessing the show, advocating for the show or selling tickets to the show are lost, Brown fears. At the same time, this historical separation was precisely the thing that worried Balme (2014), who saw it as siloising theatre off into a closed feedback loop where artists, critics, and subscriber audiences simply talk to each other, failing to link to broader social networks at all. In the larger scheme, Balme's point seems more pressing for those interested in the survival and sustainability of theatre as an impactful cultural form, if not for specific roles in the theatre.

The richest possibility of these new social media platforms is the points where texts, paratexts, expert criticism and public commentary blur, cross over, converge or prompt metalevel reflection on practice. These points are, according to mainstream media theory, the points where new forms are born. Naturally, these new forms are not likely to emerge predictably, or along a straight path of progression from conventional criticism to new commentary, to creative combinations of the two, that broaden access while at the same time fulfilling the same function that historical criticism held dear. As Briggs and Burke (2009, 61) argue, while the advent of the printing press and the newspaper was held as a means of making knowledge more accessible, the path did not run straight but rather in a zigzag, with moments of gain and loss and along the way—a zigzag pathway that the evolution of social media as a mechanism for theatre commentary and critique is likely to take too.

As demonstrated here, *Exhibit B*, *Ugly Mugs* and *Involuntary Dances* sparked scandal, controversy and debate that brought people into conversations, and that had at least some impact in the public, political or industrial spheres of theatre practice going forward. They got attention, if not on the terms that the artists wanted then on the terms that the audiences and the public at large wanted—unless, of course, *Exhibit B*, *Ugly Mugs*, and *Involuntary Dances* were intended by the artists to be taken as shock pieces from the start. The differences in the degree to which the participants saw these debates as a good chance to raise consciousness about important issues, regardless of disagreements, and thus as part of the performance itself, resulted in differences in the amount of impact each had in the public sphere as time went on. In the case of Marcalo's *Involuntary Dances*, the online debate sparked ongoing discussion in the disability performance community (Cameron 2014; Gotman 2012; Hadley 2014; Lobel 2012). In this sense it has had a lasting legacy in public sphere debates about disability, disability representation and disability politics. In the case of Bailey's *Exhibit B*, while it certainly received attention online, with a lot of press articles about it, the ongoing community and academic debate is still to emerge. To date, this is the only post hoc academic analysis of it, but current academic community sentiment suggests that there may yet be more, so it is still too early to say how withdrawal of the show has impacted on its lasting legacy in the public sphere. In the case of Brady's *Ugly Mugs*, though, the online debate appears not to have led to a lot of impact—at least not compared with other incidents in Australian theatre, such as the debate about misogyny discussed in Chap. 2, which led to roundtables, reports and policy renewal in funding agencies and flagship theatre companies. It is difficult to say whether this is because of the nature of the community engaged, the nature of the cross-connections between that community, theatre communities and other communities that might have a stake in the matter, the nature of the actions that the theatre makers took to try to forestall further scandal, or some other factor. Equally, it is difficult to say whether this is because of different notions of democracy that came to prevail among participants. With Marcalo's *Involuntary Differences*, participants resolved the matter by recourse to what Chantal Mouffe (2005, 16) has described as "agonistic pluralism", a disensus model in which democracy means different views existing in an ongoing dialogue, not a consensus model in which democracy means the decisions of the dominant majority win out. With Bailey's *Exhibit B*, withdrawing the show meant the decisions of the most vocal did win the day. Intriguingly, though, with *Ugly Mugs*, participants resolved to resolve the debate with irresolution until tempers calmed. While these examples do give us insight into the way spectators use social media to stake their claims in debate, there is clearly still more to learn about the way these practices come to be impactful in the public sphere in the short, medium and long term.

The fact that theatre makers, spectators and scholars still have much to learn about how social media can help them to make an impact in the public sphere is, as suggested in Chap. 3, one reason why some mainstage theatre companies remain cautious in their social media engagement. While most mainstage theatre companies want profile, they do not want to become objects of the sorts of social and news media debates seen in the *Exhibit B*, *Ugly Mugs* and *Involuntary Dances* examples. As Connor explains,

> [e]vidence suggests that the arts industry in the United States isn't fully prepared for this so-called redemocratization of the audience's position in the power structure of arts creation, delivery, and valuation. Some arts workers—my term for artists, presenters, producers, educators, and commentators—simply don't want the audience to take over the meaning-making process, since control over meaning (and thus value) is central to their vision of what it means to be an arts industry professional. Other artsworkers, though energized by rising audience-centered hermeneutic practices, don't know how to facilitate those practices, how to participate in them, or even when to get out of the way of them. (2013, 3)

This, Brown suggests, is why many focus their social media strategies on "feverishly filtering their feeds for 'Wow, amazing!' times 30, rather than looking for two or three discriminating reviews that actually study the work on offer, it's impact on the soul, its place among human achievements" (2013). Many mainstage theatre makers and companies still deal with social media commentary in the way they dealt with a rating, response or review in a newspaper—a focus on the simple, straightforward positive parts of the response, as the only parts that will actually make it into their annual report anyway, and a swift apology for any problems to quell sentiment until public interest moves on. Entering a world in which personal rather than professional interest holds sway, in which fellow citizens rather than famous people become influencers, trawling through the tracts of data that this makes available to assess the impact of a work remains a challenge that some companies, sponsors and other stakeholders are reluctant to tackle—especially if it might effect their reputation, and thus their future subsidy and ticket sales. For many subsidised mainstage companies, Balme therefore claims—following Janelle Reinelt (2011)—that the uncertainties around any further engagement with the online public sphere makes the prospect of deeper engagement "practically impossible" (Balme 2014, 11). Siloising different sorts of review, comment and critique into different categories, sticking with old strategies for response regardless of the category, and sticking with the most mundane sorts of response can make sense to theatre makers who simply do not yet know how to facilitate these new forms of feedback into useful paths forward for them, their stakeholders, their audiences or society at large.

Having discussed the role that social media is playing in theatre production and in theatre criticism, it is therefore worth turning to the role that social media is, or could be, playing in audience development activities more broadly—that is, the use of social media to give a glimpse into the work and working worlds of artists, artsworkers and arts organisations, as well as their supporters, in moments of mundane day-to-day activity as much as in moments of crisis.

## References


Andrews, Kehinde. 2014. Exhibit B, the Human Zoo, Is a Grotesque Parody—Boycott It. *The Guardian*, 12 September 2014. http://www.theguardian.com/commentisfree/2014/sep/12/exhibit-b-human-zoo-boycott-exhibition-racial-abuse. Accessed 5 Jan 2015.

Bailey, Brett. 2014. Yes, Exhibit B is challenging—but I Never Sought to Alienate or Offend. *The Guardian*, 25 Sep 2014. http://www.theguardian.com/commentisfree/2014/sep/24/exhibit-b-challenging-work-never-sought-alienate-offend-brett-bailey. Accessed 8 Jan 2015.

Balme, Christoper. 2014. *The Theatrical Public Sphere*. Cambridge: Cambridge University Press.

Barnes, Leslie. 2014. Ugly Mugs: "An Unacceptable Breach of Sex Workers' Privacy". *The Conversation*, 19 Aug 2014. http://theconversation.com/ugly-mugs-an-unacceptable-breach-of-sex-workers-privacy-30615. Accessed 15 Jan 2015.

Bennett, Susan. 1997. *Theatre Audiences: A Theory of Production an Reception*, 2nd ed. London: Routledge.

Bishop, Clare. 2012. *Artificial Hells: Participatory Art and the Politics of Spectatorship*. New York: Verso.

Blake, Elissa. 2010. Geeks, Tweets and Bums on Seats: How Social Media Is Shaping the Arts in Australia. *Sydney Morning Herald*. 10 July 2010. http://www.smh.com/au/entertainment/theatre/geeks-tweets-and-bums-on-seats-20100709-103g8.html. Accessed 9 Aug 2013.

Briggs, Asa, and Burke, Peter. 2009. *A Social History of Media: From Gutenberg to the Internet*, 3rd Edition. Cambridge: Polity.

Brown, Ismene. 2013. Only the Artists Can Save the Arts Critics. Culture Professionals Network. *The Guardian* 2 Aug 2013.

Butsch, Richard. 2008. *The Citizen Audience: Crowds, Publics and Individuals*. London: Routledge.

Cameron, Colin. 2014. *Disability Studies: A Student's Guide*. London: Sage.

Carson, Christie, and Peter Kirwan. 2014a. *Shakespeare and the Digital World: Redefining Scholarship and Practice*. Cambridge: Cambridge University Press.

Carson, Christie, and Peter Kirwan. 2014b. Conclusion: Digital Dreaming. In *Shakespeare and the Digital World: Redefining Scholarship and Practice*, ed. Christie Carson, and Peter Kirwan, 238–257. Cambridge: Cambridge University Press.

Carvajal, Doreen. 2014. On Display, and On a Hot Seat: Exhibit B, a Work about Human Zoos, Stirs Protest. Art & Design, *The New York Times.* 25 Nov 2014. http://www.nytimes.com/2014/11/26/arts/exhibit-b-a-work-about-human-zoos-stirs-protests.html?_r=0. Accessed 5 Jan 2015.

Collins, Eleanor. 2010. Theatre Reviewing in Post-consensus Society: Performance, Print and the Blogosphere. Reviewing Shakespearean Theatre: The State of the Art. *Shakespeare* 6.3: 330–336.

Conner, Lynne. 2013. *Audience Engagement and the Role of Arts Talk in the Digital Era.* London: Palgrave Macmillan.

Crittenden, Stephen. 2012. Now Everyone Really Is a Critic. *Global Mail* 6 Feb 2012. http://www.theglobalmail.org/feature/now-everyone-really-is-a-critic/23/. Accessed 3 Feb 2015.

Croggon, Alison. 2014a. Sex Workers and Theatre Community at Odds over Ugly Mugs. *ABC* 22 Aug 2014. http://www.abc.net.au/arts/blog/Alison-Croggon/Sex-workers-and-theatre-community-at-odds-over-ugly-mugs-140821/. Accessed 25 January 2015.

Croggon, Alison. 2014b. Ugly Mugs and the Politics of Representation. *Storify.* https://storify.com/alisoncroggon/ugly-mugs-and-the-politics-of-representation. Accessed 25 Jan 2015.

Cunningham, Harriet. 2014. Why I'm Not Going to the Opera Next Year. Daily Review. *Crikey* 8 December 2014. http://dailyreview.crikey.com.au/why-im-not-going-to-the-opera-next-year/16623. Accessed 15 July 2015.

Dotiwala, Jasmine. 2013. Training Tommorrow's Arts Journalists to Save Tommorrow's Art. Culture Professionals Blog. *The Guardian* 13Aug 2013. http://www.theguardian.com/culture-professionals-network/culture-professionals-blog/2012/jul/13/arts360-arts-journalism-training-scheme#start-of-comments. Accessed 15 Jan 2015.

Gander, Kashmira. 2014. Exhibit B: Performers in "Human Zoo"-Inspired Project Respond to Claims Production is Racist. *The Independent* 5 Sep 2014. http://www.independent.co.uk/arts-entertainment/theatre-dance/news/exhibit-b-performers-in-controversial-human-zoo-project-respond-to-claims-production-is-racist-9715394.html. Accessed 5 Jan 2015.

Gardner, Lyn. 2014. Edinburgh Festival 2014 Review: Exhibit B—Facing the Appalling Reality of Europe's Colonial Past. *The Guardian* 12 Aug 2014. http://www.theguardian.com/stage/2014/aug/12/exhibit-b-edinburgh-festival-2014-review. Accessed 5 Jan 2015.

Goffman, Erving. 1963. *Behaviour in Public Places: Notes on the Social Organization of Gatherings.* New York: The Free Press.

Goffman, Erving. 1973. *Presentation of the Self in Everyday Life.* Woodstock: Overlook Press.

Gotman, Kelina. 2012. Epilepsy, Chorea, and Involuntary Movements Onstage: The Politics and Aesthetics of Alterkinetic Dance. *About Performance* 11: 159–183.

Gray, Jonathan. 2012. Web 2.0 and Collaborative On-Line Performance. *Text and Performance Quarterly* 32 (1): 65–72.

Green, Jane. 2014. Sex Workers Protest "Ugly Mugs" at Griffin Theatre in Sydney. *Sex Lies Ductape*—Sex Worker, Activist and Random Trouble-Maker, 15 Aug 2014. http://sexliesducttape.me/2014/08/15/sex-workers-protest-ugly-mugs-at-griffin-theatre-in-sydney/. Accessed 20 Jan 2015.

Griffin Theatre. 2014a. *Ugly Mugs*. http://www.griffintheatre.com.au/whats-on/ugly-mugs/. Accessed 15 Jan 2015.

Griffin Theatre. 2014b. RESPONSE TO [Jane Green's] UGLY MUGS BLOG [endorsed by Scarlett Alliance and Vixen Collective], 13 Aug 2014. http://www.griffintheatre.com.au/blog/response-to-ugly-mugs-blog/. Accessed 15 Jan 2015.

Hadley, Bree. 2014. *Disability, Public Space Performance and Spectatorship: Unconscious Performers*. London: Palgrave Macmillan.

Hadley, Bree. 2008b. Remobilising the Monster: Modern Disabled Performers' Manipulation of the Freakshow. *MC Journal* 11.3. http://journal.media-culture.org.au/index.php/mcjournal/article/viewArticle/47. Accessed 1 June 2013.

Hird, Alison. 2014. French Exhibit B Theatre Defies Anti-racist Human Zoo Protests. *Radio France international* 7 Dec 2014. Updated 8 Dec 2014. http://www.english.rfi.fr/africa/20141207-french-exhibit-b-theatre-defies-anti-racist-human-zoo-protests. Accessed 8 Jan 2015.

Lobel, Brian. 2012. Spokeswomen and Posterpeople: Disability, Advocacy and Live Art. *Contemporary Theatre Review* 22 (1): 79–93.

Lutz, Jerry. 1974. *Pitchman's Melody: Shaw about "Shakespeare"*. Lewisberg: Bucknell University Press.

Maeres, Joel. 2015. "So Childish": Opera Australia Artistic Director Lyndon Terracini Revokes Critics' tickets. *Sydney Morning Herald* 3 Jan 2015. http://www.smh.com.au/entertainment/opera/so-childish-opera-australia-artistic-director-lyndon-terracini-revokes-critics-tickets-20150103-12hait.html. Accessed 28 Nov 2014.

Malik, Kenan. 2014. Exhbit B and Thinking for Oneself. *Pandemonium*, 28 Sep 2014. http://kenanmalik.wordpress.com/2014/09/28/exhibit-b-and-thinking-for-oneself/. Accessed 5 Jan 2015.

Malthouse Theatre. 2014. Ugly Mugs. http://malthousetheatre.com.au/whats-on/ugly-mugs. Accessed 15 Jan 2015.

Mouffe, Chantal. 2005. *On the Political*. Abington: Routledge.

Muir, Hugh. 2014a. Slavery Exhibition Featuring Black Actors Chained in Cages Shut Down.*The Guardian* 24 Sep 2014. http://www.theguardian.com/culture/2014/sep/24/slavery-exhibition-black-actors-cages-shut-down. Accessed 6 Jan 2015.

Muir, Hugh. 2014b. Barbican Criticises Protesters Who Forced Exhibit B Cancellation. *The Guardian* 24 Sep 2014. http://www.theguardian.com/culture/2014/sep/24/barbican-criticise-protesters-who-forced-exhibit-b-cancellation. Accessed 6 Jan 2015.

Myers, Sara. 2014a. Petitioning Jo Daly Executive Assistant to Sir Nicholas Kenyon (Barbican) Sir Nicholas Kenyon [To] Withdraw the Racist Exhibition "Exhibit B—The Human Zoo" from Showing at the Barbican from 23rd–27th Sep. *Change.org*. https://www.change.org/p/withdraw-the-racist-exhibition-exhibition-b-the-human-zoo. Accessed 4 Jan 2015.

Myers, Sara. 2014b. Withdraw the Rcist Exhibition "Exhibit B—The Human Zoo." *Facebook*. https://www.facebook.com/boycotthumanzoo. Accessed 4 Jan 2015.

Neutze, Ben. 2014a. Ugly Mugs—Review. *Crikey* 22 May 2014. http://dailyreview.crikey.com.au/ugly-mugs-review-malthouse-melbourne/6442. Accessed 20 Jan 2015.

Neutze, Ben. 2014b. Sex Workers Accuse Playwright of Exploitation. The Daily Review 13 Aug 2014. http://dailyreview.com.au/sex-workers-accuse-playwright-of-exploitation/10262. Accessed 20 Jan 2015.

Northover, Kylie. 2014. Sex Worker Union Member Attacks Peta Brady Play for Being "Pity Porn." *Sydney Morning Herald* 13 Aug 2014. http://www.smh.com.au/entertainment/theatre/sex-worker-union-member-attacks-peta-brady-play-for-being-pity-porn-20140813-103mty.html#ixzz3vZwHsRDp. Accessed 20 Jan 2015.

O'Mahony, John. 2014. Edinburgh's Most Controversial Show: Exhibit B, a Human Zoo, EdinburghFestival 2014, *The Guardian* 12 Aug 2014.

Page, Ruth. 2012. *Stories and Social Media: Identities and Interaction*. London: Routledge.

Palmer, Richard H. 1988. *The Critic's Cannon: Standards of Theatrical Reviewing in America*. New York: Greenwood Press.

Reinelt, Janelle. 2011. Rethinking the Public Sphere for a Global Age. *Performance Research* 16 (2): 16–27.

Sant, Toni. 2008. A Second Life for Online Performance: Understanding Present Developments through an Historical Context. *International Journal of Performance Arts and Digital Media* 4 (1): 69–79.

Sant, Toni. 2009. Performance in Second Life: Some Possibilities for Learning and Teaching. In *Learning and Teaching in the Virtual World of Second Life*, ed. Judith Molka-Sanielsen, and Mats Deutschmann, 145–166. Trondheim: Tapir Academic Press.

Sant, Toni. 2013. Theatrical Performance on the Internet: How Far Have We Come Since Hamnet? *International Journal of Performance Arts and Digital Media* 9 (2): 247–259.

Sant, Toni. 2014. Art, Performance, and Social Media. In *Routledge Handbook of Social Media*, ed. Jeremy Hunsinger, and Theresa M. Senft, 45–58. London: Routledge.

Schrum, Wesley. 1991. Critics and Publics: Cultural Mediation in Highbrow and Popular Performing Arts. *American Journal of Sociology* 97: 347–375.

Simmonds, Diana. 2015. Lyndon Doesn't Like Criticism—Who Knew! Stage Noise 2 Jan 2015. http://www.stagenoise.com/feature/2015/lyndon-doesnt-like-criticism-who-knew. Accessed 5 Feb 2015.

Singh, Anita. 2014. Human Zoo Exhibition Featuring Black People in Chains is Closed Down after Protests. Art News, *The Telegraph* 24 September 2014. http://www.telegraph.co.uk/culture/art/art-news/11118727/Human-zoo-exhibition-featuring-black-people-in-chains-is-closed-down-after-protests.html. Accessed 5 Jan 2015.

Stephens, Simon. 2010. Sarah Kane's debut play Blasted returns. *The Guardian*, 25 October 2010. http://www.theguardian.com/stage/2010/oct/24/sarah-kane-blasted. Accessed 15 Feb 2015.

Supple, Augusta. 2014. Hey. We've Gotta Galk About This—Issues in/with New Writing. Augusta Supple 14 Aug 2014. http://augustasupple.com/2014/08/hey-weve-gotta-talk-about-this-issues-inwith-new-writing/. Accessed 15 Jan 2015.

Todd, Tony, and Boitiaux, Charlotte. 2014. "Human Zoo" Exhibition Comes to Paris amid Racism Row. Culture. France 24 19 Nov 2014. http://www.france24.com/en/20141119-human-zoo-exhibition-comes-paris-amid-racism-row-france-art/. Accessed 5 Jan 2015.

Tracey, Emma. 2009. Interviews—13 Questions: Dance Artist Rita Marcalo. *BBC Ouch!* 9 Dec 2009. http://www.bbc.co.uk/ouch/interviews/13_questions_dance-Artist_rita_marcalo.shtml. Accessed 10 April 2011.

Verrent, Jo. 2009. Jo Verrent sees Rita Marcalo's *Involuntary Dances*, *Disability Arts Online* 12 Dec 2009. http: http://www.disabilityartsonline.org/?location_id1110. Accessed 10 April 2011.

Watts, Richard. 2012. Biting the Hand that Reviews You. ArtsHub 2 Sep 2012. http://performing.artshub.com.au/opinions/arts/biting-the-hand-that-reviews-you-191362. Accessed 27 Nov 2014.

Watts, Richard. 2013. How to Be a Good Audience. ArtsHub 11 Nov 2013. http://www.artshub.com.au/news-article/features/performing-arts/how-to-be-a-good-audience-193438. Accessed 27 Nov 2014.

Watts, Richard. 2014. Sex workers accuse Griffin, Malthouse of exploitation. *ArtsHub* 13 Aug 2014. http://performing.artshub.com.au/news-article/news/performing-arts/sex-workers-accuse-griffin-malthouse-of-exploitation-245304. Accessed 15 Jan 2015.

Weidner, Ashley. 2009. Social Media in Theatre. *TheatrePeople.com*, 9 August 2011. http://theatrepeople.com.au/features/social-media-theatre. Accessed 29 Nov 2014.

Wilkinson, Kate. 2009. Theatre Reviewing: Performance versus Criticism. *Style* 43: 1.

CHAPTER 5

# Social Media as Cultural Stage: Co-creation, Audience Collaboration and the Construction of Theatre Cultures

If there is an area in which social media is touted as a truly revolutionary technology, it is in audience development—attracting, interacting with and maintaining an audience for a theatre maker's work. Audience development is a term that twenty-first-century theatre makers and marketers adopt to stress the fact that marketing activities go well beyond simply telling spectators that a show is on. More than just a synonym for advertising, promoting and publicising a show to an audience, marketing is a strategic process by which an artist identifies which programmes will appeal to audiences, at which time, place and price, as well as the most appropriate channels to communicate with audiences. At its best, Joanne Kotler and Peter Scheff (1997, 31; cf. Kotler et al. 2003, 15) argue, marketing is about creating productive relationships between artists and their audiences, allowing both parties to get what they need, want or will find enjoyable, educational or provocative in the exchange. Jennifer Radbourne and Margaret Fraser agree that it is about "linking the arts with an audience" (1996, 46). Peter Steidl and Robert Hughes put it a slightly different way, arguing that marketing is about "matching products with people profitably" (1999, 4)—although, in the performing arts, that profitability can be defined in economic, cultural, educational or aesthetic terms. While early twentieth-century marketing theory emphasised the product sold to the audience, and mid-twentieth-century marketing theory emphasised the transactional process by which the product was sold to the audience, the late twentieth century witnessed a clear turn to an emphasis on audience engagement, experience and value



B. Hadley, *Theatre, Social Media, and Meaning Making*,
DOI 10.1007/978-3-319-54882-1_5

created as a result of a satisfying commercial-cum-social relationship. As the twenty-first century begins, the concept of audience as active, collaborative co-creators who have a say in the sorts of show, programme or programme politics that interest them remains core.

Indeed, it is in this marketing context that the use of the term "co-creativity" deployed to talk about artists, audiences and their relationships throughout this study was first popularised. C.K. Prahalad and Venkat Ramaswarmy (2000, 2004) used it to talk about the way producers and users of products, programmes or services work together to turn them into something suited to users' needs, interests or desires. The term has since been used by Henry Jenkins (2006) to describe the participatory, collaborative, co-creative practices that prevail on transmedia storytelling platforms. Through transmedia platforms a company can offer fans a chance to shape and share new characters, scenarios and stories based on their favourite *Dr Who* series, their favourite manga, Sailor Moon or animated cartoon series or, as noted in Chap. 3, their favourite Shakespeare play. These platforms—events, zines, websites and social media sites—take advantage of what Stephen O'Neill (2014) and Patrick Lonergan (2016) call the vernacular as opposed to virtuosic creativity of audiences. The creators of such platforms take it as read that audiences have the competence to enact dramaturgically coherent extensions to their storyworlds—to make, not merely take, meaning. To circulate it, advocate for it and even on-sell it, in a way that can eventually take the original creator out of the loop, in the way that content sharing sites such as Napster and Netflix take creators and distributors out of the loop in a commercial context, or in the way that activists take creators and distributors out of the loop by coming up with their own new campaigns in their local area in a community, experimental or political context. As O'Neill puts it, "[t]he fan paratext has its own internal formal properties and its own effects that may involve a distancing from the industry text" (2014, 13). It can, even if its connection with the original text is rather superficial, contribute to its meaning—as an advertisement for it or as a challenge to its authority (56).

As Jenkins' (2006) account of fan cultures shows, as social media has become part of the computer-mediated communication landscape over the past decade, this concept of co-creativity has become an all-pervasive part of marketing, and of popular, commercial, community and political culture as a whole. Most organisations today take make at least some effort to take advantage of digital communication technologies to collaborate with audiences, whether to sell products to them, or to agitate, activate and politicise them. From their inception, as Marc Smith and Peter Kollack note, these technologies have been characterised as having the potential to "allow people to create a range of new social spaces in which to meet and interact with one another" (1999, 3). The potential to create so-called cyberspaces in which, as Michael Benedikt (2000) claims, people can mimic, amplify or alter the communication practices—passing on information, negotiating ideas, storytelling, entertainment, sales, education and politics—that traditionally unfolded in concrete social spaces, such as homes, streets and institutions. As noted in Chap. 2, however, it was not until the emergence of Web 2.0 platforms that access to these collaborative spaces, sites and practices became available to all audiences, whether they had computer coding skills or not. This, as Don Tapcott and Anthony Williams (2006) argue, is why the social media platforms and applications that typify Web 2.0 have the revolutionary, or at least evolutionary, potential to contribute to marketing initiatives that pursue active, collaborative, co-creative relationships between artist and audience, in which both have a say in the shape of future products, programmes and services. They also have the potential to contribute to marketing initiatives that are about building communities—and, in a theatre context, building the community relationships that bring plays, performances and the institutions that produce them out of the private black box and into the public consciousness again, in the way that Christopher Balme (2014) advocates. Paige Miller (2013) agrees, arguing that social media has changed marketing more in the first few years of the twenty-first century than technologies such as the printing press, radio or television did in 50 years. "Social media is ushering in a new era of marketing," she asserts, "with new ways of reaching people, different venues for presenting information, and more opportunities to send the right message to the right person at the right time" (87). Social media sites allow theatre makers to communicate with audiences in a more direct, individuated way, and to take advantage of functions for checking in, commenting, consumer-to-consumer conversations, rating, reviewing, polling, crowdsourcing, competitions, games, gadgets and viral content to maintain their interest. It is a natural fit for theatre makers looking to make relationships with audiences, either as part of a bums-on-seats agenda or as part of bringing theatre into the broader public debate agenda. In the years following its emergence, then, articles, books, industry reports and case studies offering tips on how to take advantage of social media as part of audience development strategy have emerged (Albarran 2013; Anderson 2010; Berger 2012; Brogan 2010; Constantinides and Fountain 2008; Handley and Chapman 2012; Kerpen 2011; Lovett 2011; Mangold and Faulds 2009; Zarella 2010). It is one area in which the uptake of social media in the performing arts to produce new relationships with spectators is well-trodden territory in the literature, albeit industry rather than scholarly literature.

The fact that co-creative relations between artist and audience are now prized in audience development practice as much as in aesthetic and critical practices does not mean that they are simple to facilitate. At one level, theatre makers still face the same challenges that they have always faced in attracting, managing and maintaining audiences—the fact that theatre artists tend to create a work first then look for an audience for it, as well as the fact that the work is live, ephemeral, and not easily stored for distribution to new audiences if those first targeted do not take to it. If "the purpose of a non-profit arts organization is to expose an artist and his or her message to the widest possible audience, rather than to produce the artist and the message that the largest audiences demand," as Kotler and Scheff (1997, 20) put it, this makes cultivating co-creative relationships more challenging than it is for profit-making organisations. It is a factor in the problem that Balme (2014) identifies, where theatre becomes a private, self-servicing exercise for an existing subscriber set, rather than a public activity that engages communities in exciting ways. At another level, theatre makers also face new challenges. Creating, managing and maintaining collaborative relationships with audiences via social media is more time and labour intensive than doing this on traditional media (Meyer 2009). "The vast majority of Facebook pages associated with arts organizations", Lynne Conner observes, "aren't much different, structurally and operationally, from printed newsletters and brochures" (2013, 170). Managing them is increasingly difficult as a company's audience grows, develops or becomes diversified (Anderson 2010, 93). Tasking current marketing or administrative staff to do this—instead of making it the responsibility of artists, artsworkers and the arts organisation as a whole—can mean missed opportunities, mistakes, upset among audiences that miss more personal attention. The audience experience can suffer. Convergence between personal, social and professional lives can also be a challenge, as noted in Chap. 2, as comments that staff make to family, friends and colleagues come together with comments, congratulations, competitions and calls for collaborative creativity targeted to audiences in the same platforms. Again, the audience experience can suffer. Which can become a problem, Anderson explains, "because *the experience itself was the thing being sold*" (2010, 93, original emphasis). Because, as Conner (2013) notes, in theatre, the paratexts are as important a part of the experience as the performance texts, and in fact inseparable from them, as a part of the overall experience. Both are essential to the appeal of theatre in today's "experience economy" (Pine and Gilmore 2011).

Whatever the potentials and challenges, this is a terrain that theatre makers and companies need to negotiate. As audience development moves into the digital age, and social media becomes more important than print, radio or television in shaping public consumption practices (Mangold and Faulds 2009), theatre makers are under pressure from funding bodies, publicists and even the public themselves to implement initiatives that make at least some use of social media. This, combined with the appeal of the discourses suggesting that social media might help to make theatre more interesting, innovative and meaningful in the public sphere, or more democratic, means that most theatre makers have to use it to attract, interact with and activate their audiences.

In this chapter I look at how theatre makers are using social media in their audience development, audience engagement and evaluation of their audience engagement. I focus more on practices in Australia than I have in previous chapters because understanding a community is useful in analysing audience development activities undertaken in it, and, of course, because the US and UK contexts have been considered by scholars such as Conner (2013) and Balme (2014). The global reach of social and news media notwithstanding, issues in the USA, the UK or Europe can take time to filter through Australasia, particularly when synchronicity in conversations about live theatre is not as critical as synchronicity in conversations about globally broadcast television shows, sport or politics (Evans 2011, 162). I consider moments where activities unfold as planned, and the interactions are mundane, and moments where activities go awry, making interactions more interesting, because both are educative about how social media activity has an impact. I look for moments where a theatre maker's, company's or community's activities start to move beyond marketing in communities of association, and towards more meaningful debate among communities of affinity, as the moments where spectators start to turn into publics.

## Creating Theatre Communities Online

Computer-mediated communication technologies have always had the potential to "create new collective and individual identities as well as new environments for humaninteraction" (Downes 2005, 4). In the first few decades of mainstream computer use, though, the question of whether computer-mediated communication could create real communities—real relations between real people with real impacts in the public sphere—was hotly debated (cf. Bell 2001; Downes 2005; Holmes 1997a, b; Rheingold 1993; Smith and Kollack 1999; Sternberg 2012). According to Benedikt Anderson (1991, 6), a community is an imagined collective in which we come to believe. It is "imagined" because people cannot in practice meet all members of a community. In this sense, it is a conceptual more than a concrete experience of connection with people (Jordan 1999, 131). The question for early computer culture scholars was whether connecting online could create a real, reciprocitous, functioning community in which people "feel linked by common purpose and interest" (Downes 2005, 8). Initially, scholars argued that meeting online to discuss, debate, play or do business did not build a fully functioning community. However, Howard Rheingold (2000), the most prominent proponent of the countering point of view, argued that the main features of communities—affinities, connection, negotiation and rules—can all be manifest in online collectives as much as in offline ones. Since then, most commentators have recognised that online communities really can support conventional communities and create new sorts of communities (Bell 2001, 97–98). In the theatre industry, online communities can extend current and establish new artist-to-artist, artist-to-audience and artist-to-audience relationships, as well as create new affinities between people in a particular area, interested in a particular genre or interested in a particular entertainment, education or political outcome. These communities can make audience members feel like they are a part of the theatre-making process, and share responsibility for successes and for solving problems—whether these are the everyday problems of programme selection, promotion and impact, or the extradaily problems of dealing with floods, fires or other natural or social disasters affecting the companies.

While accepting social media as a platform where communities can emerge, grow and generate the social capital that they call on to sustain themselves, commentators today are swifter than their predecessors to acknowledge that creating communities online is a complex process, subject to powerplays, prejudices and unpredictable outside influences. Following Mark Poster (1997), most see online space as public space, a public sphere. As noted in Chap. 2, the public sphere is typified by the agora of ancient Greece. It is a space that cannot be claimed by one person, or one group. It is, by definition, a public space in which many people and groups come together to gossip, exchange information, exchange ideas and negotiate cultural norms. The public sphere has been incarnated in many spaces and places across times, cultures and contexts, "such as the agora, the New England town hall, the village church, the coffee house, the tavern, the public square, a convenient bard, a union hall, a park, a factory lunch room, and even a street corner" (1997, 217), or, in a less Western context, a ceremonial space for ritual and corroboree among Koori, Murri or Noongar Aboriginal and/or Torres Strait Islander Australians, or a marae for ritual and community relations among Aoeteroa New Zealand Maori. Today it is incarnated online on social media applications and platforms. Wherever it may be, the public sphere is critical in constructing citizens, community and society. It is, as Daniel Downes describes it, "a discursive construction subject to the rules of performance and debate" (2005, 87). It is a place where a boisterous or apathetic crowd can be turned into a public of politically active citizens (Butsch 2008). In his initial investigation of the public sphere, Jürgen Habermas (1989) worried that modern mass media was destroying face-to-face interaction that typified the development of democratic society in and through debate in the public sphere, and thus, in fact, destroying the public sphere. "He criticize[d] mass media for transforming public participation into consumerism and politics into spectacle" (Downes 2005, 87), and he sought to reclaim spaces and places for such participation. As noted, though, Habermas came in for criticism from a range of post-structuralist and post-structuralist feminist thinkers, from Jean-Francois Lyotard (1984), to Oscar Negt and Alexander Kluge(1972), Nancy Fraser (1989, 1990) and Rita Felski (1989). As Poster (1997, 218) explains, these theorists challenged Habermas's tendency to talk about reconstructing a public sphere in which rational, consensus-building debate drives the development of communal norms, without considering the way people marginalised by gender, race, class or ability might want to challenge the terms of the current public sphere, or create an oppositional counter-public sphere. Today, many see countering oppression as a more important project, in the offline public sphere, and in the online public sphere—or, if we take John Hartley and Alan McKee's suggestion that there are actually multiple public spheres (2000), the multiple public spheres that people move through in their day-to-day lives.

Many communities use social media to try to make room for more diverse points of view in the public sphere today. As discussed, for example, women Australian theatre makers have used social media to counter the idea that there is no audience for mainstage theatre written or directed by women to build community interest and investment in their cause. For these women the new relationships with fellow artists, stakeholders and spectators that social media makes possible create what Jordan calls "a more politically egalitarian debate" (1999, 2–3). One where white, heterosexual, able, male voices cannot shout down other voices the way they might have done in physical, face-to-face debates (2–3). One with as much if not more of the reciprocity, responsibility and social capital seen in offline networks. Still, as noted in Chap. 2, what David Holmes (1997a, b) has called "anomalies of reciprocity" exist in these online relationships, networks and communities. Attempts to create appealing, provocative, circulation-worthy posts, to bond members of a community, bring new members into a community or build a more inclusive community, do not always play out in predictable ways. In the case of the women theatre makers, for instance, their attempts to make room for women in Australia's modern theatrical landscape were accompanied by risks—the risk that their comments would be missed or dismissed, the risk that their case would be co-opted by counter-feminist discourses; or, indeed, the risk that their own individual contributions would be called out as unreasonable or offensive to well meaning male peers, causing harm to their reputation.

The challenge for such organisations, groups and individuals is to make their voices heard, and to make their voices circulate beyond their own centralised networks into new decentralised networks in fast-paced social media platforms where mistakes, misunderstandings and powerplays still impact on attempts to participate in debates of ideas, ideologies and issues. Whether the goal is to develop a market, a community or a more inclusive public sphere, cutting through in this context is not guaranteed. For any theatre maker or company, then, an understanding of the affordances of social media platforms, and the fact that content, frequency and timing of comments, conversations and "shares" is difficult to control, is critical to success (Brogan 2010)—or, more precisely (as this chapter will show), to a theatre maker's perceptions about the likelihood of success—perceptions that can encourage or discourage them from participating in audience development, discussion and debate through social media.

## Collaborating with Theatre Communities Online

A survey of current use of social media to create a sense of community with audiences, potential audiences and the public at large shows that practices are many, varied and, at times, very complex. "By around 2009," Sant notes, "most artists had come to realize that communicating with their target audience and loyal admirers was best done through online social media" (2014, 51). Accordingly, "[a]lmost every artist now has a presence on one or more social media sites, from Facebook and Twitter to Google+ as well as less broad reaching platforms, like MySpace, Reverbnation, and many others" (51). Almost all theatre makers and companies today at least create a profile Facebook page—linked to a more traditional website—to give industry stakeholders and society at large a sense of who they are, what they do, when, why and how. Most go further, posting information about their day-to-day work, interests, successes or current search for work opportunities as status updates on the social media platform. This is also often followed by the decision—strategic or spur of the moment—to go beyond traditional newsletter-type communications and share information about training, auditions, rehearsals and show runs that the person is involved with at the present moment.

At some points in this flow of day-to-day information about a theatre maker's or company's activities, as a show, programme or service is about to launch, theatre makers pick up the pace, frequency and diversity of their posts to social media platforms. Most circulate publicity materials, promotions or competitions to attract spectators to their show. Although it is not so prominent among individual theatre makers, most mainstage theatre companies and many independent, small and small-to-medium companies have also started using social media to promote sponsors' products, in the same way that commercial companies in other industries do in their cross-promotions. They will praise a printer, restaurant or nightclub that has played some part in producing the show, or another local company that has promoted the show, suggesting that loyal spectators, as critical co-creators of the show, season or festival, may want to support this partner by giving them more business.

Theatre makers and companies are also experimenting with crowdsourcing, not just ideas about what spectators to see but funds too, from their social media networks. They call on industry stakeholders, spectators and the public at large to become a co-creator, not just in the conversations online or the success of the show in attracting audiences, attention and reviews, but in the actual production process, as financial investors via platforms such as Pozzible or Kickstarter, often in exchange for a credit or for a ticket when the production is ready for the public.

Finally, theatre makers and companies are making use of their social media data—likes, shares, comments, or promises to contribute to a crowdfunding campaign—to evaluate the impact of their work, and argue that impact to funders, sponsors and supporters.

The Brisbane Festival—the largest festival in Brisbane—is a good example in that it follows precisely these patterns in developing its social media presence. A sizeable company by theatre industry standards, it has an online presence that includes a purpose-built website, which presents company, programme and ticket-purchase information, as well as profiles on social media platforms to present snippets of shows, hype and offers to their networks. As the festival launch comes closer in September of each year, it increases the pace, frequency and diversity of its posts. For instance, a look at its posting patterns around the September 2013 festival, programmed by Artistic Director and CEO Noel Staunton, shows a clear commitment to using the platforms regularly, and using programme activities, partnerships and bloggers to assist in generating a presence on social media platforms as part of the core business.

The online presence began with an intriguing teaser, provoked by a street art project by Stormie Mills (www.stormiemills.com/) at the festival. The teaser took the form of photos, posts and tweets about a set of giant plastic pink rabbits placed around the city—the pink of the rabbit precisely the same pink of the festival logo and thus of the banners with the festival starting to go up around the city at the same time. The rabbit was designed to make passersby stop, look and think about this strange presence on the streets—to "[e]ngage in the process, create your own stories, enjoy the respite from daily life for a second" (www.brisbanefestivalarchive.com.au/content/the-stormie-mills-project), as the festival put it. Strange, spectacular and out of place on public streets, this was a piece that encouraged people to take pictures and post them to blogs, microblogs or social networking sites. General passersby, as well as the festival itself, and a good number of the festival's presenting partners and employees, all did this. The people who knew, recognised, or realised the link to the festival linked their post to the festival's social media platforms, particularly their Twitter feed, through the hashtags #bnefest Mills, Stormie #thestormiemillsproject #sharethebunnylove. "Pink bunny watch: Kangaroo Point #thestormiemillsproject #bnefest @BrisFestival pic.twitter.com/ieEfjDuxmJ" (Penny Dahl (Cameron) *@Penn…*, Brisbane Festival Twitter, 2013). "The pink bunny has hopped into @ QUT @QUTTheCube !! @BrisFestival #bnefest ow.ly/i/3avED" (QUT SciEng Faculty *@QUTSci…*, Brisbane Festival Twitter, 2013), one said. "Have you seen our new friend on the Skywalk? We love our pink bunny & are proud to be a major sponsor of @BrisFestival #bnefest pic.twitter.com/UQZh6cyLaY" (Brisbane Airport *@Brisb…*, Brisbane Festival Twitter, 2013), posted another. Some cast this pink rabbit teaser as a sign of the transformations of city life that characterise a festival starting to be seen around town—"I really love how @BrisFestival transforms the city. Just having so many smiling ppl out and about during the week brings a great energy" (Amy Remeilkis *@AmyRemeilkis*, Brisbane Festival Twitter, 2013).

This teaser was followed by information about the programme launch, and activities that people could participate in, posted by the festival itself. The festival's posts were accompanied by others from theatre makers and companies coming to the festival. For instance, Tim Crouch, who was programmed to present his one-man show *I, Malvolio*, at the festival posted: "It's 10,000 miles to @BrisFestival So far in my journey, I have got to Osterley. #osterley pic.twitter.com/wShiOzB5kq" (Tim Crouch *@Tim Crouch1964*, Brisbane Festival Twitter, 2013). The festival's and theatre makers' posts came together with posts from friends and followers, with the public chiming into say "chookas" (an Australian theatrical term meaning "good luck with the show"), or that they were excited to see this or that as part of this year's programme. Where it suited the work, some artists also offered posts in character, controversial comments designed to create circulatory appeal beyond what a more basic post would in a busy social media feed. Crouch, for instance, posted as his character Mr Malvolio, who began by making fun of the Brisbane Festival and Brisbane itself: "'Oooh, look at me. I'm @BrisFestival Here's a pink rabbit. Here are some drunkards. Here's some degenerate art. I'm the bees knees.' #hubris", and "Brisbane—a foul-smelling river of iniquity running between banks of moral turpitude. Your judgement is nigh. @BrisFestival #timcrouch1964" (Malvolio *@MrMalvolio*,

Brisbane Festival Twitter, 2013). He mock-praised Australia's much maligned conservative then Prime Minister, Tony Abbott, a politician often criticised for his sexist, racist, ableist and elitist policies: "TonyAbbott: 'Jesus knew that there was a place for everything & it's not necessarily everyone's place to come to Oz." Here here @BrisFestival @BrisFestival brisbanefestival.com.au/events/view/i-..." and "Praise @ TonyAbbotMHR unafraid to be despised by artists/liberal lollygaggers. I'm coming to your aid @BrisFestival brisbanefestival.com.au/events/view/i-..." (Malvolio *@MrMalvolio*, Brisbane Festival Twitter, 2013). He warned Australia to beware of his wrath when he came to sort us all out: "Australia—you brood of vipers. Flee from the wrath to come. brisbanefestival.com.au/events/view/i-..." and "@BrisFestival #iwillberevengedonthewholepackofyou" (Malvolio @MrMalvolio, Brisbane Festival Twitter, 2013). Malvolio and Crouch also engaged in cross-commentary about each other's character, ambitions and future plans: "@newaudience sold he's planning a Tony Abbott support tour in 2016" and "@ newaudiencesold more Oz planned for Malv—nothing announcable yet. He has a lot to teach the antipodies. Your moral standards have slipped" (Tim Crouch @Tim Crouch1964, Brisbane Festival Twitter, 2013).

As the festival got under way, these teasers were joined with links to previews of programmed activities, interviews with programmed artists, tweets by programmed artists about arriving in the city, and other similar buzz and hype. There were calls to visit the QUT Theatre Republic—the home of La Boite Theatre Company inside the QUT campus—which, together with the Queensland Performing Arts Centre, the Queensland Theatre Company, the Brisbane Powerhouse, the more independent Metro Arts theatre space and the Spiegeltent was a main venue for festival activities. "Venture out to our new festival hub! QUT Theatre Republic promises to deliver sharp ideas and fresh new work ow.ly/nHmqp" (BrisbaneFestival *@BrisFestival*, Brisbane Festival Twitter, 2013), it posted. "@QUTtheatrerepublic is looking magical tonight! #bnefest #indie #theatre #nofilter instagram.com/p/eJ3IH_Ghv9/" (BrisbaneFestival *@BrisFestival*, Brisbane Festival Twitter 2013). There were snippets of rehearsals at this and other venues, billed as a "Sneak peek of Freeze Frame from last night's rehearsal. Instagram.com/p/eYQw2Nmhv5" (BrisbaneFestival *@BrisFestival*, Brisbane Festival Twitter, 2013). Such posts were followed by staff adding, for instance, "Standing ovation for first public showing of @BrisFestival Freeze Frame!! #bnefest pic.twitter.

com/voYg3Poc17" (Megan A *@roxiredbaroness*, Brisbane Festival Twitter, 2013). There were images of staff setting up the venues: "The @BrisFestival ticekting team hard at work at Opus!! #bnefest t.co/9sxpXP6ZTX" (Brisbane Festival retweeted Megan A *@roxiredbaroness*, Brisbane Festival Twitter, 2013). Artists like Crouch posted photos of the view from the greenroom as they arrived at the venue—"Opening night view from green room @Bris_Powerhouse @ BrisFestival Malvlio apoplectic with it all. #revenge pic.twitter.com/r4VmAIP4NP" (Tim Crouch *@Tim Crouch1964*, Brisbane Festival Twitter, 2013)—together with more bile from Mr Malvolio and more comments from Crouch about how good it was to be there, and how much Mr Malvolio was looking forward to putting Australian audiences right, now, and in subsequent real and fictional future tours.

During the run, the festival producers also posted photos, podcasts and clips that people could access from anywhere, along with reviews, including reflections on the performances from designated bloggers, reporters and reviewers at designated news outlets. At this point, posts on the Twitter feed were combined with more content on other social media platforms, such as Facebook, where longer stories with more content are possible, and more links to content sharing and streaming sites such as YouTube. The festival posted links to positive reviews, saying, for instance, "The jewel in the crown of QUT Theatre Republic is undoubtedly The Danger Ensemble's interpretation of The Wizard of Oz. The reviews are now in! Reviews of The Wizard of Oz www.brisbanefestival.com.au [8 Likes]" (BrisbaneFestival shared link, Brisbane Festival Facebook, 2013), then sharing: "Our friends at La Boite Theatre Company have created this enticing little video of the reviews of The Danger Ensemble's modern interpretation of The Wizard of Oz. The Wizard of Oz reviews www.youtube.com [8 Likes]" (BrisbaneFestival shared link, Brisbane Festival Facebook, 2013). The festival also pointed people to designated bloggers, reviewers and reporters. In some cases, these were deliberately "everyday" bloggers, designed to offer a lay perspective in combination with the professional arts reviews, and thus boost post circulation into new networks. For instance, "Wharf yard worker James Niland heads to the theatre for the first time in a long time ... and finds himself transported over the rainbow. Read his review of The Wizard of Oz, published on Brisbane Times: The Wizard of Oz www.brisbanetimes.com.au [11 Likes]" (BrisbaneFestival shared link, Brisbane Festival Facebook, 2013). In other cases, these were more "expert" bloggers, designed to offer a professional, multiperspectival and even multinational perspective, and thus, again, boost the circulation of posts on the @Brisbane Festival Twitter feed, and encourage people to click through to podcasts, previews, reviews, interviews and other content available on their sites. There was a partnership with UK newspaper *The Guardian* via its @Guardian feed on Twitter, as well as pages on its website. This platform offered podcasts in which Vicky Frost, Van Badham and Katherine Viner presented highlights, performer stories, and interviews with Staunton about the pink bunnies and other parts of the festival programme (*The Guardian* 2013), together with near-live video and blogging of the performances, exhibitions and events at the festival. The partnership with *The Guardian* gave London audiences a perspective on what was happening in Brisbane, and gave Brisbane audiences a perspective on what London audiences thought of what was happening.

Interspersed with blogs, reviews and reportage, there were efforts to spark conversations around the content, perceptions and interpretations being offered. After posting links to a review of Crouch's *I, Malvolio* on both Twitter and Facebook, for instance, "I, Malvolio review: 'This Shakespeare-inspired one-man show successfully hits the sweet spot between comedy and pain.' Bit.ly/1dqDo1f" (BrisbaneFestival @*BrisFestival*, Brisbane Festival Twitter, 2013), and "'This Shakespeare-inspired one-man show successfully hits the sweet spot between comedy and pain.' I, Malvolio performing.artshub.com.au [3 Likes. 1 Comment]" (BrisbaneFestival, Brisbane Festival Facebook, Septmeber 2013)—the festival asked Twitter followers, in the guise of a question to Mr Malvolio: "Dear @MrMalvolio, are you really 'deserving of compassion'? Bit.ly/1dqDo1f @timcrouch1964" (BrisbaneFestival *@BrisFestival*, Brisbane Festival Twitter, 2013). There were openings to conversations, though there was nowhere near the level of uptake or controversy as with the examples considered in Chap. 4.

The blogs, reviews and reportage were accompanied by celebratory comments from both industry and lay audience members, consistently retweeted by the Brisbane Festival to the @BrisFestival feed. The festival retweeted specific comments: "'I will be revenged upon the pack of you!' Tim Crouch BRILLIANT as Malvolio @BrisFestival" (Brisbane Festival retweeted Sarah Kanowski *@SarahKanowski*, Brisbane Festival Twitter, 2013) and "Awsome Sunday Jazz session! Best Washboard player ever!! @BrisFestival #spiegeltent" (Brisbane Festival retweeted Scott Bagnell

*@ssbagnell*, Brisbane Festival Twitter, 2013). It also retweeted more general praise: "Why can't it be Brisbane Festival every day!!?? Loving it Soooo much!! @BrisFestival #BrisbaneFestival" (Brisbane Festival retweeted Scott Bagnell *@ssbagnell*, Brisbane Festival Twitter, 2013). It was diligent about retweeting posts that pointed back to other parts of the feed, such as "Had a great night with Doku Rai from East Timor for @BrisFestival. Recommend you see them at Judith Wright this week pic.twitter.com/TnMITRAsUO" (Brisbane Festival retweeted Jessica Row *@Jessica_Row*, Brisbane Festival Twitter, 2013), and "Great to be @BrisFestival. For tips or to feel like you're actually [sic] here @GuardianAus live blog which is well LIVE! Theguardian.com/culture/2013/s..." (Brisbane Festival retweeted JesseCox *@BrisFestival*, Brisbane Festival Twitter, 2013).

In the midst of this running commentary, the festival posted invitations and instructions to audience members. "Planning on catching a show in the Spieglent? [sic] Then you'd better book now, because these shows are already sold out: Calexico, Emma Louise, Big Scary, Olafur Arnalds, Hungry Kids of Hungary, most La Soiree performances" (BrisbaneFestival shared link, Brisbane Festival Facebook, 2013) and "If you're heading to 'No Lights, No Lycra' tonight at Basement Late Nights in Metro Arts, here's a few tips to help you make the most of your evening: 1. Ensure you have adequate water for an hour plus of boogie-ing and bootyshakein'. 2. Please take off your shoes—sliding around ... See more Basement Late Nights www.brisbanefestival.com.au" (BrisbaneFestival shared link, Brisbane Festival Facebook, Septmeber 2013).

The invitations and instructions included ticket offers and competitions for people to take up: "We have an enews going out tommorrow. If you don't already receive them, sign up here –www.brisbanefestival.com.au/subscribe. When you subscribe you will instantly go in the draw to WIN the ultimate Final Festival Fling for you and three friends. What's the Final Festival ... See more [26 Likes. 1 Comment]" (BrisbaneFestival shared link, Brisbane Festival Facebook, 2013). The festivals own offers were regularly interspersed with partner offers, presented as part of sponsored partnerships with restaurants, pubs and clubs around the festival precincts: "Visit one of our partner restaurants and order the special Festival Flavours dish; Instagram a photo of your Festival Flavours experience and you might just win a prize. Find out how: Festival Flavours www.brisbanefestival.com.au

[11 Likes]" (BrisbaneFestival shared link, Brisbane Festival Facebook, 2013) and "Did you know, our friends at Fifth Element host Australia's largest selection of wines by the glass #festivalflavours ow.ly/oxz4w" (BrisbaneFestival *@BrisFestival*, Brisbane Festival Twitter, 2013). There were also posts pointing to other performing arts producers, though these were more in the weeks following the run of the festival. For instance, "Attention performers & producers—expressions of interest are now open for next year's @anywherefest—get on it—anywherefest.com/2014-eoi/" (BrisbaneFestival *@BrisFestival*, Brisbane Festival Twitter, 2013), followed by "@BrisFestival Thank you muchly for the retweet. You all moved from festival recovery mode to planning mode yet? :-)" (Anywhere Festival *@anywherefest,* Brisbane Festival Twitter, 2013) and "@anywherefest Our pleasure. :) And yes, it's onwards and upwards to 2014!" (BrisbaneFestival *@BrisFestival*, Brisbane Festival *Twitter*, 2013). The partners reciprocated, presenting the festival with opportunities to retweet other groups and organisations, such as Ausdance, ABC Arts and Map Magazine's tweets promoting or praising their programmes.

As the festival wound up there were thank yous, reviews, wraps, top-ten lists and other posts looking backwards or looking forward to the next year's festival. For instance, "@VirginAustralia sent me to the @ BrisFestival last weekend, and it was a blast! Here are the TOP 10 things I did: virginaustraliahighflyer.tumblr.com" (Brisbane Festival retweeted Cameron Ernst *@cameronernst*, Brisbane Festival Twitter, 2013).

As this summary shows, the Brisbane Festival developed its own dramaturgy of social media posts, provocations and prompts to try to engage audiences with the festival experiences. There was, at least at that iteration of the festival, little by way of posts offering insights into the development of the works in the weeks, months or years leading up to the festival. As a large-scale festival that offers "something for everyone" in its programming—mainstage events, fringe events and community events in its programming, though the prevalence of community events was less in the first programme by Noel Staunton than it was under the previous director, Lyndon Terrancini (Hadley and Gattenhof 2011)—Brisbane Festival is a producing as well as a presenting organisation. It commissions and co-produces new works, it circulates calls for local, national and international presenters to pitch new work, particularly for its fringe programme, and it co-creates work with communities, as well as presenting existing mainstage work sourced at arts markets and festivals, and existing roaming work sourced through agents. In this sense, it could theoretically offer more insight into developmental processes, decision, and work in progress prior to its run each year than it typically does, to develop a sense of collaborative curation or consultation with audiences. This may be because programmes are not fixed prior to launch, or kept secret prior to launch, because in Australia the example of the Adelaide Festival of the Arts in 2000, in which director Peter Sellers promised great partnerships with communities who became disappointed when this did not come to fruition (Caines 2008), looms large in the national memory. The Brisbane Festival, like many of the major producers, may be fearful that even a tentative mention of something on social media could be taken as a promise, and thus be a disappointment if it does not come to pass. Accordingly, posting about developmental processes seemed to be left to independent, experimental and fringe artists in the programme. The festival's social media presence picks up post launch, with posts, prompts and links from different perspectives in funny, informational, quaint or provocative formats. Everyday and expert bloggers, reviewers and reporters are set up to respond, and to ensure circulation beyond Brisbane theatre community networks into new networks—global theatre communities or non-theatre communities—if not to offer actual conversations about content.

The dramaturgy of social media posts engages audiences with the festival and the festival experience. Independent artists programmed within the festival seemed to pick up on this dramaturgical structure—for instance, having been included in the Brisbane Festival in 2013, independent Brisbane theatre company Motherland in the following months continued to follow through with these types of post, in smaller ways, posting updates, programmes and pitches to support sponsor products: "Check out the e-program for Motherland. tiny/cc/MotherlandProgram metroarts.com.au" (Motherland, Motherland Facebook, 2013). "If you're coming into the city early (or hangign around) to see Motherland—here's a special offer from Pig'n'Whistle. [1 Like] ☺" (Motherland, Motherland Facebook, 2013).

As standard content flow for many theatre makers and companies on social media platforms, this content is worth interrogating in light of Sant's (2014) and Conner's (2013) comments about major theatre companies being slow to produce, disseminate or promote their work through social media. For Sant, while most theatre makers have set up a profile on one or more platforms, "very few make any special effort to interact with their fans" (2014, 51). Given that companies like the Brisbane Festival are clearly making the effort to interact online, what Sant may be pointing to here is the gap between transmitting information and more productive types of interaction via social media platforms. While mainstage theatre makers and companies use social media platforms to transmit information, or send congratulations and plugs for partners, Sant's comment suggests that this may not amount to an effort to engage in discussion, debate and collaboration that goes beyond marketing into meaningful, impactful conversations. Clearly, many mainstage theatres do use social media to build interest, investment or hype when a programme is ready for an audience. While there is interactivity involved, though, it can be rote in its formats, and it can flow mainly within centralised networks of fellow producers, partners and stakeholders in the industry. It is thus at the selective rather than the productive end of the interactivity spectrum. It does not necessarily deploy social media to present a record of creative process, seek stimuli for a project or call a community into issue-driven debate. For Sant, and others who share her views, moving beyond chookas to meaningful, impactful conversations is still more common among independent, experimental or activist artists than among mainstage artists, among individuals rather than mainstage companies.

Sant's comment thus raises questions about whether a social media presence such as that presented by the Brisbane Festival goes beyond association and into actual community. The Brisbane Festival is clearly conscious that it needs something beyond its own posts on its own programme content to create the sort of conversational and circulatory appeal that engages existing and expanded networks in the work, let alone in issues or ideas. It works to engage with others, via teasers, provocations of the sort that Crouch creates when he has Mr. Malvolio mock Brisbane, the bunnies, the Australian prime minister and so on, everyday and expert bloggers, and partnerships with other companies locally, nationally and internationally. It is successful but, for commentators like Sant (2014), perhaps successful up to a point, in that this mainly results in formulaic conversations and congratulations, raising the question of what it would take in this city, this context and this theatre culture to move beyond these basic conversations into broader community debate.

## Brisbane Theatre Culture Debate

Although Brisbane as a sub tropical city is a laid back, suburban, beach-and-bush culture, at least compared with other Australian capitals such as Sydney and Melbourne, or international capitals such as London and

New York, the evidence suggests that there are issues and incidents that will spark fast-paced, heated, passionate debate and protest, both offline and online.

The best-remembered example of this more productive public debate in the twenty-first century so far has been the fast-paced, furious and passionate discussion that unfolded in 2010 after a series of policy, production and commercial incidents caused the Brisbane theatre community to consider the health of its practices compared with those of other cities in Australia. The debate happened in 2010, as Brisbane theatre scholars Paul Makeham, Joon-Yee Kwok and I were analysing the health of Brisbane's theatre ecology—mapping the paths to success of particular practitioners, productions and companies—via records in the Australian government-funded AusStage database discussed in Chap. 3 (Makeham et al. 2012). The online conversations that unfolded were thus of interest, and we collected them to track, code and analyse. The data shed light on just how active Brisbane's theatre and broader communities could be in public debate, and how this debate could help the community to advocate for ideas, practices and changes to practice.

As Makeham, Kwok and I acknowledged at the time (2012), this debate came about as a result of a range of incidents in Brisbane's theatre and broader culture rather than a single isolated incident, show or season. After massive shifts in infrastructure, support and policy surrounding theatre in Brisbane over the past couple of decades (Gill 2010), John Baylis's *Mapping Queensland Theatre* report, which contained significant criticism of the local theatre ecology, had just been published (2009; Makeham et al. 2012). At the same time, a series of more mundane issues popped up. There were a couple of controversies. There was, as noted in Chap. 2, one about Facebook comments on Brides of Frank's erotic writhing with homewares in a performance at the Matilda Awards for Excellence in Brisbane Theatre in 2010, which appeared on Katherine Lyall Watson's Performing Arts blog on OurBrisbane.com. There was a decision to tear down Brisbane's iconic Regent Theatre, which, though a row over an old cinematic theatre rather than a live theatre venue, raised issues about attitudes to culture and cultural resources in the city. Most pertinently, there was the fact that Brisbane was "passed over" for Sir Ian McKellen's production of *Waiting for Godot*, apparently as a result of the lack of an appropriate venue in Brisbane, compared with Sydney or Melbourne (Makeham et al. 2012). Former leader of the conservative right-leaning opposition and then Shadow Arts Minister Jean-Paul Langbroek remarked that "[u]nder [then Premier Anna] Bligh and [leftist] Labor, Brisbane is a one-town show, a cultural desert" (cited by Turner 2010a). The issue sparked the passion of a broad set of interested parties in debates that played out in the online comment sections of *Courier Mail*—Brisbane's main, if often much maligned, newspaper—the online comments sections of *Brisbane Times*, and major Brisbane theatre blogs such as Kate Foy's *Groundling*, Sean Mee's *Reasonable Death*, and Katherine Lyall Watson's *Our Brisbane—Performing Arts Blog* (Makeham et al. 2012). At the height of the debate, in March 2010, these sites all drew comment (considered, conflicted, contentious, abusive, acknowledged and anonymous, all the characteristics of social media communication noted since Chap. 2) about the state of Brisbane's performing arts sector from artists, audiences and the public. At the time, these online conversations were characterised by concern about Brisbane's theatre culture, about Brisbane's attitudes towards its theatre culture, and about Brisbane's apparent inability to stop recycling the same old laments about its theatre culture and move forward in constructive, creative new ways.

To understand the heat that the debate generated, it is necessary to understand the part that the "cultural cringe" plays in Brisbane culture, and broader Australian culture, as public spheres. Living in a colonised country, Australians harbour a complex set of anxieties about the value of their arts, cultural and creative products, and, indeed, all its products. Contested notions of "cultural cringe" (Phillips 2006), cross-cultural comparisons, and various commentaries on the excellence, entertainment value or educational merit of Australia's performing arts is standard fare for our national newspapers and weekend magazines. As a smaller, more suburban city, Brisbane is particularly susceptible to such anxieties and replays of such debate.

In a general sense, government and social support for Brisbane theatre in fact tends to follow what fellow arts programme evaluator Sandra Gattenhof and I have pointed to as national Australian trends (Hadley and Gattenhof 2012). There have been amateur theatres such as Brisbane Arts Theatre and La Boite Theatre Company operating in Brisbane since the early twentieth century. In what Ruth Rentschler (2002, 21–32) calls the "Foundational" stages of Australia-specific arts policy in the 1950s, 1960s and 1970s, a state-supported mainstage company—the Queensland Theatre Company—emerged in Brisbane.

The emphasis shifted towards professional performing arts of excellence that replicated something of the culture of mother England's stages. In the 1970s and 1980s, with the emergence of the Australia Council for the Arts, this emphasis on English cultural traditions gave way to a greater emphasis on self-created, community, multicultural and indigenous theatre. This, in the climate of corruption, cronyism and oppression that prevailed under corrupt conservative politician Joh Bjelke-Petersen's 20-year reign as Premier of Queensland, led to a flourishing of street, subversive and political theatre by companies such as the Popular Theatre Troupe and Street Arts Community Theatre (Capelin 1995). It also led to the growth of significant expertise in theatre for schools, children and young audiences among Brisbane artists, from La Boite's children's theatre programmes, to the touring Grin & Tonic Theatre Troupe, to community cultural development companies such as Contact and Feral Arts, to major youth programming initiatives such as the 2High Festival (cf. Fotheringham 1992; Milne 2004). In the late 1980s and early 1990s policy, industrial and production practices picked up on the professionalisation, nationalisation and internationalisation agenda that emerged via the *Creative Nation* (1994) cultural policy. Brisbane has staged major events such as World Expo 88, established a new arts precinct at the Queensland Performing Arts Centre on the Brisbane River, and other venues such as the Brisbane Powerhouse, the Judith Wright Centre for Contemporary Arts and Metro Arts. It now has Queensland Theatre Company, a second mainstage theatre company in La Boite Theatre Company and a host of high-performing independent theatre outfits—from physical theatre company Zen Zen Zo, to circus company Circa (formerly Rock'n' Roll Circus), musical theatre companies Harvest Rain, Oscar and Blue Fish, and contemporary theatre companies 23rd Productions, The Escapists and the Dead Puppet Society (cf. Makeham et al. 2012). Brisbane's independent companies are regularly acknowledged as leading examples of innovation (Croggon 2010), and are benefiting from increased emphasis on production platforms, producers, emergent companies and emergent practitioners in current local, state and national cultural policy agendas (Australian Government 2011). Indeed, in Baylis's *Mapping Queensland Theatre*, the then emerging wave of independent artists and companies was described as essential to the "well-being of Queensland theatre" (2009, 20), and a critical part of the way forward to an entertaining, successful and sustainable body of practice in Brisbane and beyond. Baylis advocated producing partnerships and producer hubs, where mainstage companies shared resources with these new, independent and emerging companies, to better support this essential element of Brisbane's theatre landscape (Baylis 2009; Makeham et al. 2012). This legacy, and this potential, together with the set of practices emerging as Brisbane moved forward from what Raymond Gill calls "Brisbane's [image of] corrupt cops and even more corrupt bagmen politicians rul[ing] the frontier town of XXXX beer and barbeque" (2010), has led some to lay claims to Brisbane as a cultural capital.

Yet even in this context where the work has clearly been evolving decade by decade—and was, in some periods at least, strongly engaged with broader public sensibilities in a corrupt political climate—criticisms, anxieties and "cringes" about Brisbane's lack of culture continue. Baylis's *Mapping Queensland Theatre* brought these anxieties to the fore again by describing a situation in which Brisbane's contribution to Australian theatre is failing to live up to what might be anticipated on a per capita basis (Baylis 2009, 4; 28; Makeham et al. 2012), in which there are significant gaps in terms of training, presentation platforms and career pathways, and a situation in which the context, conditions and critical mass for excellent theatre is "not yet in place in Queensland", and quality work is therefore "rare" (Baylis 2009, 28; Makeham et al. 2012). These criticisms prefaced almost every report, article and response that came out as Brisbane returned in 2010 to debates about strengths, weaknesses and support needed for its current theatre culture. In "Is Brisbane Australia's New Cultural Capital?" (2010), for example, Raymond Gill quotes then Premier Anna Bligh arguing a clear plan for Brisbane's culture—a criticism that sits next to quotes from then incoming Brisbane Festival director Noel Staunton describing how the city's culture has evolved past looking to Sydney or Melbourne, and quotes from then outgoing Queensland Theatre Company Director Michael Gow, citing the odd opinions and attitudes that southerners continue to hold about Brisbane's culture. Running in between there were long replays of the best and worst of Brisbane in the Bjeilke-Peterson era.

In 2010 the presence of social media platforms that had not been part of this network or community before provided artists, arts organisations and audiences with a new platform for debating the status, confidence, voice and value of Brisbane theatre culture in a new way. Makeham, Kwok and I collected and analysed comments and conversation around the article that seemed to spark much of this wave of debate: "Is

Brisbane Brisvegas—or a Cultural Desert", published by Tonya Turner in *Courier Mail* on 17 March 2010 (2010a). Tapping into these issues, the conversations had much more dramaturgical complexity than the more day-to-day conversations in the case of the Brisbane Festival described above, although there was still a roteness of a sort in the repetition of oft-cited criticisms of the city's culture.

In the course of 120+ individual comment threads over about 24 h—not the thousands of comments that the works considered in Chap. 4 drew, but still a significant number for a small city such as Brisbane—artists, audiences and the public presented a variety of viewpoints on the issue about the lack of arts infrastructure to support major touring shows raised in the article, and on the broader set of issues about Brisbane arts culture that this issue points to. Many of those responding argued that Brisbane has a tendency to tear down its arts infrastructure that is not beneficial to building the city's culture. A small proportion argued that this sort of behaviour means that Brisbane is indeed "boring", and Brisbanites need to stop tearing things down and instead start building things up to overcome this. "Brisbane could certainly do more to encourage culture" (Julia H, via Turner 2010a), one participant said. "Brisbane has been fighting to shirk the 'cultural backwater' claim for years, don't let there be even more reason for the name to stick" (Erin Kennedy, via Turner 2010a), another agreed. "Let's be honest—Brisbane has always been a cultural desert" (Leith "Squashedbeak" Lynagh, via Turner 2010a), some complained. "The words 'culture' and 'Brisbane' are mutually exclusive. That's unless you are referring to the "Booze and Bash" culture of the Valley or the Boofhead culture of Lang Park" (Mal Arkey, via Turner 2010a). this meant that, unless you mean police beating up activists, drunks and drug addicts in nightclub precinct Fortitude Valley, or boorish behaviour from sports fans, similarly drunk or drugged, at rugby league football venue Lang Park, Brisbane really struggles to build rather than tear down culture. "Brisbane has no soul, there is nothing to do in this boring town" (Russ, via Turner 2010a), some posters said. "Brisbane's cultural scene is dire" (Lesley Carey, via Turner 2010a), others agreed. Comparisons with real cultural capitals such as Sydney and Melbourne came out again and again. "Brisbane is so boring, after visiting a real city like Melbourne" (Morally Thin, via Turner 2010a). "While Brisbane is making some progress in terms of its cultural identity ...We cannot possibly compete with such cultural hubs as Melbourne and Sydney when we choose to let important artistic landmarks …go to waste" (Mike Lepre, via Turner 2010a). Accordingly, because it is letting cultural landmarks and opportunities go to waste, "Brisbane really is boring and gentrified. I get embarrassed at times!!!!" (Listless, via Turner 2010a). While the boorish, booze-driven behaviour of the 1970s and 1980s might be changing, with yuppies moving into the inner city, including the precincts around the Valley, and the Lang Park venue, these Brisbane residents are not more cultured than the previous residents. All this means is that "Brisbane is miles behind. The people are miles behind. Hardly anybody has a rigorous education in the various art forms because it's simply not cool during school" (Jarrod Schindler, via Turner 2010a). "Brisbane lacks energy, creativity and individual thought. Maybe it is that way because Langbroek's political ancestors destroyed any individuality Brisbane had" (Barry, via Turner 2010a). The conservative Jean-Paul Langbroek's political ancestors, in the corrupt Joh Bjeilke-Peterson regime of the 1970s and 1980s, have sapped the city of creativity, energy and enthusiasm for culture, even to this day. "I am utterly disgusted … We might as well be back living under JB" (Towers, via Turner 2010a) .

As these criticisms played out, a number of posters claimed that the situation needed to be addressed now or artists would continue to move south to Sydney and Melbourne. "[A]s a teacher, [I] see drama students opting to go to Melbourne or Sydney to study and to act, because Brisbane won't come to the party [and this breaks my heart!]" (Erin Kennedy, via Turner 2010a), one said. "All the people in the Arts are leaving, and will continue to leave in droves to other cities and countries because just like everyone else, they get tired of butting their heads against the brick wall that is Bligh" (Shannon A, via Turner 2010a), another agreed. "Brisbane actually did have a few [venues]—until the Bjeilke-Peterson government sanctioned their destruction and in doing so robbed this city of some proud iconic cultural landmarks. It's such a shame and an ongoing embarrassment that Queensland governments continue to treasure economics and sports over arts and culture" (Helen Cassidy, via Turner 2010a), yet another lamented. For many, though, the likelihood of Brisbane being able to change in the still-problematic political climate remained remote. "Most certainly a cultural desert," one put it.

> Instead of asking "Why? What can we do to change it?", politicians and parochial locals scream and cry yelling "No we're not!" The only way to grow, to develop, is to listen to criticism, and respond accordingly (which also means explaining sometimes why the criticism is wrong). Mind you

> with Dumb and Dumber in parliament, that ain't going to be happening any time soon :]. (Michael B, via Turner 2010a)

There were contrary points of view. A small percentage of posts noted that Metro Arts, Judith Wright Centre of Contemporary Arts, Brisbane Powerhouse and Brisbane Arts Centre offer venues in Brisbane even if they are small ones:

> We have a lot of theatres, a lot of excellent live music venues ... a fantastic Gallery of Modern Art, a fantastic State Library, a bunch of smaller galleries floating around the city (if you bother to look), the only free antiquities museum in Australia at UQ, an exciting cultural complex at QUT KG with art galleries, theatres and studios in which people are actively creating "culture". (Dr Rob, via Turner 2010a)

"There is QUT theatre, The Roundhouse theatre, The Brisbane Powerhouse, QPAC, UQ Schonell Theatre ... It is just that some places are better known than others" (Theatre, via Turner 2010a), another agreed. Someone else still argued: "i like the cultural facilities we have in brisbane. i subscribe to the opera and ballet and also attend other events that interest me when they come to brisbane. i've lived in melbourne and sydney also and i don't think we suffer by comparison. in fact, i think we're extremely lucky here in brizvegas. love ya queensland :)" (genie, via Turner 2010a), echoing well-recognised marketing terms such as "Brisvegas" and slogans like "Love you Queensland" in the process.

Others concurred: "We are in fact a very lucky city and for our population we are exposed to 1st class cultural experiences" (Rick O'Shea, via Turner 2010a), and

> People who think Brisbane is a desert just don't have a clue! There is so much to do, with some of the world's finest artists (visual, musical, and performing) regularly performing here—but the local media are generally more interested in promoting sport and rock concerts. Come on!! Not everyone cares what is happening with the Broncos this week!! (Jeff, via Turner 2010a)

Some suggested that, if those participating in the debate, particularly the general public, would just go out and look, there was a lot to experience. "[G]et out from in front of your television, take your friends and venture off the verandah or deck into a real theatre—you will enjoy the new experience" (Towers, via Turner 2010a).

A small percentage linked this debate to more metalevel discussions about the "ecology" of theatre culture (Makeham et al. 2012) and Brisbane's concept of good culture, compared with concepts of good culture that might apply elsewhere. "My Brisvegas, it is all in perceptions" (milo, via Turner 2010a), one said. "This story, and the comments in response to it, says far more about people's prejudices than about Brisbane's culture or lack thereof" (Col, via Turner 2010a), another agreed. The problem for such posters was that people were letting southern notions of good culture from Sydney or Melbourne, or, even worse, northern notions of good culture from international hubs in London or New York, blind them to the good things happening in Brisbane. "[W]hat people class as culture demonstrates their prejudices more than anything" (Dr Rob, via Turner 2010a), these posters suggested, so in this sense it might be perceptions rather than practices that needed to change. "Just because I don't like what you like it doesn't make you better than me—the arrogance of some of the 'cultured' folk on here is quite sad" (Gav, via Turner 2010a), another put it much more bluntly. "Think about it, culture exists in all human populations. Saying that a group of people doesn't have culture is like saying there's no weather today ... But that won't stop the snobs and elitists from subscribing to their divisive dribble..." (JD, via Turner 2010a), another agreed. "Having lived in and out of Brisbane over the last 20 years, my personal experience is that people would rather spend their social time at home ... That doesn't mean we're uncultured, just means we value different things in life compared to other cities in the world" (J.J. Rambo, via Turner 2010a). Following this same logic, some participants in the debate said they were happy to celebrate Brisbane culture just as it is. "So what if Brisbane remains a country town and back water? I like it that way" (tina, via Turner 2010a), such posters put it.

As analysis of this segment of the broader debate reveals, people in Brisbane are interested in big-picture debates about arts, culture and heritage, and support for them as critical components of a functioning public sphere. Much of the debate aligned with the criticisms in the Baylis report, *Mapping Queensland Theatre*, affirming the need for more government support, more venues, more diverse venues, more audiences for risky work in particular, more audiences for work in general, and thus more opportunities for artists to stay in Brisbane (Makeham et al. 2012). In a sense, as Sean Mee put it, "Much of Baylis' report was already known territory, at least anecdotally, by most active participants in Queensland theatre" (Mee 2010). The question, for a lot of those participating in the public debate in 2010 was how to deal with it, without rehashing the same debates again, and again and again, without any forward movement in them.

The patina of negativity cast across Brisbane theatre culture actually did have impact—in the industry and in the public sphere. It led to a follow-up in subsequent press and online commentary throughout 2010. In an article about Michael Gow's resignation as Artistic Director of the QTC shortly after, Gow made reference to the idea that Brisbane theatre is "middle of the road" and a bit boring because audiences only go to what they know—an idea that came up in much of the debate—and, apparently, 82% of those participating in an attached online poll agreed (Feeney 2010a). In her own online blog, former Queensland Theatre Company Chair Kate Foy read this not in terms of a "middle-of-the-road" penchant for the predictable but in terms of the way the "cultural cringe" leads communities to undervalue their own cultural product. Foy (2010b, original emphasis) noted that, while the conversations represented both the "cultural cringe *rampant*" (the ungrounded idea that one's own culture is lesser than others) and the "cultural cringe *reversed*" (the ungrounded idea that one's own culture is greater than others), the conflict between these two perspectives was often simply recited again and again in a way that gets us nowhere. For Foy, the online exchanges were an example of a kind of ritual rehearsal of an all-too-familiar set of concerns about venues, funding, audiences and artist exodus. "With very few exceptions the tone [was] downbeat, the tune is repetitive," Foy noted, the constant refrain being that "the theatre system—the model for institutionalised theatre—is broken" (2010a). This meant "that more of the current commentary [was] focusing on what's *wrong* with the state of the theatre as an industry than on what's *right*. Moreover, the criticism [was] rarely com[ing] with suggestions on how to change matters" (2010a). The important thing for Foy was to call out the roteness that characterised much of the conversation—as readily as the roteness of chookas and congratulations can characterise more day-to-day marketing conversation—and to find a way to move forward.

While Foy was clearly correct that a lot of these conversations got bogged down between counter-perspectives—shame and pride, tradition and future, legacy and innovation—and recycled comments about the problems without pointing to solutions, there were some glimpses of paths forward here too. These were, as the analysis by Makeham,

Kwok and I (2012) suggested, not in the posts that looked backwards with shame or the posts that look forward with pride—the cringe rampant and the cringe reversed—but in those that raised points about the specificity of Brisbane's culture. As indicated above, a small number of posters noted that being different from Sydney or Melbourne is not a bad thing, and that Brisbane does have its own culture whether it is the sort of culture a given poster is interested in or not. Indeed, some noted that claims about the need for "historical" playhouses and plays devalues what is already happening—in both the literal and artistic sense of the term—in an unhelpful way. "I think cities are all about a wide variety of options" (Alan, via Turner 2010a), one poster put it. It is therefore frustrating that governments "tak[e] the 'one size fits all' QPAC [Queensland Performing Arts Centre] approach where all you see is the same performers over and over again," another said. "No wonder the culture becomes stifled" (Tristan Currie, via Turner 2010a). The aim, these people believed, should not always be bigger, better, more like Sydney, or more like Melbourne. "Big is not always better. The amount of amazing small theatre and music productions on in Brisbane in any given week, is outstanding … and I am from Melbourne" (Theatre, via Turner 2010a). In Brisbane there may well be interesting work happening—for example, the stylised aesthetic of Australian Gothic plays by authors such as Stephen Carleton, Linda Hassall and the Dead Puppet Society; the do-it-yourself downstyle work of companies such as The Good Room; or the physical theatre of companies such as Zen Zen Zo. It may simply be, as these posters suggested, that there is not a lot of media interest about this work compared with large-scale, spectacular or "significant" pieces such as the Sir Ian McKellan production. But even if Brisbane audiences prefer smaller works, works based on evocative, stylised or everyday aesthetics, works in unconventional spaces and places, or works that happen in places outside conventional city theatres, this does not necessarily mean that Brisbane is uncultured. It is, these posters said, about "perception" (milo, via Turner 2010a) and "prejudices" (Col, via Turner 2010a). "Just because I don't like what you like it doesn't make you better than me" (Gav, via Turner 2010a), they argued. Just because Brisbane theatre is not like Sydney's or Melbourne's does not make it better or worse. If this is true, then Brisbanites' anxiety about their theatre culture may not in fact be about alienation as the cited source of much of Australia's initial "cultural cringe" from colonisation forward (Ashcroft, Griffiths and Tiffin 1989, 9–10). It may instead be about the fact that Brisbane's populations are developing a different set of aesthetic, symbolic and social tastes around which a sense of what Pierre Bourdieu (1986) calls "cultural capital" has still to develop. If what particular populations or subpopulations in Brisbane are interested in—be it mainstage theatres, musicals or smaller events in converted spaces, public spaces, suburbs or beaches—had already developed cultural capital, interstate or internationally the story might be very different.

This sentiment was also captured by some of the expert commentators in "Stage Fright" (2010b), *Courier Mail* Arts Blog's follow-up to the Tonya Turner article that captures this wave of concern about Brisbane theatre culture. "[T]hings have changed in the theatre," Andrew Ross of the Brisbane Powerhouse said. "The borders between drama, circus, physical theatre have all blurred a lot ... [and] there's been, in some cases, too much effort put into trying to preserve what are perceived as traditions, and keeping things the same rather than allowing things to change" (*Courier Mail* arts blog 2010). Building capital around non-traditional forms might be a better path forward, particularly given the problematic and oppressive cultural, sexual, racial and ableist cultural politics that main traditional theatrical forms have been party to perpetuating in one way or another.

These conversations, if analysed with an eye for the pointers that artists, audiences and the public were providing about potential futures, suggested that at least some Brisbanites feel that size, scale and spectacle are not the only or the best determinants of a satisfying theatre culture for them. They were in effect suggesting, as Makeham, Kwok and I (2012) argued in our published analysis of this and other aspects of Brisbane theatre culture at the time, that the performing arts are perhaps best viewed from an ecological point of view. From this perspective, the performing arts are an "ecology", an ecosystem made up of policy makers, organisations, artists, audiences, the media and other stakeholders, and it is relationships rather than specific elements within the system that enable its health. Traditionally, policy makers have, as Cathy Hunt and Phyllida Shaw articulate it, "concentrate[d] on individual companies or an individual artist's practice rather than the sector as a whole" (2007: 5, 43; Makeham et al. 2012). The focus has all too frequently been on single specific indicators of success (e.g. the massive 2000-seat theatres that might have brought *Waiting for Godot* to Brisbane) rather than overall indicators of a satisfying culture (e.g. the small-scale stages, spaces and productions that some audiences appreciate just as much). An ecologies approach, on the contrary,

> concentrates on engagements, energies and flows as signs of health, and thus sustainability, in a system. Ecological thinking enables policy makers, practitioners and scholars to go beyond debate about the presence of activity, the volume of activity, and the fate of individual agents as signs of health or non-health of a system. In an ecologies context, level of activity is not the only indicator of health, and low activity does not necessarily equate with instability or unsustainability. (Makeham et al. 2012)

From this point of view, a network of specific small players rather than a massive spectacle may be more aligned with the way Brisbane people want to engage with the performing arts, and this would be fine, fruitful and worth celebrating.

The online debate thus ultimately demonstrated that, in Brisbane, interests differ, and that there is a will, at least in some sections of the public sphere, to try valuing what is distinctive and working well, whether it is large-scale, spectacular, traditional or not, and whether it compares to what works well elsewhere or not. There is a will to valorise the specificity of our culture as a driver of our theatre culture, rather than constantly feel the pressure to spend so much time looking forward or backward that we fail to see the interesting new theatrical beasts emerging in our own cultural landscape. In the three years following this debate, the push to support production hubs, producers and pathways for small, independent practitioners foreshadowed in the Baylis report, as one of the factors that sparked the debate, did tap into this interest in supporting what is emergent in our own ecology. The connections between mainstage, independent stage, students and others were strengthened with new programmes and initiatives—for example, a new World Theatre Festival at Brisbane Powerhouse celebrating a very DIY aesthetic, a new Anywhere Theatre Festival celebrating pop-up performance practices in public spaces and places, and scratch and independent programmes in mainstage venues. The angst that brought about the big debate died down.

The incidents in 2010 sparked more debate than anything that happened in 2011, 2012 or 2013. Interestingly, though, three years later in 2013—at about the same time as the Brisbane Festival iteration in 2013 above—there was another set of incidents that would, at least at the surface, have seemed worthy of another major debate. There was a change in government. The population in Brisbane, and in Queensland more broadly, voted to be rid of the Labor government led by Anna Bligh that drew such scathing critique among some of the commentators cited here. They voted for a Liberal National Party government, led by Campbell Newman and others such as Jean-Paul Langbroek, and in fact provided this culturally, socially and economically conservative new government with a majority much larger even than Bjeilke Peterson's majority in the National Party's heyday in the 1970s and 1980s. The new government immediately began to cut support for arts and cultural programmes, and, in particular, for the production hubs, producers, pathways, partnerships and advocacy services for small, independent, experimental or emerging youth artists that had allowed Brisbanites to try valorising the interesting creators in their own unique ecology in the years since the 2010 debates. The language of "support" for "sustainable" and "socially useful" practice went out, and the language of "investment" in practice with "strong economic returns" came in (Jabour 2013). The bureaucrats went around major, small-to-medium and independent companies telling them to expect big cuts when the next policy and funding protocol came; that they would not all survive, and that they would need to rationalise, merge and minimise costs to have any chance of to stay around in any form at all. In effect, the debt-busting of the new government brought the Brisbane theatre community back to support for big, mainstage providers with the best chance of bringing in stars from overseas, and showing benefits for big audiences.

Given the debate above, this would have seemed to be a good spark for another discussion, debate or protest campaign. This time, however, while there were a few posts lamenting the loss of companies, particularly youth theatre companies, and a few attempts to create debate, petitions and mainstream press interest, the volume of these, and the volume of commentary on these, was far less than that seen in the previous social media debate. Rather, the response was to whisper behind the scenes rather than shout on the social media stage. There were whispers in corridors and at the close of committee meetings, as well as in classrooms, restaurants and foyers where theatre lovers tend to congregate, but very little news or social media commentary on the changes coming. There were a few media stories about the bumbling then-arts minister Roz Bates, who had to be sacked, as a result of personal indiscretions more than anything to do with the policy, but nothing of the sort of substance that was reflected in the 2010 debate.

This seems strange, given the stakes of the issue, together with the fact that press articles, reports and resources offering advice about how to make use of social media to connect with, reconnect with or activate communities had in fact increased exponentially in 2010, 2011 and 2012. Analysis of the seasons, incidents and issues in the Brisbane theatre community in 2010 shows that the players clearly did have the desire and ability to leverage social media to take moments of controversy, misunderstanding or concern and use them to spark debate that had at least some impact in the public sphere. They were able to use social media to create meaningful communities of affinity in times of controversy, as much as to create communities of association in times of calm. Yet in 2013 they did not. There were a few posters who tried to spark the sort of debate that goes beyond a show itself, and into what the show, the season, the institution and the players that support it mean for culture as a whole, but this time the spark did not take.

It would, at one level, be easy to put this down to lack of confidence, fear of possible consequences, and the fraught feelings about the political, policy and industrial climate at the time. The social field can frame and dictate the possibilities for discussion and debate on social media platforms, regardless of the technology and the player's skill in using the technology. The fact that what Sant (2014), Westbrook (2014) and others cast as a stalling of uptake of social media platforms in theatre came at the same time as an exponential increase in articles, report, and resources offering advice about how to make use of social media to connect with, reconnect with or activate theatre communities in 2010, 2011 and 2012, does, though, raise further questions. Since examples such as the online controversy around *Involuntary Dances* in & discussed in Chap. 4, and the online controversy of Brisbane and more broadly Australian theatre culture in 2009 and 2010 discussed in Chaps. 3, 4 and this chapter, there has been an explosion of industry-based commentary on the uptake of social media in the theatre. This changes the context in which later examples, such as *Exhibit B*, *Ugly Mugs* and the more recent Australian theatre funding cuts, sit. The advice about how to use social media in the theatre—focusing strongly on theatre marketing, audience development and assessment—is, as noted in the Introduction, not matched by critique of the usage or the advice. This advice has proliferated ahead of actual practices, which is notable, given that advice clearly did not outpace practice with the uptake of the printing press, lighting, projection or other technologies that have impacted theatre practice over the years. In this sense, though, the theatre companies' response to online criticism of *Exhibit B* and *Ugly Mugs* did at some level remediate the "do not fight back against bad press too strongly" advice of the old theatre criticism age, theoretically flagging a lack of understanding, learning or innovation in the new form. The theatre companies' and communities' lack of response to these latter prompts may in fact also be a result of following the latest advice about how to act and interact on social media. This advice-outpacing-practice situation could be taken as a sign of how revolutionary the uptake of social media in theatre has the potential to be. Alternatively, though, it could be taken as a sign that theatre makers may be too aware of expert recommendations about how to engage with the practice to leap headlong into it. This in turn raises questions about whether advice about how to engage with audiences via social media risks returning us to the closed-circuit conversations in centralised communities of association that fail to connect with the broader public sphere that Balme (2014) was concerned about, stalling rather than sparking the potentials of engagement with the new platforms. For this reason, the advice is worth interrogating, not just in terms of its ability to support marketing but also in terms of its ability to support the more meaningful and extended engagement that theatre makers—at least not-for-profit, educational, community and experimental theatre makers—claim to value.

## Common Advice for Collaborating Online

The explosion of interest in social media means that many consultants are offering advice about how to engage with it effectively. The advice is often based on case studies as much as core principles, and guides theatre makers in developing a profile, a network of friends, followers and advocates, a system of tags, topics or themes to help filter information in a way relevant to those followers, and strategies for dealing with different audiences, whilst avoiding mistakes. According to Michael Nabarro (2013), this sort of knowledge sharing is critical. It allows an industry composed of a lot of independent, small and small-to-medium companies to make the most effective use of, and meet audience expectations around that use of, emerging technologies. While performing arts organisations often have strong brands, which make them seem strong, well resourced and reputable, Nabarro (2013) argues that this can be both a benefit and a drawback when it comes to social media. "It means that often they are expected to behave—digitally—like much bigger, consumer-facing organisations that have the ability to invest in new technology on a continuous basis" (2013), he notes. This means that managing expectations, and pooling resources that tell people how to manage expectations, as much as managing practices, processes and relationships online per se, is critical to survival. It is a lesson that the press suggests some theatre companies are currently learning the hard way. In 2013, for instance, the press covered a case where the Belvoir Theatre—the same one that sparked debate about Australian theatre culture's misogyny—was chastised for asking fellow artsworkers and audiences to crowdfund $10,000 of a $100,000 tour of its production of *Peter Pan* to New York because it was in receipt of so much more funding than most Australian companies already (Blake 2013). Then in 2014, the press covered a case where Plaza Media ran into similar trouble when it called for professional dancers to work free of charge in a video that Sydney Dance Company's Rafael Bonachela was choreographing for Kylie Minogue in a few days time, and was chastised for exploiting artists (*Sydney Morning Herald* 2014; Puvanenthiran 2014). Such incidents perhaps explain why research on early-uptake crowdfunding, commissioned by ArtSupport Australia, the philanthropic arm of the Australia Council for the Arts, shows that though people may "want to feel part of the cultural process, either for genuine reasons or for social kudos" (Eliezer 2012), getting them to pledge to online crowdfunding platforms can still be difficult. As a result, the advice that is informing theatre makers online is often about caution, care and managing expectations, as much as anything else.

The advice around this is prolific. There are at least a dozen different recommendations that come up again and again in reports, advice columns and comments on the topic of connecting with theatre audiences through these technologies. Some recommendations come up frequently—in particular, the advice associated with building a presence, a profile, a network of friends, followers and advocates, and a dramaturgy of engagement that goes beyond the 'buy my tickets' posts that can leave audiences bored and disappointed. Some recommendations come up less frequently, especially in the largely industry-based to date advice literature available to theatre makers and companies—in particular, advice associated with responding to mistakes, misunderstandings and mixed opinions that might confuse sponsors, supporters and funders. In all cases, though, it is about managing expectations and maintaining control to facilitate engagement without making people feel confused, concerned or angry about shows, seasons, issues or the industry.

### *Building an Accessible Presence Online*

The first advice for theatre makers and companies looking to create an online presence typically relates to access and adoption patterns among target audiences. As computer-mediated communication theorist David Bell (2001, 132) notes, education, economic status, gender, race, class, disability and other factors can mean that technologies are not available or accessible to everyone in an audience. Moreover, even if such technologies are available, an audience—as a collection of individuals, rather than a coherent or organized group—can vary in their adoption and participation patterns. A person's personality traits, social interests and professional needs can, as discussed in Chap. 2, and as Teresa Correa, Amber Willard Hinsely and Homero Gil de Zúñiga agree, be "crucial factors leading them to engage in this participatory media" (2010). Accordingly, theatre makers are advised, it is not necessarily as simple as saying that young people will participate more and older people will participate less, or saying that extroverts will participate more and introverts, lurkers, voyeurs and privacy-oriented people will participate less. Certainly, extrovert tendencies can correlate with higher rates of participation among young users. At the same time, though, introvert tendencies can correlate with higher rates of participation among middle-aged and older users—not because they love socialising or have a lot of time for it, like the young users, but, paradoxically, because they find offline socialising emotionally taxing and prefer online forms. Some users will love the interaction and make an art of it—for instance, those involved in the "quantified self" movement discussed in Chap. 3. Other users will not love it but will make the effort because personal, social or professional networks demand it. Others will join, then friend or follow a few fellow users, Daniel Trottier (2012, 77) notes, more because of peer pressure, or a desire to claim the user name before another can, than because of any real intent to participate. Others still will avoid it altogether because it does not appeal, or because they have problems with the breakdown in face-to-face relationships that it is reported to represent. As Leo Becker and Klaus Schoenbauch (1989, 10–11) note, media theorists have now spent a century studying adoption, participation and time-allocation patterns in relation to new media, and tested a number of theories—uses, gratifications, and a variety of psychological, cultural or economic motivations—to try to understand them. They have looked at the way the desire to express oneself, entertain oneself or others, educate oneself or others, engage with others personally, socially or professionally, enable choices for others (as in traditional theatre commentary), or advocate (as in traditional theatre commentary and audience development) underpins conscious or unconscious decisions to watch or participate in media practices. They have discovered that adoption and participation patterns are always more complex, uncertain and hard to tie to any cause-and-effect logic than can be explained by any of these types of theory in isolation.

What this anxiety about adoption patterns means is that, even in countries with high adoption rates—including, as noted in Chap. 2, the US, the UK, Western Europe, Australasia and parts of Asia—theatre makers are told they cannot assume that fellow artists, stakeholders, supporters, spectators, media partners or other audiences will want to connect with them online. They are told they can never be sure whether they are engaging a mass or a vocal minority, a subscriber set, a single-time spectator or somebody who has never seen a show. They can never be sure whether they are engaging people who have seen the posts they shared days, weeks or months ago, or missed them because they went by too swiftly in a fast-paced communication environment, or because they do not check their accounts frequently.

The advice, therefore, is to avoid assuming that social media platforms can replace other marketing, promotion and engagement strategies (Brogan 2010; Mangold and Faulds 2009)—to make it part of an integrated marketing plan, and an integrated marketing assessment and metrics plan, in which other online and offline strategies still play a part, and predictable determinants of success, results, and reciprocity still apply. This can require extra resources if both staff for social media marketing and those for standard marketing are required, or it can result in redundancy if theatre makers are simply replicating content across online and offline platforms to market shows or try to create meaningful conversations about shows, seasons and the industry.

### *Building an "Authentic" Brand Profile*

The next set of advice is about the way theatre makers construct an authentic profile, identity or brand across social media platforms. For the most part, the public, as well as professionals in public-facing fields such as the arts, culture, entertainment or politics, are aware that social media allows them to build their personal, social or professional brand. They are aware that "the celebrity stories told on Twitter are carefully constructed performances," as Page puts it, "rather than a genuine presentation of back stage identity" (2012, 163). In spite or perhaps because of this acknowledgement of identity's artificially constructed nature, online users devote a lot of time, effort and energy to constructing their profile, identity or brand (Heer and Boyd 2005). The work to create what Downes (2005, 77) calls complex, prosthetic Others of themselves—extended presences or telepresences—is more complex than any character that any actor creates on film, television or other traditional media. It is done through texts, images, interactions, emoticons and other features designed to develop a face, front or brand on a platform where textual, visual and video rather than physical cues dominate as the clues or markers of everything from gender, race, class and ability, to profession, to trustworthiness (85). "[T]hrough profiles," Trottier argues, "the logic of brands extends to personal identities" (2012, 58) as people work to build up a perceived-to-be-reliable picture of who and what they are.

This anxiety about inauthenticity and the artificiality identities on social media platforms, Page (2012, 163) argues, makes the ability to tell a story in a reliable, authentic manner all the more important. The ability to claim authenticity and thus authority is, as noted in Chap. 4, critical to success in engaging with others online. The advice for theatre makers, then—whether independent or working in a company—is to devote time to building a branded profile across multiple platforms that conveys their intentions with sincerity and a sense of reliability. The commentators warn that without this, colleagues, stakeholders and audiences will not want to connect with them and come into the trusting reciprocal relationships that create social capital with them.

Theatre makers are therefore advised that engagement through social media should, as through any other medium, convey real, clear and consistent messages about a theatre maker's or company's philosophy, purpose for creating work, processes and products. Unless the theatre maker is speaking as a character performing on the online platform for entertainment purposes—as Crouch's Mr. Malvolio did—they should avoid deceit marketing, or massaging the truth to link to popular topics or trends purely to try to gain traction into new networks. Theatre makers are told that if they send false, deceitful or offensive messages about who they are, what they do and what they want to do with others too many times—whether deliberately or accidentally—people will not want to connect with them.

In this sense, theatre makers are advised to connect with their online social networks as they would with their offline social networks—to treat them as real networks, fostering real relationships, by transmitting real information to friends, rather than just bombarding people with "buy this" messages that seem unthought out and, at times, overdone to the point that they become "spam" (Altes 2009; Gentry 2009). To think of social media as merely a marketing, promotion and publicity tool is, as Fee Plumley, Digital Programs Officer at Australia Council for Arts, says, a "mistake" (cited by Blake 2010). Carly Severn, Digital Programs Coordinator for the San Francisco Ballet, agrees: "If you simply push out marketing messages, people don't like it" (cited by Mackrell 2012). This, commentator Blake clarifies, is because

> Twitter users don't like the hard sell. No one wants to read "buy tickets now." And no one enjoys a one-way broadcast from someone who never replies to your comments and doesn't bother to follow you in return. For Twitter to work it has to be a two-way exchange and that requires thought, energy and time (2010).

The same advice is offered in relation to most social media platforms, not just Twitter but Facebook, LinkedIn and YouTube too. The advice, it seems, is to market a brand without strongly marketing a brand.

Where this becomes tricky is when theatre makers find themselves having to enact what Alan Albarran (2013, 12) calls a "horizontal-vertical integration", conversing both with peers in horizontal network relations and with industry stakeholders, sponsors and spectators in more hierarchical or vertical network relations, in the same space and time. In 2009, for instance, casting agent Daryl Eisenberg caused controversy when she tweeted scathing comments about artists auditioning for a new show being created for the New York Musical Theatre Festival. "If we wanted to hear it a different way, don't worry, we'll ask" (cited by Itzkoff 2009), she said. "If you are going to sing about getting on your knees, might as well do it and crawl towards us … right?" (cited by Itzkoff 2009). Eisenberg had form for having made similar comments on social media platforms during prior audition processes: "Seeing #70 right now. I'm tired. My ears are bleeding" (cited by Itzkoff 2009), "Holding your foot above your head IN YOUR HEADSHOT is a BAD IDEA!" (cited by Itzkoff 2009) and other such comments. Although this might have been an authentic representation of Eisenberg's identity, authority and conversations at the casting director's table, when shared with actors, audiences and other stakeholders it became a scandal. This was made worse by Eisenberg's response, stating that "[t]here is NO rule/guideline against Twitter/Facebook/MySpace/Friendster. Freedom of speech. Ever heard of it?" (cited by Itzkoff 2009), and so failing to acknowledge that she might have been pushing the boundaries of professional propriety in her online self-performance. When these conversations—some frontstage, some backstage and some bridging the boundary between the two—are visible to too many of a theatre maker's networks and communities at once, this case shows, the context collapse can cause trouble.

### *Balancing Frontstage and Backstage Information*

The challenges that this presents lead to the next set of advice. On these platforms, theatre makers are told, they are called on to share a unique new combination of stage, sidestage, and backstage information about themselves as the aesthetic, critical, marketing, audience development and assessment domains of their work come together. It is a unique new challenge for the impression management practices that people may excel at in other parts of their personal, social or professional lives (where the conversations stay separate) but which they are new to in their online lives (where conversations start to come together in the same space, place and time). This is particularly the case if they have the proclivity to share things that could be considered controversial, offensive or sensitive. In one publicised case, for instance, Devin Alberda, a dancer with the New York City Ballet, known for developing his social media persona through what Fiona Mackrell calls "sometimes subversive commentary" (2012), commented on a drunk-driving charge that his boss, Peter Martins, was facing. "Thank goodness riding the subway while intoxicated isn't a misdemeanor or offense #don'tfireme" (cited by Mackrell 2012), he said. The post led the dancer, the company and the dancers' union into a debate about appropriate behaviour online. The fact that Alberda's post was seen as personal rather than professional criticism was particularly problematic. Again, though, Alberda's "#don'tfireme" response was criticised for not acknowledging that he had pushed the boundaries of professional propriety in his online self-performance.

Theatre makers are typically advised that they need to cultivate at least some capacity to talk not just about their work (the sales pitch) but around the work (social relationships) to succeed. "If companies want to attract new audiences, they have to jump in [online] and chat about the minutiae of what's going on," Plumley advises. "Audiences are not just interested in a celebrity onstage. They really want to know how the show works, how the set was made, how it was cast, and who's doing the lighting and what goes wrong sometimes" (cited by Blake 2010). This advice is cast as particularly critical for artforms that are perceived as elitist or inaccessible to a lay audience, such as opera, dance or experimental work, the theory being that even if lay audiences cannot understand the symbolic and choreographic systems that drive abstract classical dance, they can find appeal in the virtuosity, vitality and athleticism of the performer and the work they do to develop that athleticism (Mackrell 2012) . By engaging with audiences via social media platforms, performers are said to provide audiences with a sense of themselves as real people, doing real things, both frontstage and backstage—to produce the personality, authenticity and authority that can amplify the conversational and circulatory appeal of posts on social media. However, as the Eisenberg and Alberda examples show, this wider circulation of hitherto hidden opinions can have a real impact on personal and professional relationships if it jars with community expectations.

### *Empowering Staff, Stakeholders and Spectators*

Most of those offering advice on social media strategies suggest that the need to share personal, social and professional information and show interest in other colleagues, companies and audience members' information across multiple fast-paced online platforms means that simply adding social media to a low-level administrator's responsibilities (in a company), or acting only a few days before a show (in the case of an independent artist), can be among the biggest "mistakes" that theatre makers can make. Commentators recommend making social media engagement a part of all roles, and setting aside time and resources for this, as well as having digital specialists such as the "Geek in Residence Program" that Australia Council for the Arts funding programmes provide for a select few companies. Equally critical, most say, is empowering staff to take on the role. Both individual theatre makers and companies are advised to set out guidelines, principles and practices suited to their own work, and the sorts of self-expression that will best support their work, as well as to train all staff members to use the platforms well (Berger 2012). This includes distinguishing between conventional marketing, celebrity marketing, and what really works for real theatre makers and companies looking to create communities online—theatre makers and companies who, by and large, are not in the same celebrity influencer sphere as those working in film, television, games or politics.

### *Ethics, Etiquette and Netiquette for Staff, Stakeholders and Spectators*

When guidelines, principles and training programmes come into play, they lead to a "netiquette" policy for staff, stakeholders and spectators to provide clear instruction on etiquette and ethics online. This, it is suggested, should include instructions on where boundaries lie with regard to stage, sidestage and backstage information, what sorts of information staff can and cannot share, and what sorts of other companies' staff they can or cannot connect with online. These instructions are designed to prevent a staff member from sharing too much about a company's internal management problems, politics or personality conflicts, connecting to racist, sexist or ableist groups, or creating a conflict of interest with regard to a grant agency. Which, it is feared, would lead to the same sort of scandal, controversy or campaigning seen in the *Exhibit B*, *Ugly Mugs* or *Involuntary Dances* examples in Chap. 4, or the more industry-based examples in Chap. 5. As Franscisco Pérez-Latre (2013, 50) observes, most of these issues already existed in prior media, communication and marketing paradigms, but their visibility on social media is new. Putting explicit rather than implicit rules in place is recognised as a necessity for theatre makers and companies in the digital age. The industry tends to be small in any given city or country, with much movement of staff between companies and much pressure of convention to comment on each other's work, the argument goes. A policy can guide people regarding what messages can be conveyed through "company" sites, what can be conveyed through "personal" sites and what is best left unsaid, as well as how to comment or support without appearing to endorse controversial or counter-to-interest ideas.

The perils of letting internal policies around issues such as casting received press coverage in a recent case, for instance, when producer John Frost's call to casting agents to find performers with better Twitter profiles—which they felt would help create a better social media presence during the run of their Rocky Horror Show production—was shared on social media by blogger Toby Francis. This sparked the anger of would-be-musical theatre performers looking for work.

[N]ever mind the fact that 10,000 Twitter followers means jack diddle shit in regards to being able to sing, dance, and act, using the number of Twitter followers to decide who is good enough for an audition doesn't mean anything because you can buy 10,000 followers for $70 AUD. (True fact, check it here.) It literally doesn't even mean what these casting people think it means (Francis 2013a).

"Agree" (Mark, Arparna7496, Josh, and Caroline Shanks, via Francis 2013a), many of his followers said. Some raised questions about whether he was vilifying Frost without knowing the full story (Domina Breeze, via 2013a), or if he would be better to acknowledge that in a failing industry this might be necessary (Morrison McGreggor, via 2013a), but most felt his comments were fair. Francis was offered the opportunity to republish a version of his blog piece on ArtsHub that week (Francis 2013b), and he got a link to his piece on *Australian Theatre Online* (AussieTheatre.com 2013).

### *Connections Over Content*

With these principles in mind, when it comes to making decisions about what to share, when and how, most commentators advise theatre makers to remember the distinctive features of social media communication. As noted in Chap. 2, content, context, character, and conversational and circulatory appeal are all considered important factors in facilitating successful networking through social media, where success is defined in terms of follows, friendings, likes, shares and further circulation of the message as others comment or come into the conversation. The research suggests that when users make a decision to connect online, the status of the person sharing the information, the size of their network and the scope of their influence across networks are as important as the content of the information. In their study of media sharing site Vimeo, for instance, Katarzyna Musia and Sastry Nishanth (2012) found that there were few instances where members of a network liked the same videos, suggesting that the choice was based more on who they were than on what videos they wanted to share. Accordingly, their advice for theatre makers and companies looking to succeed in social media marketing is to remember that connections with colleagues in the industry, stakeholders, audiences and other interested or interesting parties comes first. Circulating information about one's own products thus comes second. If theatre makers do not make the effort to find the right people to follow, and encourage the right people to follow them, creating a user-friendly community that people want to be a part of, they are warned, their messages about their shows will not get much attention. Here, good partners and good relations with partners are characterised as critical to creating the right networks and, in turn, the right sorts of connection, tag, topic and filter in the feeds to appeal to the right sorts of audience.

### *Creating Filters, Folksonomies and Taxonomies*

When connecting with communities, networks and influencers, theatre makers and companies are told that they are setting up filtering systems that determine what comes through their feed. As Alan Cann, Konstantia Dimitriou and Tristram Hooley have advised, "[t]he process of building, curating, and filtering useful networks is a skill which needs to be practiced" (2011, 9). This filtering—via the sites on which a theatre maker does or does not have their profile; via their links, likes and friends; via their tags and hashtags; and via active reading to select the posts, phrases, topics and content they will choose to engage with—is seen as critical. Algorithms in the software record this and use it to create new relations, networks and content, and to recommend new connections or content to the theatre maker and their audiences. Accordingly, they can help or hinder a theatre maker's efforts to make their profile and their posts visible to their audiences. In reality, of course, these algorithms are popularity based, and this means that they are not always perfect, so odd connections can lead to unpredictable consequences. For example, as O'Neill (2014, 70) notes in his study of Shakespeare on YouTube, non-European adaptations do not show up in searches without the addition of racial adjectives such as African, Asian or Pacific. This, he says in his study of how Shakespeare fans create communities of practice online, is not to cast "algorithms as a sinister form of artificial intelligence" (37); it is to note that the technological and social factors that work together to drive their recommendations can be subject to contradictions, paradoxes and points of concern that can affect users' engagement with content in potentially unpredictable ways.

Cann, Dimitriou and Hooley (2011) call the filters that people set up within their social media profiles and platforms as a result of links, likes, follows and hashtags "folksonomies" rather than taxonomies because they come from the ground up in the network, not necessarily from deliberate decision making. The challenge for theatre makers is to create folksonomies that filter the information in a feed in a way that will work for the artist, for their audience and for every member of their audience if they have a mixed audience where interests, roles and even languages differ. If the thematic and social tags that drive a theatre maker's social media page do not work well, they may not come up on searches, or come up in their target spectators' feeds, meaning that they may not attract new audiences, via the rippling out effect as content moves through expanding circles of new audiences, because the filters or categories are not interesting, popular or sufficiently well understood. In this way, folksonomies—consciously or unconsciously constructed—impact on what sorts of content, comment, conversation and co-creation opportunities gain traction within a theatre maker's networks.

Usually the advice is that theatre makers and companies should follow relevant people, posts and topics, and use relevant tags, as widely as possible, while at the same time avoiding jumping on the bandwagon of a hashtag, topic or theme simply because it is popular, if the relation to their work is too tangential. To do this will only undermine the filters informing what comes up in their and their audiences' feeds, making connecting to their network a less appealing prospect, they are told. Such advice becomes a sort of algorithmic gatekeeper.

### *Creating Content Relevant to Form and Platform*

Although connections are important, theatre makers are advised that content still matters too. The first piece of advice that commentators offer in relation to content is that it should be relevant, interesting and, above all, tailored to each social media platform that a theatre maker or company uses (Mackrell 2012). If content is too long, too text based or too visually based to suit the platform in question, theatre makers are told, it will not have conversational and circulatory appeal, even within a well-functioning network with good tags, topics and filter systems.

### *Creating Content Relevant to Followers*

The next piece of advice in relation to content is that it should be relevant to the specific followers, friends and potential future audiences that it is targeting. In some cases, theatre makers are told, it may be necessary to segment a company's market (Pérez-Latre 2013, 49), making more specific niche pages or conversation portals for specific audiences, such as schools programme audiences, which have different needs, interests and desires from mainstage audiences. This can allow a theatre maker or company to engage new communities without alienating existing ones, and without creating conflict, tension and clashes when communities converge. This is cast as critical because one audience member's views on a topic may be antithetical to another audience members views—as a result of experience, expectations, politics or other factors. While other casting agents might appreciate jokes about auditionees, for instance, would-be actors, their friends, their families and their audiences might misunderstand, misinterpret or be offended by them. The consequences of this in these personally, socially, professionally and technologically convergent social media platforms are potentially dire. What Simon Cooper (1997, 95) has called an "ecological" awareness of all of the parts within a complex whole is recommended.

### *Connecting Across Platforms*

The next piece of advice that commentators offer in relation to content is a reiteration of the first two, with a new emphasis, and is the suggestion that theatre makers and companies should avoid sending out the same messages across two, three, four or more social media platforms. "[M]any social media users utilize multiple forms of social media," David Goff notes (2013, 18). Accordingly, selecting the right messages for the form, platform and followers, and presenting them in specific ways—optimised for blogs, microblogs, social networking sites or mobile users—is again recommended to theatre makers as a way to avoid repetitive regurgitation of the same message, or irrelevant messages that alienate some audience members.

### *Reciprocity*

Although theatre makers and companies may start using social media mainly out of a desire to get the message about their own work out, most commentators maintain that reciprocity—two-way conversation, plus commenting on and sharing other people's content—is critical to success. "We're living in a new participatory culture where dialogue (versus monologue) is paramount," as Gentry puts it (2009, 1). A monologue about oneself, or a marketing sales pitch, without openings out to more meaningful conversations, is said to be best avoided. The advice therefore is to friend others, follow others and share their content in the hope that they will reciprocate. This way, a theatre maker or company can hope to become a hub in a network, a home of dialogue, debate, or at least useful information about what is happening across a sector—across all musicals, mainstage programmes or live art programmes in a city—which is more appealing than a monologue. It is cast as critical for theatre makers who want colleagues, competitors, stakeholders and spectators to return the favour, respond and develop the relationship. Indicating possible courses of action, calling for a response or creating motivation to respond through resonance, humour or revelation are all recommended to encourage others to treat social media as an environment in which dialogue rather than monologue should prevail.

### *Cultivating Advocates and Connectors*

Most commentators advise theatre makers and companies to actively look for what might be called "advocates", "connectors" or influencers—people who will promote their work—within their networks (Berger 2012). These people are important because they help to develop the networks, the tags, the topics and filter systems, the dialogue and all of the features critical to success outlined above (Pérez-Latre 2013, 48). The best ambassadors, they are told, tend to be skilled at doing it, without overdoing it, in a way that more passive users are not.

### *Taking Responsibility for Mistakes, Misunderstandings and Mischief Making*

One of the most appealing aspects of developing an audience through social media is the fact that it can allow theatre makers and companies to "listen in" on what others—stakeholders, competitors and spectators—are saying (Constantinides and Fountain 2008). This said, the old adage about eavesdroppers not always liking what they hear about themselves does apply. The "unpleasant" things that a practitioner or company hears about themselves can come about as a result of terms, ideas or ideologies that do not match up or mean the same things to different communities of users. A major company might not see taking advantage of crowdfunding, calling for free labour or recounting funny stories about failed auditions in the same terms as independent and individual theatre makers. Such negative messages can come about as a result of efforts to construct an edgy, subversive, satirical character that do not come off;

they can come about as a result of accuracy becoming a victim of speed, or social media participants' tendency to pounce on an issue whether they know the facts or not; they can come about as a result of mischief makers or trolls deliberately creating scandal, controversy or trouble through disinformation disrupting information—for example, as noted in Chap. 2, mischief makers deliberately transporting content or comments from one context to another because they know it will cause a controversy. More simply, they can come about as a result of the proliferation of content that lacks substance or integrity, and is thus seen as spam. These issues all mean that, when a theatre maker or company listens in, they may find themselves labelled in ways they do not like. "Even if the accusation is unfounded," Judith Donath notes, "being branded a troll is quite damaging to one's online reputation" (1999, 45), as is being branded unethical, superficial, too sales oriented or a spammer.

As noted in Chap. 4, the advice for theatre makers and companies when this happens has historically been to avoid arguing back—at least in theatre criticism circles. The heat, passion and rage that come across can create fights, and can lead to abuse and anti-social conduct. On the surface, this advice seems to contradict the notion that the advantage of building a community online is that all players can discuss, debate and co-create ideas that may come to be the dominant ones in the future. The trick, commentators claim, is to be savvy about when to respond and how. As Karene Altes argues, "the structure of social media relies on the freedom of individuals to interact without hierarchy" (2009, 47). Simply editing out posts that are critical—not posts that are racist, sexist, ableist and thus criminal communications that do, as Janet Sternberg (2012, 8) says, need to be dealt with swiftly—is typically ineffective, mainly because it reintroduces hierarchy into the community (or, rather, reintroduces awareness that hierarchies exist in this online community as much as in any offline community). At the same time, however, simply letting such posts pile up, without responding, is also problematic because it reintroduces into the community a sense of a monologue rather than dialogue. For this reason, many recommend (in an audience development context if not necessarily in a critical or aesthetic context) that a theatre maker at least offers a non-response response to criticism. That is, they recommend saying that they are sorry the person had a bad experience, and asking them to get in touch so it can be discussed offline. In this way there is a dialogue of a sort, even if it is not a deep one.

Analysing audience development and engagement activities in this chapter suggests that doing this in an audience development context is as hard as, if not harder than, doing it in the aesthetic and critical contexts discussed in Chaps. 3 and 4—that there can be a temptation to shut down meaningful debate, or at least a reluctance to test the notion that reputation can remain intact during the course of such debate. On one level, the fact that theatres are doing this suggests that the advice relating to the non-response response is useful and can achieve the desired outcome, if that is to return to calm, congratulatory, formulaic conversations. On another level, though, the advice can be less useful if the desired outcome is to facilitate truly co-creative conversations.

### *Making Metrics Count*

Another aspect of social media that many theatre companies and makers are taught to fear is the fact that challenging comments, criticism and conflict are visible to all—not just spectators, but sponsors, funders and the public at large. Many worry that this might become part of a set of "big data" that will impact on their ability to secure sponsors, supporters and government subsidy in the future.

Certainly, new online technology has raised issues of privacy; surveillance by individuals, institutions or competitors in the market; and measurement and control. Accordingly, as Nabarro notes, it is not surprising that "[t]echnology has since the days of the first electronic box office been a way of gathering data to support the case for subsidy of the arts" (2013), individually, and as an industry. Social media technology is useful in gathering data to support the case for subsidy because it can show who attends what, when, where and why; help set benchmarks; and help monitor performance against those benchmarks via social media informatics and metrics. It a powerful—and thus potentially anxiety-inducing—tool to gauge as well as generate audience appeal and loyalty.

As John Lovett (2011) explains, social media metrics can include counting visits, likes, follows, friends, posts, reposts and pace of circulation, as well as comparing trend data in an industry or an area to establish or evidence a company's percentage or share of traffic. It can also, less commonly, include content or narrative analysis of comments and connections, and influence patterns. It can therefore, as Nicole Kelly (2010) notes, be used to measure both exposure (number of friends or followers in a theatre maker's network) and engagements (volume of comments, conversations, likes, shares and circulations). This data about traffic, exposure, engagements and influence can be correlated with sales data to give a picture of a theatre maker's or company's success or influence. With the right software, these important metrics can be reported on and visualized in a whole range of different maps, charts and graphs. Indeed, as noted in the Introduction, visualising the so-called "big data" sets that social media creates is one of the most popular topics in studies in the area.

If this data is used internally for continuous improvement, most theatre makers and companies are comfortable with it. If it is used externally for surveillance and judgement, then comfort levels start to slip. Though social media posts fly by fast, they do not completely disappear, and this creates concerns that supporters, sponsors and funders will not see mistakes in their bigger context as part of the continuous improvement and innovation process, only as faults, or as reasons to withdraw funding. In a commercial context, this may not be a major problem—users might see a bad review or rating but they cannot demand that a commercial company share all its data—but in taxpayer subsidised practices, sponsors can demand all data to justify continued subsidy.

> As Trottier suggests, then, social media are a risky opportunity for business. Like institutions and individuals, they are changing their practices in response to the exponential increase in visibility of their clients and markets. But they are also made visible to their clients when users upload opinions, reviews and experiences with their products and services. (Trottier 2012, 18)

If information is visible, surveillable and measurable by all stakeholders, it becomes difficult to exercise the sort of self-presentation, front and face strategies that Goffman (1963, 1973) describes, except, of course, by minimising, excluding, siloising and separating practices so that data sets are bounded and become almost impossible to see as a whole. This may be why aesthetic, critical and audience development practices on social media platforms so rarely connect. The co-creative work of spectators during the show, or in the tweet seats in the stalls, is not connected up with reviews, reflections on marketing success or sales figures, so as to avoid creating a whole that adversely impacts on reputation.

This issue is among the least discussed in advice about theatre makers' use of social media. Certainly, there are guides and workshops giving advice about using social media to measure audience engagement.

There are, however, few focusing on how to avoid falling prey to the temptation to keep conversations on social media superficial, siloised and separate so that they do not generate the contradictory data that might be mistaken by stakeholders for a reason to defund a theatre maker or company, rather than simply as stimulus for a continuous improvement process.

The advice at this point in time is the same as that offered at the start of any measurement, metrics or evaluation process. In any business, management, marketing or audience development context, theatre makers and companies are advised to be specific about what sort of data will be an indicator of success. If worried that measurement will not reflect a positive result, a theatre maker is advised not to set this as a primary indicator of success. For example, not-for-profit companies are advised to set community, cultural or educational rather than economic goals as indicators of success.

### *Recognising When Less Is More*

In light of the sheer volume of concerns cited in the advice that circulates at this stage, the last common piece of advice for those developing audiences via social media is that sometimes less can be more (Berger 2012). For many theatre makers and companies, setting up a clear, well-scoped and interesting plan for social media strategies, and expectations to match, is cast as a necessity. "This kind of viral word of mouth—as scary as it is positive—is potentially marketing gold for arts companies but it must be nurtured rather than exploited," as Blake (2010), puts it. Yet, as Nabarro (2013) notes, theatre makers and companies do not always have the capacity to nurture this activity the way commercial companies in other industries do. Accordingly, theatre makers are sometimes advised to start in small, specific areas of the work so that they are less likely to encounter complexities, contradictions and conflicts that they do not have the capacity to handle. The question is whether theatre companies can do this without losing the discussion, debate and dialogue in a community, so that their sites start to come across as what Goff (2013, 39) has called a "walled garden", where all the hierarchies of conventional monologic communication media are still mostly maintained. This is something that theatre makers have managed in an aesthetic context, as noted in Chap. 3, by taking a transmedia approach to co-creativity in value-add products, programmes and platforms, reducing risk to core programmes. The strategies by which this might be achieved in the critical contexts discussed in Chap. 4, or the audience development contexts discussed in Chap. 5, remain rather less clear.

## Contested Concepts of Access, Inclusion and Democracy

The advice offered here—on everything from audience diversity to developing an appealing profile, to managing multiple stakeholder communities, through tags, topics, content and network connections, to dealing with misunderstandings, mistakes, mischief and anomalies of digital reciprocity, to dealing with "big data"—is based on a set of assumptions. The main assumption, it seems, is that theatre companies and makers want to make use of social media. It appears, however, that there is also an assumption that theatre companies and makers want to do so without becoming the scandal, or the example of something that went wrong, for spectators, sponsors and society at large to judge. In this sense, the volume and range of advice on offer may explain why controversies and complaints about unconsenting involvement in experiments stand out as the exception rather than the norm when theatre makers engage with social media for their day-to-day audience development activities, as in the case of the Brisbane theatre community examples cited above.

The advice is clearly useful for those looking to avoid problems on platforms where anomalies of digital reciprocity mean that artist–artist, artist–audience and audience–audience relationships do not always play out in predictable ways, and where problems are much more surveillable, recordable and trackable than in past media paradigms. The fact that advice is outpacing practice—at least in the marketing, audience development and assessment domains—seems, however, to be creating a that these platforms could become "walled gardens" where dialogue is more rote than revolutionary. The advice for addressing the anxiety that these new media platforms create is tending to constrain theatre makers' practice before they have had a chance to experiment with it. Theatre makers take well-meaning and great-from-a-marketing-perspective advice to build a profile, brand and beneficial connections, and to share a set of authentic onstage, sidestage and backstage content, but this can result in bounded content and conversations. They heed warnings that social media demands dialogue not monologue. However, heeding these warnings often results in dialogue that registers as a selective surface level of interactivity, designed to appeal to current centralised networks of current artists, audiences and stakeholders, not a more productive level of interactivity, designed to activate debate across new decentralised networks or communities. As a result—as commentators such as Sant (2014) have claimed—there seem to be few mainstage theatre companies and makers going further, staging dialogue in a truly co-creative and constructive way, with a whole range of different audiences, with a view to changing culture.

A lack of desire, or a lack of dramaturgical skill to move through debates, declare viewpoints and make meaningful discourse, are not necessarily the factors forestalling wider debates here. As the controversy around *Involuntary Dances* in 2009 discussed in Chap. 4, and around Brisbane and broader Australian theatre in 2009 and 2010 discussed in Chap. 5, demonstrate, there are cases where the self-performances of artists, audiences and the public at large online have sparked attention, action and at least some sort of legacy in the public sphere. It has happened in theatre culture as much as in US politics in the lead-up to the election of Barack Obama, or in Middle Eastern politics in the lead-up to the Arab Spring. However, it has not necessarily happened frequently. In Chap. 4 I suggested that the fact that the producers remediated traditional responses to non-traditional criticism may have been one reason why the *Ugly Mugs* scandal simple petered out. In this chapter it seems it is not always remediation of old forms but also sometimes application of advice for new forms that may be a factor forestalling the emergence of more meaningful engagements. In other words, this well-meaning advice about how to engage with artists, audiences and the public at large online may consciously or unconsciously be advocating a type of two-way interaction designed to defuse debate, and develop consensus, via mundane rather than meaningful conversations.

The advice to theatre makers looking to use social media for audience development, marketing and assessment seems to push them to self-surveillance, so they do not unwittingly become examples of worst-case scenarios for others to critique. In doing so, it seems to push them towards collegiality, conciliation and consensus building with those who question them—by filtering them out of their feeds, setting up special feeds, limiting content or, when things go wrong, saying sorry for the offence and suggesting they speak offline straightaway. These practices seem designed to stop tension, discomfort and fraught conversations while maintaining a sense of dialogue rather than monologue—a response that may actually be limiting responsibility for the broader cultural impacts of the work, or at least limiting the ability to respond in a larger ideological sense.

As the examples in the later chapters of this book show, willingness to continue working through identity construction, anecdotes, claims and counter-claims, and also acknowledge the tenseness of the encounter, is related to the potential productivity of the encounter. It is a characteristic of examples that lead to ongoing conversation or legacy in the public sphere. Where this willingness to continue a tense conversation comes to prevail in aesthetic, critical or audience development activities, participants push past defining democracy in terms of majority, consensus and resolving antagonism into a conclusion, and towards defining democracy in terms of the capacity to exist in a fraught relationship with each other for days, weeks, months or years to create the conditions of possibility for new ideas to start permeating the public sphere. As Balme (2014, 9), following Chantal Mouffe (2005), has argued, this is not the norm in the West, where notions of democracy tend to be defined in terms of consensus, not in terms of creating an ability to live with a range of different attitudes, opinions or worldviews in an agonistic but not antagonistic dialogue. Democracy tends to be defined in terms of assimilation, not in terms of accommodating differences in a separate-but-together, same-but-different, unified-but-diversified community. Saying sorry, stopping the show or promising to set out a new policy for the next show, season or initiative seems to be a strategy that serves mainly to shut down sparks of debate before they can develop into longer-running conversations in which participants might actually start to negotiate new norms. While this might work well for marketing, and for creating the engaging experiences that the average citizen consumer today enjoys more than the old transaction-oriented marketing of the past, it seems it works less well for facilitating more meaningful conversations. It thus works less well for making a theatre ecology lively, healthy and evolving, and for making a theatre that is impactful on the larger cultural ecology as it lives and evolves.

What this analysis shows, then, is that the consensus notions of democracy that underpin much advice about social media tend to close off the weak ties or bridges between players that allow conversations to circulate out across decentralised networks on social media platforms. The disensus notions of democracy tend to hold open the weak ties or bridges between players, and thus the possibilities for meaningful and impactful conversation across networks. The former might be good for creating bonding capital between people who already know each other, enjoyable experiences and better-functioning existing communities. It may not be as good for creating bridging capital between people who might want to come to know or have influence on each other, and to engender culture-changing experiences, which transform the form, nature and functioning of communities.

In a social media context, keeping both bonds and bridges open is necessary to leverage the hubs, spokes, ties and networks that give users the power to influence individuals, institutions and societies—the power to go beyond likes, shares and statements of love or hate, and to spark into more substantive conversations, actions or consequences. Advice based on maintaining bonds within a community without necessarily making new bridges out to new communities is useful for marketing but less useful for meaningful impact in the public sphere because, while the bounded conversations may be appreciated by communities of affinity who already have high stakes in the matter, they are less likely to draw the attention of the looser communities to become audiences, stakeholders or advocates too. Accordingly, adopting the former approach over the latter may limit a theatre maker's chance to become a hub in the production, dissemination, reception and debate about theatre. This, ironically, may mean that if and when an issue comes up, they are more likely to become fodder for rather than facilitator of debate about a significant social issue—as happened in several of the controversies analysed here—not because a theatre maker has not learned enough about the affordances of social media platforms, but, paradoxically, because they have learned just enough to leave conversation bounded, without becoming critical of those boundaries.

That a lack of experimentation, engagement and participation in public debate is most prominent among mainstage theatre companies, and comes from concerns about losing subsidy, is undoubtedly true. Mainstage theatre companies say they want to be part of public debate, but, paradoxically, they also often want to avoid being part of that debate because the line between facilitator and focus of that debate is thin, and because taking a stand can risk offending the government that funds them. In a social media context, though, that fear of losing funding is driven by the discourse in the press, industry reports and recommendations about the uptake of social media that dictates bounded rather than open forms of dialogue. These recommendations reduce the possibility that theatre makers will get involved in democratic action that goes beyond transmedia marketing, up voting, down voting and bounded dialogue designed to build consensus on social media platforms to activities that build new communities and cultures on these platforms. The opportunity to turn audience development, marketing and assessment activities into more meaningful conversations is lost, but, in this case, it seems it is lost by the uptake of the very advice that purported to be leading people towards it. This may be a concern for mainstage theatre companies and makers, their audiences and their other stakeholders. It will likely be a bigger concern for independent, community and activist theatre makers, audiences and communities looking to agitate for cultural change

To date, theatre makers do not seem to have found an equivalent of the transmedia marketing practices that make space for experimentation in aesthetic style by means of social media in the critical, audience development, marketing and assessment domains. In these latter domains, a space in which mainstage theatre companies and makers might attempt these sorts of experiments in a non-public way, or at least a not-part-of-primary-programming way, has yet to emerge. Ironically, it has often been funding bodies that have been at the forefront of attempting to create such spaces, with little success to date as a result of the advice coming through at the same time as the funding. Identifying what it might take to prompt mainstage theatre companies, makers, audiences and communities to take a leap of faith and try something different, contrary to the most well-meant advice, is difficult. However, this may be the main manoeuvre necessary to make social media a platform for conversations that go beyond marketing into more meaningful cultural engagement for mainstage, as much as for independent, community and activist, theatre makers and companies.

## References

Albarran, Alan B. (ed.). 2013. *The Social Media Industries*. London: Routledge.

Altes, Karene. 2009. Social Media: Young Professionals Effect Change in the Workplace. *Journal of Property Management* 74 (5): 44–47.

Anderson, Benedikt. 1991. *Imagined Communities: Reflections on the Origin and Spread of Nationalism*. London: Verso.

Anderson, Eric. 2010. *Social Media Marketing: Game Theory and The Emergence of Collaboration*. Portland: Springer.

Ashcroft, Bill, Gareth Griffiths, and Helen Tiffin. 1989. *The Empire Writes Back: Theory and Practice in Post-Colonial Studies*. London: Routledge.

AussieTheatre.com. 2013. Producer tools, AussieTheatre.com. http://aussietheatre.com.au/forums/topic/producer-tools. Accessed 9 June 2014.

Australian Government. 2011. National Cultural Policy Discussion Paper. Department of Prime Minster and Cabinet—Office for the Arts 2011, 1 Oct 2011. http://culture.arts.gov.au/discussion-paper. Accessed 13 Aug 2013.

Balme, Christoper. 2014. *The Theatrical Public Sphere*. Cambridge: Cambridge University Press.

Baylis, John. 2009. Mapping Queensland Theatre. *Arts Queensland*. http://www.arts.qld.gov.au/docs/mapping-queensland-theatre-report.doc. Accessed 10 Sept 2011.

Becker, Leo B. and Schoenbach, Klaus, B. 1989. When Media Content Diversifies: Anticipating Audience Behaviour. In *Audience Responses to Media Diversification: Coping with Plenty*, ed. Lee B. Becker, and Klaus B. Schoenbach, 1–27. Hillsdale: Lawrence Erlbaum Associates.

Bell, David. 2001. *An Introduction to Cybercultures*. London: Routledge.

Benedikt, Micheal. 2000. 'Cyberspace: First Steps. In *The Cybercultures Reader*, ed. David Bell and Barbara M Kennedy, 29–44. London and New York: Routledge.

Berger, Christopher. 2012. *The Social Media Strategists: Build a Successful Program from the Inside Out*. Boston: McGraw-Hill.

Blake, Elissa. 2010. Geeks, Tweets and Bums on Seats: How Social Media Is Shaping the Arts in Australia. *Sydney Morning Herald*. 10 July 2010. http://www.smh.com/au/entertainment/theatre/geeks-tweets-and-bums-on-seats-20100709-103g8.html. Accessed 9 Aug 2013.

Blake, Elissa. 2013. Belvoir Rattles the Pan, and Some Miss the Magic. *Sydney Morning Herald* 7 Aug 2013. http://www.smh.com.au/entertainment/theatre/belvoir-rattles-the-pan-and-some-miss-the-magic-20130807-2rf9w.html. Accessed 5 Jan 2015.

Bourdieu, Pierre. 1986. The Forms of Capital. In *Handbook of Theory and Research for the Sociology of Education*, ed. John C. Richardson, 241–258. New York: Greenwood.

Brogan, Chris. 2010. *Social Media 101: Tactics and Tips to Develop Your Business Online*. Hoboken: Wiley.

Butsch, Richard. 2008. *The Citizen Audience: Crowds, Publics and Individuals*. London: Routledge.

Caines, Rebecca. 2008. *Troubling Spaces: The Politics of "New" Community-Based Guerrilla Performance in Australia*. PhD thesis, University of New South Wales, Sydney, Australia. http://www.unsworks.unsw.edu.au/primo_library/libweb/action/dlDisplay.do?vid=UNSWORKS&docId=unsworks_2403&fromSitemap=1&afterPDS=true. Accessed 5 Jan 2015.

Capelin, Steve (ed.). 1995. *Challenging the Centre: Two Decades of Political Theatre*. Brisbane: Playlab Press.

Cann, Alan, Dimitriou, Konstantia, and Hooley, Tristram. 2011. Social Media: A Guide For Researchers. *Research Information Network*. Accessed 5 Jan 2015. http://www.rin.ac.uk/social-media-guide. Accessed 5 Dec 2012.

Cooper, Simon. 1997. Plenitude and Alienation: The Subject of Virtual Reality. In *Virtual Politics: Identity and Community*, ed. David Holmes, 93–106. London: Sage.

Correa, Teresa, Willard Hinsely, Amber and Gil de Zúñiga, Homero. 2010. Who Interacts on the Web?: The Intersection of Users' Personality and Social Media Use. *Computers in Human Behaviour* 26.2: 247–253.

Conner, Lynne. 2013. *Audience Engagement and the Role of Arts Talk in the Digital Era*. London: Palgrave Macmillan.

Constantinides, Efthymios and Fountain, Stafan J. 2008. Web 2.0: Conceptual Foundations and Marketing Issues. *Journal of Direct, Data and Digital Marketing Practice* 9.3: 231–245.

Croggon, Alison. 2010. Now For Something Different. *The Australian* 7 Dec 2010. www.theaustralian.com.au/news/arts/now-for-something-different/story-e6frg8n6-1225966594569. Accessed 16 Jan 2015.

Donath, Judith S. 1999. Identity and Deception in the Virtual Community. In *Communities in Cyberspace*, ed. Mark A. Smith, and Peter Kollack, 29–59. London: Routledge.

Downes, Daniel. 2005. *Interactive Realism: The Poetics of Cyberspace*. Montreal: McGill-Queens University Press.

Eliezer, Christie. 2012. Crowdfunding Survey: Why Some Aussie Projects Fail. *The Music Network* 1 Aug 2012. http://www.themusicnetwork.com/music-news/industry/2012/08/01/crowdfunding-survey-why-some-aussie-projects-fail/. Accessed 13 Dec 2014.

Evans, Elizabeth. 2011. *Transmedia Television: Audiences, New Media and Daily Life*. London: Routledge.

Felski, Rita. 1989. *Beyond Feminist Aesthetics: Feminist Literature and Social Change*. Boston: Harvard University Press.

Feeney, Katherine. 2010a. Gow Happy to Leave "Middle of the Road". *Brisbane Times* 28 April 2010. http://www.brisbanetimes.com.au/entertainment/gow-happy-to-leave-middle-of-the-road-20100428-tr8c.html?rand=1272500089595. Accessed 13 Jan 2015.

Fotheringham, Richard. 1992. *Community Theatre in Australia*. Sydney: Currency Press.

Foy, Kate. 2010a. Is there Anything Right with the Theatre? *Groundling* 10 Jan 2010. http://katefoy.com/2010/01/is-there-anything-right-with-the-theatre/. Accessed 10 Sept 2011.

Foy, Kate. 2010b. Brisbane: Wanted—A Cultural Reality Check. *Groundling* 20 March 2010. http://katefoy.com/2010/03/brisbane-wanted-a-cultural-reality-check/. Accessed 10 Sept 2011.

Francis, Toby. 2013a. Australian Musical Theatre's Got Talent. *Robojustice Superfighter* 22 July 2013. http://robojusticesuperfighter.com/2013/07/22/australian-musical-theatres-got-talent/. Accessed 15 Jan 2015.

Francis, Toby. 2013b. Twitter and The X Factor are the New Casting Couches. *ArtsHub*, 23 July 2013. http://au.artshub.com/au/news-article/opinions/performing-arts/twitter-and-the-x-factor-are-the-new-casting-couches-196094. Accessed 15 Jan 2015.

Fraser, Nancy. 1989. *Unruly Practices: Power, Discourse and Gender in Contemporary Social Theory*. Minneapolis: University of Minnesota Press.

Fraser, Nancy. 1990. Rethinking The Public Sphere: A Contribution to the Critique of Actually Existing Democracy. *Social Text* 25 (26): 56–80.

Gentry, James K. 2009. The Social Networking Revolution: You Can't Afford to Ignore Social Media. *Accounting Today* 23 (16): 42.

Gill, Raymond. 2010. Is Brisbane Australia's New Cultural Capital? *Sydney Morning Herald* 16 Oct 2010. http://www.smh.com.au/entertainment/art-and-design/is-brisbane-australias-new-cultural-capital-20101015-16np5.html. Accessed 10 Sept 2011.

Goff, David H. 2013. A History of the Social Media Industries. In *the Social Media Industries*, ed. Alan B. Albarran, 16–45. London: Routledge.

Goffman, Erving. 1963. *Behaviour in Public Places: Notes on the Social Organization of Gatherings*. New York: The Free Press.

Goffman, Erving. 1973. *Presentation of the Self in Everyday Life*. Woodstock: Overlook Press.

Habermas, Jürgen. 1962/1989. *The Structural Transformation of the Public Sphere*. London: Polity.

Hadley, Bree, and Sandra Gattenhof. 2012. Brokering Evaluations of Partnerships in Australian Community Arts: Responding to Entrepreneurial Tendencies. *Journal of Arts and Communities* 4 (3): 231–249.

Hadley, Bree, and Gattenhof, Sandra. 2011. *Creating Queensland, Creative Communities Partnership—Major Brisbane Festival and Australia Council for the Arts*. Brisbane: Queensland University of Technology. http://eprints.qut.edu.au/54833/. Accessed 1 June 2013.

Handley, Ann, and C.C. Chapman. 2012. *Content Rules: How to Create Killer Blogs, Podcasts, Videos, eBooks, Webinars*. Hoboken: Wiley.

Hartley, John, and Alan McKee. 2000. *The Indigenous Public Sphere: The Reporting and Reception of Indigenous Issues in the Australian Media, 1994–1997*. Oxford: Oxford Unviersity Press.

Heer, Jeffrey, and Danah Boyd. 2005. Vizster: Visualizing Online Social Networks. In *Information Visualization, 2005. INFOVIS 2005. IEEE Symposium on*, 32–39.

Holmes, David. 1997a. Virtual Politics—Identity and Community in Cyberspace. In *Virtual Politics: Identity and Community*, ed. David Holmes, 1–25. London: Sage.

Holmes, David. 1997b. Virtual Identity: Communities of Broadcast, Communities of Interactivity. In *Virtual Politics: Identity and Community*, ed. David Holmes, 26–45. London: Sage.

Hunt, Cathy, and Phyllida Shaw. 2007. *A Sustainable Arts Sector: What Will It Take?*. Strawberry Hills: Currency House.

Itzkoff, Dave. 2009. Casting Director Tweets at Tryouts, to Negative Reviews.Theater. *New York Times* 14 Aug 2009. http://theater.nytimes.com/2009/08/15/theater/15tweet.html?_r=0. Accessed 19 Aug 2013.

Jabour, Bridie. 2013. Smart Arts? Finance First on New Arts Board. *Brisbane Times* 7 Feb 2013. http://www.brisbanetimes.com.au/queensland/smart-arts-finance-first-on-new-board-20130207-2e0t6.html#ixzz2SZoT7KwJ. Accessed 3 Feb 2015.

Jenkins, Henry. 2006. *Convergence Culture: Where Old and New Media Collide*. New York: New York University Press.

Jordan, Tim. 1999. *Cyberpower: The Culture and Politics of Cyberspace and the Internet*. London and New York: Routledge.

Kelly, Nicole. 2010. 4 Ways to Measure Social Media and It's Impact on Your Brand. *Social Media Examiner*. http://www.socialmediaexaminer.com/4-ways-measure-social-media-and-its-impact-on-your-brand/. Accessed 19 Dec 2011.

Kerpen, Dave. 2011. *Likeable Social Media: How to Delight Your Customers, Create an Irresistible Brand, and Be Generally Amazing on Facebook (and Other Social Networks)*. New York: McGraw-Hill.

Kotler, Phillip, and Joanne Scheff. 1997. *Standing Room Only*. Boston: Harvard Business School Press.

Kotler, Phillip, Stewart, Adam, Brown, Linden, and Armstrong, Gary. 2003. *Principles of Marketing*. NSW: Pearson Education.

Lonergan, Patrick. 2016. *Theatre & Social Media*. London: Palgrave Macmillan.

Lovett, John. 2011. *Social Media Metrics Secrets*. Hoboken: Wiley.

Lyotard, Jean-Francois. 1984. *The Postmodern Condition: A Report on Knowledge*. Manchester: Manchester University Press.

Mackrell, Judith. 2012. Dancing with the Digits. *Sydney Morning Herald* 2 Aug 2012. http://www.smh.com.au/digital-life-news/dancing-with-the-digits-20120802-23hrt.html. Accessed 19 Aug 2013.

Makeham, Paul, Hadley, Bree and Kwok, Joon-Yee. 2012. A Value Ecology Approach to the Performing Arts. *MC Journal*, 15.3. http://journal.media-culture.org.au. Accessed 1 June 2013.

Mangold, W.Glynn, and David J. Faulds. 2009. Social Media: The New Hybrid Element of the Promotional Mix. *Business Horizons* 52 (4): 357–365.

Mee, Sean. 2010. The Baylis Report: Don't Look Back. *The Death of Reason*, 20 May 2010. http://areasonabledeath.blogspot.com/. Accessed 10 Sept 2011.

Meyer, Marc. 2009. Give More and Get More out of Social Media. *Communication World* 26 (6): 48.

Miller, Paige. 2013. Social Media Marketing. In *The Social Media Industries*, ed. Alan B. Albarran, 86–104. London: Routledge.

Milne, Geoffrey. 2004. *Theatre Australia (Un)limited: Australian Theatre since the 1950s*. Amsterdam: Rodopi.

Mouffe, Chantal. 2005. *On the Political.* Abington: Routledge.

Musia, Katarzyna and Nishanth, Sastry. 2012. Social Media: Are They Underpinned by Social or Interest Based Interactions? In *Proceedings, Simplex /12—Proceedings of the Fourth Annual Workshop on Simplifying Complex Networks for Practitioners*, 1–6. New York: ACM.

Nabarro, Michael. 2013. How Technology is Transforming the Theatre Box Office. Culture Professionals Network, *The Guardian* 12 Aug 2013. http://www.theguardian.com/culture-professionals-network/culture-professionals-blog/2013/aug/09/technology-theatre-box-office-digital?INTCMP=ILCNETTXT3487. Accessed 19 Aug 2013.

Negt, Oscar and Kluge, Alexander. 1972/1993. *The Public Sphere and Experience: Toward an Analysis of the Bourgeois and Proletarian Public Sphere.* Minneapolis: University of Minnesota Press.

O'Neill, Stephen. 2014. *Shakespeare and YouTube: New Media Forms of the Bard.* London: Bloomsbury.

Page, Ruth. 2012. *Stories and Social Media: Identities and Interaction.* London: Routledge.

Pérez-Latre, Francisco. 2013. The Paradoxes of Social Media: A Review of Theoretical Issues. In *The Social Media Industries*, ed. Alan B. Albarran, 46–59. London: Routledge.

Phillips, Arther Angel. 2006. *A.A. Philips on the Cultural Cringe*, Melbourne: Melbourne University Publishing.

Pine, B.Joseph, and James H. Gilmore. 2011. *The Experience Economy*, 2nd ed. Boston: Harvard Business Review Press.

Poster, Mark. 1997. Cyberdemocracy: The Internet and the Public Sphere. In *Virtual Politics: Identity and Community*, ed. David Holmes, 212–228. London: Sage.

Prahalad, C.K., and Venkat Ramaswarmy. 2000. Co-opting Customer Competence. *Harvard Business Review* 78 (1): 79–87.

Prahalad, C.K., and Venkat Ramaswarmy. 2004. *The Future of Competition: Co-Creating Unique Value With Customers.* Boston: Harvard Business Review Press.

Puvanenthiran, Bhakthi. 2014. Call for Free Kylie Dancers Stumbles. *Sydney Morning Herald* 25 April 2014. http://www.smh.com.au/entertainment/music/call-for-free-kylie-dancers-stumbles-20140424-377a0.html. Accessed 19 Jan 2015.

Radbourne, Jennifer, and Margaret Fraser. 1996. *Arts Management: A Practical Guide.* St Leonards: Allen and Unwin.

Rentschler, Ruth. 2002. *The Entrepreneurial Arts Leader: Cultural Policy, Change and Reinvention.* St Lucia: University of Queensland Press.

Rheingold, Howard. 1993/2000. *The Virtual Community: Homesteading on the Electronic Frontier.* Cambridge: MIT Press.

Sant, Toni. 2014. Art, Performance, and Social Media. In *Routledge Handbook of Social Media*, ed. Jeremy Hunsinger, and Theresa M. Senft, 45–58. London: Routledge.

Sloss Performing Arts Company. 2011. MUSE OF FIRE: Shakespeare at Sloss. http://www.shakespeareatsloss.org/MUSE_OF_FIRE/Home.html. Accessed 19 Aug 2013.

Sloss Performing Arts Company. 2011. Call For Participation: MUSE OF FIRE: Shakespeare at Sloss. Facebook. http://www.facebook.c0m/#!/group.php?gid=99211185718&v=info. Accessed 19 Aug 2013.

Smith, Marc A., and Peter Kollock. 1999. Communities in Cyberspace. In *Communities in Cyberspace*, ed. Mark A. Smith, and Peter Kollack, 3–25. London: Routledge.

Steidl, Peter, and Robert Hughes. 1999. *Marketing Strategies for Arts Organisations*. Sydney: Australian Council.

Sternberg, Janet. 2012. *Misbehavior in Cyber Places: The Regulation of Online Conduct in Virtual Communities on the Internet*. Lanahm: University Press of America.

Tapcott, Don, and Anthony D. Williams. 2006. *Wikinomics*. New York: Portfolio.

Trottier, Daniel. 2012. *Social Media as Surveillance: Rethinking Visibility in a Converging World*. Abingdon: Ashgate Publishing Group.

Turner, Tonya. 2010a. Is Brisbane Brizvegas—Or a Cultural Desert? *Courier Mail* 17 March 2010. http://www.couriermail.com.au/entertainment/is-brisbane-brizvegas-or-a-cultural-desert/comments-e6freq7f-1225842056993?pg=1. Accessed 10 Sept 2011.

Turner, Tonya. 2010b. Stage Fright: Debrief. *Courier Mail* 17 May 2010. http://blogs.news.com.au/couriermail/arts/index.php/couriermail/comments/stage_fright_debrief/. Accessed 10 Sept 2011.

Westbrook, Cathy. 2014. How to stage theatre's online future, *The Guardian* Theatre blog with Lyn Gardiner, Monday 14 April 2014. Available online http://www.theguardian.com/stage/theatreblog/2014/apr/14/stage-theatre-online-future.

Zarella, Dan. 2010. *The Social Media Marketing Book*. Sebastapol: O'Reilly Media.

CHAPTER 6

# Conclusion

In her book on *Audience Engagement and the Role of Arts Talk in the Digital Era*, Lynne Conner says: "I believe that much will be gained from travelling the social media universe in search of information about the ways in which people are talking about their arts experiences" (2013, 170). Much, she contends, will be gained by finding ways to further enable artists to engage with the arts via these platforms. In his book *The Theatrical Public Sphere*, Christopher Balme expresses similar sentiments, sharing the interest in social media platforms that "enable, at least in principle, more intense forms of feedback between theatres and their publics" (2014, 48). Though they take their discussions in different directions, these authors share an interest in shaking up theatre cultures that they suspect have become all too stagnant. Although I share their interest in spectators, audiences and shaking up stagnant theatre cultures, I have, in *Theatre, Social Media and Meaning Making*, taken my own travels in the social media universe in search of examples of the ways in which theatre makers, critics and audiences are using platforms to connect with the public sphere in a different direction again. I have looked at the aesthetic, critical and audience development possibilities that social media presents. I have looked for moments where meaningful engagement between artists, spectators and societies has started to emerge. I have found them but, at the same time, not found them in places where I might have anticipated them too. Moving through the examples mentioned in this book, I have recognised that industry-based articles, recommendations and advice have outpaced both practice and academic



B. Hadley, *Theatre, Social Media, and Meaning Making*,
DOI 10.1007/978-3-319-54882-1_6

attention to that practice. This is the gap I have sought to address here. Instead of constructing or reciting recommendations to help theatre companies and makers use social media technology, I have considered the reports, case studies and recommendations available and, more critically, considered the way these may or may not contribute to the new ways of negotiating meaning that advocates of social media in the theatre desire.

In the course of the journey, I have considered a range of practices, performance texts and para-performance texts. I have drawn from onstage works such as Adam Cass's *I Love You Bro*, Liesel Zink's *Various Selves* and The Builders Association's *Continuous City*, to live and as live broadcasts by the National Theatre, to immersive, telematic, networked and participatory performances making use of Second Life, Upstage, Twitter, Facebook and other branded or bespoke social media platforms, including Paul Sermon's *Telematic Dreaming*, Blast Theory's *Desert Rain*, Ian Upton's *Ritual Circle*, the RSC and Mudlark's *Such Tweet Sorrow*, the RSC Google Creative Lab's *A Midsummer Night's Dreaming*, Punchdrunk's *Sleep No More*, New Paradise Laboratories' *Fatebook: Avoiding Catastrophe One Party at a Time*, Jeffrey Cranor's tweet plays, La Pocha Nostra's *Ethno-Cyberpunk Trading Post*, Wafaa Bilal's *Domestic Tension*, Brian Lobel's *Purge*, Sarah Rodigari's *Reach Out Touch Faith* and @Platea's *Co-Modify*. From archives, such as Hemispherica and AusStage, to anti-archives, such as *Anarcha*. I have examined debate about specific theatre shows, such as *Exhibit B*, *Ugly Mugs* and *Involuntary Dances*, and debate about theatre-industry issues, such as the role of critics, the role of women, the role of people of colour, and the health of local theatre ecologies, not to mention the surprising lack of debate about what would seem to be equally discussion-worthy shows and issues. I have taken note of praise and potentialities, but also of caution from commentators such as Toni Sant (2008, 2009, 2013, 2014) and Cathy Westbrook (2014), who ask why all the energy and enthusiasm has not led to a wider range of practices, at least in mainstage and mainstream contexts. I have suggested that the most interesting practices emerge when performance texts and para-performance texts meet and mix in interesting ways, whether on platforms such as UpStage, when paid professional critics start to cite public commentary on Twitter or Facebook as a source, or when small stories about a city missing out on a touring show tip over into bigger discussions about that city's theatre culture. I have suggested also that experimentation on social media platforms is necessarily more public than experimentation in a creative development, fringe festival, or even simply a closed rehearsal room. While mainstage theatre companies and makers have found a useful space for aesthetic experimentation in special projects that serve as a sort of transmedia marketing for their primary programming, similar spaces for critical, audience development, marketing and assessment experimentation are less easy to find in the highly public world of social media platforms. The burden for taking risks that might transform practice thus often falls to independent, community and activist theatre makers, whose livelihood is less tied to risks, successes and failures in this regard. This, together with a host of other factors, is impacting the zigzag pattern of uptake of social media in the theatre. This in itself is par for the course with the emergence of any new technology that has the potential to impact on theatre production, distribution or reception. The fact that the amount of advice about how to take advantage of social media is outpacing the practice—and thus, potentially, prompting theatre makers to plan out and pull back from the promise that Connor (2013), Balme (2014), Sant (2008, 2009, 2013, 2014) and others see in the platforms before the many much talked about but in fact less often seen problems arise—is less par for the course. It is, I have argued, difficult to think of another case where advice about how to use a technology has outpaced practical experimentation with that technology in the theatre, and, as a result, has had the potential to impact on the parameters of experimentation, in precisely this way.

The fact that mainstage theatre companies' and makers' concerns about the challenges of using social media in their production, distribution, marketing and audience development practices may be leading them to limit the types of interactivity they become involved into marketing-oriented conversations is not necessarily a problem or a point of criticism. As I noted in Chap. 3, there is good marketing and there is less good marketing, and a number of the examples in Chaps. 3, 4 and 5 represent innovations in making the marketing-driven experience of engagement with mainstage theatre texts and paratexts more exciting. This said, the difference between marketing conversations and more meaningful cultural conversations may point to a need for mainstage theatre companies, and makers in particular, to be clearer about the impact they desire, and the discourses about the impact they desire, when they make use of social media. Do mainstage theatre companies and makers want to be facilitators of these big cultural debates about gender, race, class, (dis) ability, culture, politics or the environment? Do they want to be facilitators of these big cultural debates, as well as fodder or exemplars for others facilitating these big cultural debates? Do they want to facilitate these debates as part of every show, season, initiative and communication, in the way some independent, activist and netactivist artists who work with communities marginalised by gender, race, class or (dis)ability do every day? The answer, for many, may be no, not always. Instead, in much of their core programming, mainstage theatre companies and makers may be looking to present work that entertains, evokes emotion or extends the aesthetics of the theatre form they work in, not necessarily to educate, empower or agitate for cultural change. If so, these sorts of theatre maker and company may be in need of a new language to describe what so many are currently describing as the democratisation of theatre and theatrical meaning making by means of social media.

In many cases, when mainstage theatre makers and companies today say they are using social media to democratise their practice, and the meanings their audiences make of their practice, they are pointing to the fact that they are offering increased access and interactivity of a certain type, and at a certain level, because that is what today's active citizen consumers want when they engage with arts, culture or anything else in their lives—all today's active citizen consumers, but most especially those who have been alienated from participation in arts, culture or anything else in their lives in the past or not. In the first decades of the twenty-first century, we are witnessing what Joseph Pine and James Gilmore (2011) describe as a shift from a product-, knowledge- or even information-driven social economy to an experience-driven social economy. A paradigm in which everyone wants every encounter with every company—from their local theatre company, to their shopping centre, to their bank—to be an engaging, entertaining, easy or fun one in which they feel they are an important part of the encounter in which they find themselves. In which their presence, participation and part in meaning making matters. Enabling these sorts of experiences is meaningful, impactful and valuable. Many of the reports, recommendations and tips on offer for theatre makers looking to make use of social media to connect with, reconnect with or build their audiences enable them to do this in better, newer and more innovative ways than they may have done in the past. This is not, however, the same as activating communities for the purpose of democratising culture, access and meaning making at a much larger level.

This being the case, there is a need for new terminology to differentiate between "democratisation" as the practice of making accessible engaging and interactive experiences in which people feel they are an important player in the encounter and "democratisation" as making meaningful impact in a culture's form and functioning in a larger sense. This new terminology would help theatre companies to manage the different expectations of the different imagined communities present on social media platforms, with their different ideas about democracy, access, meaning making and the best means of enacting them. Based on this book's survey of current practice, the discourse of "democratisation" and "democratising" access for audiences is often being used to describe practices that make the mainstream audience member's role in the theatre industry more active, engaged and engaging—as distinct from practices that make room for non-mainstream audience members historically excluded from theatre, and excluded from society at large, as a result of gender, race, class, or (dis)ability. In mainstage theatre, the latter is not, or at least is not always—outside education programmes, community programmes or other initiatives that currently take place outside the core programmes of large companies—the main aim. In mainstage theatre, practitioners are not necessarily "democratising" theatre access, culture and meaning making in this sense. Moreover, they may be adopting advice, recommendations and practices about the use of social media platforms that at best do not facilitate and at worst forestall the possibility of this, risking alienating some of their audiences. This may not be a problem in and of itself, but it will become a problem if theatre companies, makers, consultants or funding agencies continue to use a term as contested as "democratisation" in a casual way. The problem, at present, is more the result of the persistent use of heavily loaded terms such as "access", "inclusion" and "democratisation" in the reports, recommendations, advice articles and guides that have proliferated ahead of practice, and ahead of critical attention to both the practice and the advice about the practice, rather than the theatre makers and companies themselves. It will only improve with more detailed attention being paid to the practice, and the advice about the practice, which can differentiate between the different notions of democratisation, access and inclusion in meaning making, and different desired impacts of so-called democratisation, access and inclusion in meaning making, in play here.

I hope that *Theatre, Social Media and Meaning Making* has taken the first step in this direction, offering an analysis of theatre and social media that looks beyond the discourse surrounding the practice into the strategies, manoeuvres and techniques theatre makers and companies are actually using, and what they are actually achieving, and why.

## References


Balme, Christoper. 2014. *The Theatrical Public Sphere*. Cambridge: Cambridge University Press.

Conner, Lynne. 2013. *Audience Engagement and the Role of Arts Talk in the Digital Era*. London: Palgrave Macmillan.

Pine, B. Joseph, and Gilmore, James H. 2011. *The Experience Economy*, 2nd ed. Boston: Harvard Business Review Press.

Sant, Toni. 2008. A Second Life for Online Performance: Understanding Present Developments through an Historical Context. *International Journal of Performance Arts and Digital Media* 4 (1): 69–79.

Sant, Toni. 2009. Performance in Second Life: Some Possibilities for Learning and Teaching. In *Learning and Teaching in the Virtual World of Second Life*, ed. Judith Molka-Sanielsen, and Mats Deutschmann, 145–166. Trondheim: Tapir Academic Press.

Sant, Toni. 2013. Theatrical Performance on the Internet: How Far Have We Come Since Hamnet? *International Journal of Performance Arts and Digital Media* 9 (2): 247–259.

Sant, Toni. 2014. Art, Performance, and Social Media. In *Routledge Handbook of Social Media*, ed. Jeremy Hunsinger, and Theresa M. Senft, 45–58. London: Routledge.

Westbrook, Cathy. 2014. How to stage theatre's online future, The Guardian Theatre blog with Lyn Gardiner, Monday 14 April 2014. Available online http://www.theguardian.com/stage/theatreblog/2014/apr/14/stage-theatre-online-future.

# Bibliography


Adorno, Theodor. 1975. The Culture Industry Reconsidered. *New German Critique* 6: 12–19.

AusStage. n.d. AusStage Australian Theatre Database. http://www.ausstage.edu.auwww.ausstage.edu.au. Accessed 13 Aug 2013.

Boorsma, Miranda, and Hans van Maanen. 2010. View and Review in the Netherlands: The Role of Theatre Criticism in the Construction of Audience Experience. *Journal of Cultural Policy* 9 (3): 319–335.

Boyd, Dana, and Ellison, N. B. 2007. Social Network Sites: Definition, History, and Scholarship. *Journal of Computer-Mediated Communication* 13.1: 210–230

Brisbane Festival. 2013. The Stormie Mills Project. Brisbane Festival Archive. http://www.brisbanefestivalarchive.com.au/content/the-stormie-mills-project. Accessed 5 Jan 2015.

Clarke, Elly, 2011. Elly Clarke Tracing Mobility. *Plan B*. http://www.planbperformance.net/index.php?id=exhibitions. Accessed 18 Aug 2013.

Croggon, Alison. n.d. *Theatre Notes*. http://theatrenotes.blogspot.com.au/. Accessed 2 Feb 2015.

Croggon, Alison. 2009. Women in Theatre—Philip Parsons Memorial Lecture. *Theatre Notes* 19 November 2009. http://theatrenotes.blogspot.com.au/2009/11/women-in-theatre-philip-parons-memorial.html. Accessed 16 January 2015.

D'Cruz, Glenn, and Gorkem Acaroglu. 2014. Digital Performance Futures in Australasia. *Australasian Drama Studies* 65: 5–11.

Duggan, Maeve, Ellison, Nicole B., Lampe, Cliff, Lenhart, Amanda, and Madden, Mary. 2015. Social Media Updated 2014. Pew Research Centre, 9





B. Hadley, *Theatre, Social Media, and Meaning Making*,
DOI 10.1007/978-3-319-54882-1

January 2015. http://www.pewinternet.org/2015/01/09/social-media-update-2014/. Accessed 13 Dec 2015.

Feeney, Katherine. 2010b. No Courage: Qld Theatre "Falling Behind". *Brisbane Times*, 29 April 2010. http://www.brisbanetimes.com.au/entertainment/stage/no-courage-qld-theatre-falling-behind-20100429-tuuk.html. Accessed 10 Sep 2011.

Giannachi, Gabriella. 2007. *The Politics of New Media Theatre*. London and New York: Routledge.

Guardian, The. 2013. "Podcast—Episode One", Brisbane Festival Theatre Blog. *The Guardian* 15 September 2014. http://www.theguardian.com/culture/australia-culture-blog/audio/2013/sep/15/festival-podcast-brisbane-audio-art?view=desktop. Accessed 3 Feb 2015.

Guardian, The. 2014. Exhibit B: Is the "Human Zoo" Racist? The Performers Respond. Guardian Stage. *The Guardian* 5 Sep 2014. http://www.theguardian.com/culture/2014/sep/05/exhibit-b-is-the-human-zoo-racist-the-performers-respond. Accessed 6 Jan 2015.

Haber, Ben. 2008. Employee Fired for Facebook Comment. *RaceTalkBlog*. http://racetalkblog.com/2008/06/30/employee-fired-for-facebook-comment/. Accessed 28 Nov 2014.

Herbert, Kate. 2014. Theatre Review: Ugly Mugs, Malthouse Theatre. *Herald Sun* 21 May 2014. http://www.heraldsun.com.au/entertainment/arts/theatre-review-ugly-mugs-malthouse-theatre/story-fni0fcgk-1226926025595?nk=353bc0922591f3e4e8f036899a844554. Accessed 15 Jan 2015.

House, Brian. 2012. *Quotidian Record*. Eyebeam Gallery New York. http://www.eyebeam.org/taxonomy/term/7011. Accessed 19 Aug 2013.

Jenkins, Henry. 1992. *Textual Poachers: Television Fans and Participatory Culture*. London and New York: Routledge.

Jenkins, Henry. 2011. Transmedia 202: Further Reflections. *Confessions of an Aca-Fan: The Official Weblog of Henry Jenkins* 1 August 2011. http://henryjenkins.org/2011/08/defining_transmedia_further_re.html. Accessed 19 Aug 2013.

Lobel, Brian. 2011. *Purge*. http://www.blobelwarming.com/purge.html. Accessed 19 Jan 2015.

Mills, Stormie. n.d. *Stormie Mills.com*. http://stormiemills.com/. Accessed 5 Feb 2015.

Radio France Internationale. 2014. Protesters Stop Exhibit B "Human Zoo" Performance at Paris Theatre. *Radio France international* 28 November 2014. Updated 29 November 2014. http://www.english.rfi.fr/africa/20141128-protesters-stop-exhibit-b-human-zoo-performance-paris-theatre. Accessed 5 Jan 2015.

Royal Shakespeare Company. 2011a. RSC Transformation: The Vision. http://www.rsc.org.uk/transformation/vision/default.asp. Accessed 19 Aug 2013.

Royal Shakespeare Company. 2011b. *Such Tweet Sorrow*. http:// www.suchtweetsorrow.com. Accessed 19 Aug 2013.

Shrum, Wesley. 1991. Critics and Publics: Cultural Mediation in Highbrow and Popular Performing Arts. *American Journal of Sociology* 97 (2): 347–375.

Simmonds, Diana. 2014. Ugly Mugs—Review. *StageNoise* 24 July 2014. http://www.stagenoise.com/review/2014/ugly-mugs. Accessed 15 Jan 2015.

Surowiecki, James. 2005. *The Wisdom of Crowds*. Colección: Anchor Books.

Sweeney, Kathleen. 2010. Transmedia Remix. *Afterimage* 38 (3): 2.

The Builders Association. n.d. *Continuous City*. http://www.thebuildersassociation.org/prod_continuous_info.html. Accessed 19 Aug 2013.

Woodhouse, Cameron. 2014. Ugly Mugs Explores Harrowing Realities of Sex Work. *Sydney Morning Herald* 21 May 2014. http://www.smh.com.au/entertainment/theatre/review-ugly-mugs-explores-harrowing-realities-of-sex-work-20140522-zrkc4.html. Accessed 15 Jan 2015.

# Index





B. Hadley, *Theatre, Social Media, and Meaning Making*,
DOI 10.1007/978-3-319-54882-1

## C

## Q



## R

Kolibri 360 GmbH
Ferdinand-Jühlke-Straße 7
99095 Erfurt, Deutschland
produktsicherheit@kolibri360.de